Bureaucrats, Politicians, and Peasants in Mexico

Bureaucrats, Politicians, and Peasants in Mexico

A Case Study in Public Policy

MERILEE SERRILL GRINDLE

UNIVERSITY OF CALIFORNIA PRESS

Berkeley · Los Angeles · London

University of California Press
Berkeley and Los Angeles, California

University of California Press, Ltd.
London, England

Copyright © 1977 by
The Regents of the University of California

ISBN 0-520-03238-1
Library of Congress Catalog Card Number: 76-7759
Printed in the United States of America

For Steven, June, and Douglas

Contents

List of Tables and Figures

Text Tables

Appendix Figures

Acknowledgments

This book is a result of ninety-seven interviews with high and middle level public officials in Mexico. The names of these individuals, all of whom gave courteously and openly of their time and energy to answer my questions, cannot be listed here without violating the anonymity of their responses. However, their generosity and helpfulness cannot go unacknowledged; I am sincerely grateful to them for the graciousness with which they received me and the insights they shared with me.

More specifically, I wish to express my gratitude to Licenciado Gustavo Esteva, who enriched my appreciation of CONSUPO's role in rural Mexico and who provided many opportunities for me to speak with officials within and without the agency.

His collaborators, Ingeniero Ignacio Argaez and Ingeniero Carlos Montañez, spent many hours educating me in the realities of Mexican agricultural development. Without this instruction, the present work could not have been written. I am greatly in their debt for the patience and kindness they showed me.

In addition, many of the regional coordinators of CONSUPO's Field Coordination Program added to my education by introducing me to local communities and their development problems. The dedication of these individuals and their sympathy with the problems of *ejidatarios* and other rural inhabitants in Mexico impressed me greatly. To them also I wish to express my thanks.

Wayne A. Cornelius of MIT provided invaluable guidance and standards of rigorous scholarship during the preparation of this book. Myron Weiner and Harvey Sapolsky, also of MIT, offered helpful criticism and encouragement on numerous occasions while the study was in progress. Licenciado Fernando Solana of CONASUPO enabled me to begin the research in 1974, and José Luís Reyna of the Colegio de México provided intellectual assistance during my stay in Mexico. A good friend, Nancy Peck Letizia, assisted in the preparation of the manuscript with efficiency and cheerfulness. A grant from the Social Science Research Council and the American Council of Learned Societies made the field research financially possible. While I alone am responsible for errors in facts or interpretations which appear here, the efforts of all these individuals and institutions are gratefully acknowledged.

Throughout the field work and preparation of this study, Steven Hale Grindle has been a constant source of encouragement, understanding, and perspective. His ready humor and unfailing patience have contributed to the completion of this work in ways too diverse to list, on occasions too numerous to count. I am deeply appreciative of his willingness to share in this work.

MSG
Wellesley, Massachusetts

Glossary of Acronyms

ACONSA   Abastecedora CONASUPO, S.A. de C.V.: CONASUPO Provision Co., a subsidiary of CONASUPO, part of DICONSA system.

ADA   Almacenes de Depósitos Agropecuarios: Agricultural Warehouses, a Venezuelan agency charged with storage of supplies of agricultural products.

ANDSA   Almacenes Nacionales de Depósito, S.A. de C.V.: National Storage Warehouses Co., taken over by CONASUPO and administered by BORUCONSA.

ARCONSA   Almacenes de Ropa y Calzado CONASUPO, S.A. de C.V.: CONASUPO Clothing and Shoe Stores, a CONASUPO subsidiary, part of DICONSA system.

BORUCONSA   Bodegas Rurales CONASUPO, S.A. de C.V.: CONASUPO Rural Warehouse Co., a subsidiary of CONASUPO.

CECONCA   Centros CONASUPO de Capacitación Campesina: CONASUPO Peasant Training Centers, a subsidiary of CONASUPO.

CNC   Confederación Nacional Campesina: National Peasants Confederation, peasant sector of the PRI.

COCOSA   Comité Coordinador del Sector Agropecuario: Agricultural Sector Planning Committee.

CONASUPO   Compañía Nacional de Subsistencias Populares, S.A. de C.V.: National Staple Products Co.

DICONSA Distribuidora CONASUPO, S.A. de C.V.: CONASUPO Distributing Co., CONASUPO subsidiary with responsibility to oversee the following subsidiaries of CONASUPO:

DICONSA Central
DICONSA Metropolitan
DICONSA Northwest
DICONSA North
DICONSA South
ACONSA
ARCONSA

ECA Empresa de Comercio Agrícola: Agricultural Market Industry, Chilean agency charged with regulating prices of basic consumer goods.

EPSA Empresa Peruana de Subsistencias Alimenticias: Peruvian Food Marketing Agency.

IDEMA Instituto de Mercadeo Agropecuario: Institute for Agricultural Marketing, Colombian agency charged with regulating prices of basic consumer goqds.

ICONSA Industrias CONSUPO S.A. de C.V.: CONASUPO Industries Co., a CONASUPO subsidiary.

INPI Instituto Nacional de Protección a la Infancia: National Child Protection Institute.

ISI Import substituting industrialization.

LICONSA Leche Industrializado CONSUPO, S.A. de C.V.: CONASUPO Processed Milk Co., a CONASUPO subsidiary.

MACONSA Materiales de Construcción CONASUPO, S.A. de C.V.: CONASUPO Construction Materials Co., a CONASUPO subsidiary.

MICONSA Maíz Industrializado CONASUPO, S.A. de C.V.: CONASUPO Processed Corn Co., a subsidiary of CONASUPO.

PRI Partido Revolucionario Institucional: Ministry of Agriculture.

SAG Secretaría de Agricultura y Ganadería: Ministry of Agriculture.

SRA Secretaría de Reforma Agraria: Ministry of Agrarian Reform. (Until 1975, this ministry was a federal department: DAAC, Departamento de Asuntos Agrarias y Colonización, for simplicity, referred throughout by its current name, even when referring to periods prior to its elevation to ministerial rank.)

SRH   Secretaría de Recursos Hidráulicos: Ministry of Water Resources.

SUNAB   Superintendencia Nacional de Abastecimento: National Supply Agency, Brazilian agency charged with regulating prices of staple products.

TRICONSA Trigo Industrializado CONASUPO, S.A. de C.V.: CONASUPO Processed Wheat Co., a subsidiary of CONASUPO.

UNAM   Universidad Nacional Autónoma de México: National Autonomous University.

Glossary of Non-English Terms

apoyo push, help.

arquitecto architect, title for a person who has a B.A. degree in architecture.

cabide de emprego (Portuguese) coathanger of jobs, a term for an individual who maintains several jobs or sinecures at the same time.

cacique local or regional strongman, often a traditional, informal leader of Mexican communities, sometimes serving in official capacity (see Bartra, 1975; Cornelius, 1975: Chap. 6; Friedrich, 1969; Ugalde, 1973).

camarilla clique, faction.

campesino peasant, person from rural area.

chamba a piece of good luck, a job.

compadre coparent (a child's godfather), ritual kin, close friend.

compadrazgo compaternity.

confianza trust, confidence.

coyote a hoarder, exploiter, middleman, broker, go-between.

ejidatario legally recognized member of an *ejido*.

ejido officially recognized agrarian community, holding collective title to the land.

equipo,   team, little team.
equipito

Graneros   The People's Granaries, rural warehouses built by CONA-
del Pueblo   SUPO in late 1960s.

huesito   little bone, a job or other tangible evidence of influence
gained for purely political reasons.

ingeniero   engineer, title for a person who has a degree in agronomy
or engineering.

ingrejinha   (Portuguese) little church, a term for a group of loyal
followers.

jefe máximo   the most important leader, boss.

licenciado   title for a person who has a B.A. in the humanities or
social sciences or a law degree.

município   municipality, a geopolitical unit corresponding to a
county in the United States.

nome   (Portuguese) name.

padrinos   political godfathers or patrons.
políticos

palanca   lever, a term used to imply influence.

patrones   patrons.

panela,   (Portuguese) saucepan, little saucepan, a term for a
panelinha   political clique.

políticos   politicians, usually in disparaging sense.

quemado   burned, a term for those who have made political errors
and who are in disfavor, at least temporarily.

sexenio   six-year term of administration in Mexico.

técnicos   technocrats.

tienda   "company store" found frequently on haciendas in pre-
de raya   revolutionary Mexico.

trampolim   (Portuguese) springboard.
trampolín   springboard.

1

Introduction

This is a book about the policy process in Mexico. In the following chapters, the evolution of a single policy is traced from the inauguration of a new federal administration in late 1970 to mid-1975. During this period, government leaders became interested in new policies, broad national objectives were specified, and subsequently, numerous official agencies established plans to achieve these goals and attempted to put new programs into operation. This study will describe the activities of one important federal agency as its officials created and pursued a new policy for rural development. The manner in which priorities for national concern are established; the mobilization of support for policy options; the political, economic, and social factors which intervene in the realization of national goals; and the variables that influence the allocation of public resources are among the topics which are explored in depth in the following pages.

The scope of these concerns means that this is also a book about bureaucracy. In Mexico, the administrative apparatus of the national government is central to the processes of formulation and implementation of public policy. It also has a key role in the satisfaction of demands made upon the political system, the management of economic development, and the provision of social welfare benefits to the population. Moreover, the regulatory, welfare, and entrepreneurial activities of the centralized administration have a profound impact on the daily lives of Mexicans; the masses of the population increasingly receive their political experiences from contact with representatives of the national bureaucracy rather than from party officials or local notables. In spite of their importance, however, few scholars have examined how public administrative bureaus are organized in Mexico, how they expand, how they interact with other agencies, what motivates their employees, and how operative decisions are made on a day-to-day basis. Within the context of a single case study, the research to be reported provides a perspective on these aspects of bureaucratic behavior in Mexico and suggests their relevance to the study of public administration in other Third World countries.

Because of its concern with policy and bureaucracy, this is necessarily a book about elites. The individuals in question here are members of the public administration; they are middle and high level officials who have important responsibilities for establishing and achieving the goals of the political regime. In their daily activities, these bureaucrats interact with each other, with other members of the political and bureaucratic elite, and with recipients of government services. The patterns of their interactions provide the framework within which bargaining, negotiation, choice, demand making, and the allocation of government resources occur. Therefore, central to an understanding of the governing process in Mexico is a discussion of the influences on these middle and high level administrators as they analyze problems, propose solutions, seek to ensure that preferred policies receive adequate and timely financial and political support, and oversee the distribution of goods and services to the population.

Finally, this is a book about political life in Mexico. Profoundly affected by the change of political and administrative leadership which occurs every six years at the national level, political events in that country involve a subtle process of elite bargaining, coercion, and accommodation within the context of presidential dominance, administrative centralization, and official party control. The consequences of this system for the making and processing of demands on the government and the resolution of conflict are vital to the maintenance of the current regime. The following work therefore offers insight into the political processes that have engendered a high degree of elite cohesion and mass integration in a system often characterized by authoritarian and exploitive relationships.

The Bureaucracy in Mexico

The question which unites the four themes of policy, bureaucracy, elites, and system is a simple one: How do characteristics of the Mexican political regime affect the functioning of a bureaucratic agency as its officials participate in the tasks of formulating and implementing public policy? The significance of this topic can best be appreciated through a brief consideration of the extent and power of the bureaucratic apparatus in Mexico. The catalogue of responsibilities ascribed to the state in Mexico—and Latin America generally—go far beyond those traditionally considered functions of government in the United States and Western Europe, and the role of the federal bureaucracy in the organization and management of public life is accordingly more central. Governmental activism in the definition of major national problems, constraints on inputs into the policy formulation process, and the responsibility for carrying out government plans are three factors which significantly enhance the power and influence of its middle and upper echelon officials.

The Activist State

As in other countries of Latin America, in Mexico the state has historically been zealous in matters concerning economic development and the welfare of its citizens. The roots of this activism have been traced to Spanish imperial rule, but the responsibilities of the government and the extensiveness of its services have increased markedly since the Revolution of 1910 and especially since the presidency of Lázaro Cárdenas (1934-1940).[1] The Mexican federal bureaucracy is currently composed of 18 regular ministries and departments of state, 123 decentralized agencies, 292 public enterprises, 187 official commissions, and 160 development trusts.[2] Together, the last four categories, including over 750 organizations, are responsible for a wide range of government activities, from the exploitation of oil to the management of the nationally owned airlines, from the production of steel to the provision of low cost consumer goods at the retail level, from the stimulation of rural industries to the administration of various cultural foundations.

With this large number of federal agencies, all of which administer numerous programs, it is not surprising that the economic or social rationale for the activities of some of them is tenuous. Recently, a critic of government involvement in business concerns pointed out that

> The State participates in, among other things, six firms which manufacture stoves, refrigerators, and other domestic appliances, seven which manufacture cardboard boxes, paper bags, announcement cards, and paper forms; it manufactures, sells, and distributes desk supplies; it owns a soft drink bottling plant, a dish factory, a bicycle manufacturing

1. On the historical roots of bureaucratic activism in Latin America, see Hanson (1974) and Sarfatti (1966). On Mexico, see Carrillo Castro (1973). See Appendix B for tabular data on the growth of the Mexican bureaucracy.
2. In contrast, the *United States Government Manual, 1975-1976* lists 17 executive offices, boards, and councils, 11 departments, 59 agencies, 6 quasi-official agencies, and 64 other boards, committees, and commissions in the United States federal bureaucracy.

plant, six textile mills, an airline, fifteen holding companies whose social objectives range from the administration of buildings to the construction of hotels, buildings, homes, warehouses, factories, developments, and urban housing units; it runs a factory which produces balanced animal feed, a television channel, eighteen firms dedicated to theater administration, a casino, three woodworking shops, a firm which makes synthetic rubber, another which makes doorlocks, and a luxury housing development in the Federal District (Hinojosa, 1974: 6).

Nevertheless, it has been widely recognized that the government is also greatly responsible for the rapid growth of the economy in the postwar years, the increase in agricultural export production, and the generally high rate of industrialization which the country has experienced.[3] More than a decade ago, for example, Vernon emphasized the centrality of the government to economic development:

> The Mexican government has worked itself into a position of key importance in the continued economic development of Mexico. It governs the distribution of land, water, and loans to agriculture; it mobilizes foreign credits and rations the supply of domestic credit; it imposes price ceilings, grants tax exemptions, supports private security issues, and engages in scores of other activities that directly and immediately affect the private sector (1963: 188).

Investments to stimulate economic development have accounted for an average of 45 percent of the total expenditures of the federal budget since 1940 (Wilkie, 1967: 32–33, 1974: 211).

Similarly, the activities of the government in the provision of social services are also extensive. The Constitution of 1917 recognized the responsibility of the national government to sponsor the advancement of the welfare of workers and peasants in the realms of education, health, working conditions, and urban and rural services. Gradually, the ideological commitment of the regime to these activities has been transformed into a series of provisions benefiting a limited but expanding sector of the low income population. Currently, about 20 percent of the federal budget is expended by a bewildering number of agencies and ministries to achieve the social goals declared by the Constitution (see Economist Intelligence Unit, 1975; Wilkie, 1974: 211).

In fact, so extensive is the role of the government in the daily life of its citizens and so pervasive its economic presence, that Mexico can be characterized as a "patrimonial state," a term which has been used to describe other Latin American polities.[4] The patrimonial state is typified by extensive state enterprises coexisting and supportive of the private

3. See Glade and Anderson (1963), Hansen (1971: Chap. 3), Reynolds (1970), and Shafer (1966) for descriptions of the role of the public sector in Mexican development.

4. Discussions of politics in patrimonialist systems are found in Greenfield (1972), Pike and Stritch (1974), Purcell (1975), Roett (1972), Rudolph and Rudolph (1974), and Schmitter (1971).

economic sector, comprehensive responsibility for the provision of welfare services, often provided in the absence of overt popular demands for them, and functionally organized clientele groups dependent upon and even formally attached to the regime in power.[5] Policy making in a patrimonial state is the exclusive prerogative of a small elite and is characterized by limited informational inputs, behind-the-scenes bargaining and accommodation, and low levels of public discussion and debate. Not only does the government of such a state claim responsibility for a wide range of activities; it also tends to reserve important policy making roles for the public administration.

The Policy Making Role

In the past, much research on bureaucracy in Mexico and elsewhere in Latin America has taken as an implicit model the Weberian image of a value-neutral, hierarchically organized body of rule applicators who are responsible for carrying out the administrative functions of the state. As a result, several considerations of the bureaucracy have listed the impressive number of ways in which Latin American public administrations do not measure up to the norms described by Weber—those of standardized regulations directing behavior, prescribed official duties accruing to institutionalized positions, stable hierarchical chains of command, security of tenure, and advancement strictly on the basis of merit and training.[6]

The recognition that many Latin American bureaucracies do not achieve the standards set by Weber, or that they do in fact conform to these norms but with unexpected consequences for the pursuit of public goals, has led a number of scholars to adopt the "sala" model of administration proposed by Riggs (1964). General aspects of bureaucracy in Latin America—formalism, "price indeterminacy," personalism, lack

5. Jaguaribe (1968: 144), critical of the patrimonial nature of the Brazilian regime, has coined the phrase "cartorial state" (translated as sinecure or paper-shuffling state) to describe a system in which the government is pervasively and often obstructively involved in the direction of the society and the economy. Esman has applied the concept of the "administrative state" to Latin America: "The administrative state as an ideal type is one in which the state is the dominant institution in society, guiding and controlling more than it responds to societal pressures, and administrative (bureaucratic) institutions, personnel, and values and style are more important than political and participative organs in determining the behavior of the state and thus the course of public affairs" (1972: 62).

6. Generally, public administrations in Latin America have often been excoriated for being overly centralized, overburdened by meaningless paper work and rules, unresponsive to public needs, staffed by inadequately trained personnel, and inevitably corrupt. The reasons for these inadequacies have often been considered to be procedural and organizational, and, as such, subject to alleviation and correction by more rational command structures and more efficient procedures of operation. See Hanson (1974), Henry (1958), Kriesberg (1965), Pan American Union (1965), Quinn (1972). For a review article, see Pinto (1969). For general perspectives on development administration in Third World countries see Heady and Stokes (1962), Montgomery and Siffin (1966), Thurber and Graham (1973), Waldo (1970).

of well-defined role structures—are cited as characteristics of societies not yet fully institutionalized or developed (see Daland, 1967; Denton, 1969; Gomez, 1969). The transition from traditional societies to modern ones, according to Riggs and others, causes the bureaucracy to deviate from Weber's model. This formulation continues to be the major theoretical alternative to applications of the classical ideal type, but, like the Weberian model, it remains wedded to the conceptualization of bureaucracy as an administrative and rule-applying body.[7]

Some scholars, however, have questioned the completeness of this view of the bureaucracy in Mexico and Latin America. It has become clear in a number of case studies that the functionaries of the public administration are not simply neutral (or corrupt or particularistic or traditional) rule applicators but are also active and interested participants in policy formulation and rule making.[8] Of course, the contribution of the public administration to policy making has been increasingly recognized in many other countries and is generally attributed to the increased complexity and functions of government in twentieth century society.[9] Nevertheless, a number of conditions in Latin America make this role especially salient.

First, because of strong traditions of presidential dominance, elected bodies of representatives such as the national legislatures often have a peripheral and secondary place in policy making processes. Moreover, political parties and interest groups are frequently not the interest aggregating agencies which many studies have led us to expect. Rather, they tend to be groupings of vertically organized, leader-follower alliances which depend for their maintenance not on the pursuit of general policy goals but on the particularistic application of already formulated policy (see especially Chalmers, 1972). In other cases, military or caudillo-type rulers have inhibited the development of broadly aggregative and policy-oriented parties and interest groups, emphasizing instead the paternalist and directive role of the governmental apparatus in the solution of societal problems. Thus, by design or by default, the administrative apparatus in Latin America often has ascribed to it almost the entire task of defining public policy.

Indeed, in Mexico the public administration is largely isolated from the pressure of the legislative or judicial organs of government as well as from the programmatic and organized influences of party or interest associations. Presidential dominance of the legislature is complete; all

7. Ilchman (1965) and Parrish (1973) provide useful critiques of Riggs.
8. This is evident in studies by Benveniste (1970), Greenberg (1970), Kaplan (1969), Leff (1968), Purcell (1975), and Schmitter (1971).
9. See especially the articles by Eckstein, Ehrmann, Grosser, and Waltz reprinted in Chaps. 6 and 8 of Dogan and Rose (1971). See also Chapman (1959), Mayntz and Scharpf (1975), Suleiman (1974). On the same phenomenon in the United States, see Lowi (1967), Mosher (1968), Rourke (1969: Part 1), Seidman (1970).

executive proposed bills are approved by the legislature, and when not approved unanimously—which is the case in 80 to 95 percent of the votes in recent years—they are normally opposed by less than 5 percent of the members (González Casanova, 1970: 19, 201). The executive also maintains ultimate control over the semi-public interest associations, such as those of businessmen and industrialists.[10] Additionally, the dominant political party, the PRI (Party of the Institutionalized Revolution), is currently considered to be a mechanism for mobilization, communication, and control in the hands of the top political elite, as opposed to the interest aggregator and articulator it was perceived to be in earlier conceptions.[11] While it is true that high ranking party officials are influential participants in elite decision making, they do not act as independent spokesmen for specific programmatic alternatives, supported by ranks of committed followers.

Public policy in Mexico, therefore, does not result from pressures exerted by mass publics, nor does it derive from party platforms or ideology, nor from legislative consultation and compromise. Rather, it is an end product of elite bureaucratic and political interaction which occurs beyond the purview of the general public and the rank and file adherents of the official party. Individuals who do regularly participate in policy making, in addition to the President and top party leadership, are usually identified in some way with the bureaucracy. The public administration, then, is of key importance in the process of designing and articulating public policy in Mexico.

The Policy Implementing Role

A third characteristic of the bureaucracy in Mexico, in addition to its active participation in the society and economy and its function as policy maker, is its more traditional role of policy implementor. Of course, numerous factors impinge on the implementation process, from the organizational capacity to provide goods and services at the time and place they are required to the perceptions and interests of individual bureaucrats at the moment of making a discrete decision. Any one of a variety of factors can be singled out as fundamental in determining whether a policy is implemented or not. In all cases, however, activating the various programs and instruments specified to achieve the goals of a policy is the responsibility of bureaucratic bodies. Middle level public administrators, bureaucrats who generally have little or no influence in overall policy making, are, therefore, crucial to the implementation and rule application process. Among Latin Americans themselves, the most

10. The Mexican private sector and business organizations are described and analyzed in Purcell and Purcell (1976), Shafer (1973), and Vernon (1963).

11. This perspective is affirmed in Anderson and Cockroft (1966), Brandenburg (1964), Hansen (1971), Tuohy (1973). For a different interpretation, see Scott (1964).

frequently cited reason for the failure to implement new policies is the behavior of the public officials charged with instituting the programs. Thus, one frequently hears of agricultural extensionists, public health doctors, and government bank officials who will not perform their functions unless first offered a "tip." One hears of public works which are appropriated for the personal benefit of powerful individuals or interests. And one hears of systematic exploitation of powerless groups for political or economic ends. Students of Latin American politics have regularly attributed inefficiency, corruption, partisanship, conservatism, lack of responsiveness, and vested interests to the personnel staffing the administrative agencies of government.[12] These are all characteristics which impede the implementation of public policy and which indicate the importance of the administrators themselves in the policy process.

Much of the input of the rule applicators takes place far from the vigilant eyes of the high level officials ultimately responsible for program results. Frequently, imperfect channels of communication, defective administrative and informational systems, and lack of awareness of local conditions mean that bureaucrats at the operational level have great latitude to distribute the resources they control through their official positions. And the day-to-day demands for individualized decision making, rule application, and resource allocation may significantly affect whether or not the overall policy is implemented as intended; numerous instances of rule stretching may even aggregate into a failure to achieve national priorities and policies.

At the same time, however, the resource distribution activities of the bureaucrats may figure centrally in the maintenance of regime stability through the accommodation of diverse demands on the political system. In Mexico, for example, through the timely and calculated provision of goods and services, lower level political elites maintain their ascendance and bind their popular followings to the regime. The bureaucratic resources are useful to attract political support and coopt potential opposition. Moreover, regional and local politicians, dependent upon the largesse of the federal government, may be prevented from engaging in independent activities. Frequently, too, resources are readily provided to businessmen and industrialists for the purpose of encouraging economic expansion, minimizing organized opposition, and mitigating some of the individually felt sting of general governmental policies (see Purcell and Purcell, 1976). In short, the implementation role of the bureaucracy is vitally important to both the policy process and to the maintenance of regime stability in present-day Mexico.

---

12. For recent examples, see Fagen and Tuohy (1972), Hanson (1974), Johnson (1971), Petras (1969), Scott (1966), Stinchcombe (1974).

The Study

The political importance of the bureaucracy cannot be questioned; its active involvement in the society and its policy functions are reason enough to devote time and energy to a study of this institution. In the chapters to follow, Mexico's staple commodities marketing agency, CONASUPO (National Staple Products Company), is described and analyzed in depth. A case study of a single bureaucratic agency is useful because it encourages consideration of the contextual variables which influence and constrain individual and group behavior, factors which are frequently overlooked in less intensive but more inclusive research on organizations.[13] In addition, a case study is valuable for purely descriptive purposes. While numerous books and articles on Mexico make it one of the most thoroughly studied and documented political and economic systems in Latin America, most investigation in the past has been oriented toward the role of the PRI, the institution of the presidency, or private-public sector relationships. With the important exception of Greenberg (1970), there exist no thorough studies of how bureaucratic institutions in Mexico function or become involved in the policy process.

A number of considerations intervened in the choice of CONASUPO as the site for the research. It is a large federal agency with geographically and functionally extensive activities, employing more than 8,300 individuals and operating a network of installations throughout the entire national territory. Its annual budget in 1975 was almost five times larger than the Ministry of Agriculture, its principal functional rival, amounting to nearly 5.4 percent of the total federal budget. In terms of its political impact, CONASUPO is of singular importance to the government because of the magnitude and variety of resources it has to distribute. The specific activities engaged in by CONASUPO are central to the goals of national development. Especially since 1971, when a significant policy reorientation occurred within the agency, the thrust of its programs has been to achieve an increase in agricultural production, a control on inflation, a more equitable distribution of income among the population, and the integration of marginal sectors of the population into the national economy. These are all policy goals which were stressed by the Echeverría administration (1970–1976).

Moreover, because of its extensive national constituency of beneficiaries, CONASUPO is an important agency in terms of its contributions

13. For example, Ames states, "Organizations possess special attributes differentiating them from ordinary collectivities. The core of an organization lies in the common network of social relations binding together its members. Understanding the behavior of either individuals or the organization as a whole necessitates understanding this network" (1973a: 4). Blau (1957) expands upon this point. Examples of research on bureaucracies in Latin America which are more inclusive are Daland (1972), Hopkins (1967), Petras (1969), Silva Michelena (1967).

to political stability. Its personnel work closely with government and party officials to achieve the political goals of the regime, and the agency plays a significant part in marshaling the support of large segments of the population for the regime (see Alisky, 1974). Its marketing activities, especially in urban areas, have often served as public evidence of the Mexican regime's concern for its low income population. In a survey of six low income neighborhoods in 1970, for example, over 70 percent of the respondents had made use of the agency's network of stores (Cornelius, 1973: 225–226). The relative stability of the Mexican political system since 1940 is due in no small part to the efforts of distributive and symbolic programs such as those carried out by CONASUPO. In reality, CONASUPO is more important to the solution of fundamental national problems than many regular ministries of the government. Because of this, the agency during the Echeverría administration attracted a corps of politically mobile individuals. Its middle and upper level administrators were all highly qualified and considered by Mexicans themselves to exemplify the "new wave" of technically skilled public officials who came to the fore under Echeverría. For these reasons, the agency provides insight into Mexican political life.

Rural development policy has been singled out from a number of public policy areas in which CONASUPO is involved. The rural development policy options pursued by the agency constitute the most important change which has affected the organization since the early 1960s when it was reorganized and expanded. Moreover, the policy reorientation which occurred in 1971 and 1972 was the paramount objective which was pursued by the agency's leadership under the Echeverría administration. Such an important change provides impressive opportunities for investigating how policy support is mobilized and manipulated internally and how impediments to policy implementation arise and are dealt with. The rural development policy of CONASUPO is also of interest because it coincided with a shift in the policy of agricultural development pursued by the government in general. Therefore, it offers insights into the broader process of sectoral policy making in Mexico.

In this study, the public bureaucracy is conceived as an arena in which bureaucrats seek to achieve certain personal and public goals. These goals can be reached most efficiently by entering into implicit exchange relationships with others. In Mexico, informal exchanges tend to become long term commitments between individuals of different hierarchical levels and to pyramid into networks of exchange alliances, resembling the patron-client relationships described by anthropologists and political scientists. An explanation of bureaucratic behavior based on exchange processes and a model of the patron-client linkage as it is relevant to the Mexican elite is presented in the next chapter of this study.

Following the theoretical discussion, Chapter 3 places the study of CONASUPO within the context of the Mexican political system. Because of the extensive turnover of virtually all high and middle level personnel which accompanies the change of political administrations, the pursuit of career mobility is a crucial determinant of bureaucratic behavior there. Insecurity of job tenure encourages officials to become involved in personal alliances in order to ensure future career mobility. In CONASUPO, the patterns of career management vividly demonstrate the existence of informal alliances which are fostered by characteristics of the political environment in Mexico. In the agency, it was possible to observe and analyze the methods for obtaining employment, the means used by office chiefs, department heads, and division managers to recruit able and loyal subordinates, and the use of public positions to enhance the power of the agency and of its top level administrators. These patterns had an influence on the policy process, which is described in Chapters 4, 5, and 6.

A case study of the formulation of a rural development policy and the mobilization of support for it is presented in Chapter 4. As indicated previously, between 1971 and 1973, CONASUPO underwent a significant internal reorganization and reorientation of its goals and priorities. New emphasis was placed on the agency's impact in rural areas, and a comprehensive agency-wide policy for integrated rural development was devised. The policy made demands on the loyalties, responsiveness, and interests of all major components of the agency. This chapter demonstrates that personal alliance structures, both within the agency and between its high level functionaries and other political actors, were mobilized to bring about the policy change.

In Chapters 5 and 6, the scene shifts to another aspect of the policy process: implementation. In these chapters, the responsiveness of officials to central policy directives is analyzed at both the national and the state level. At the national level, the record of policy responsiveness was affected by both career-based alliances and dependence on the central office for the allocation of resources necessary to achieve the goals of individual units. More important to this study, however, are the state offices maintained by CONASUPO throughout Mexico. The state representatives and the offices under their responsibility were the primary units for implementation of the rural development policy at the local level. These state offices were the immediate targets of pressures and demands for the allocation of resources from a number of different constituencies such as the central organization of CONASUPO, its various subsidiaries, the state governor, and locally important political and economic figures and interests. The need to answer these demands meant that frequently nationally determined policies were diluted or redefined at the state level in order to achieve more short range problem solving and conflict resolution. However, it will be shown that those states where CONASUPO offices were staffed by individuals directly dependent on central office leadership for continued career mobility opportunities were the states in which most effective implementation of central priorities occurred.

In Chapter 6, a second means to achieve faithful policy implementation, the Field Coordination Program, is described and analyzed. The Field Coordination Program was the major alternative to the state offices for delivery of the rural development scheme to the local level. Although the program was a small and fledgling unit within CONASUPO, the activities of its participants demonstrate important aspects of the interaction of elites and low status actors in Mexico. It will be demonstrated that public officials, working at the grass-roots level, acted as intermediaries between the low income clients of the agency and the institution itself in order to achieve more rapid and adequate delivery of services. The program demonstrates the pervasiveness of personal alliance structures in Mexico and the extent to which these are mobilized to solve individual problems. It also signals the function of bureaucratic personnel when they act as brokers between powerless groups and the government in the presentation of demands and the channeling of information.

Finally, Chapter 7 returns to the broader subjects of the Mexican political system and Mexican development and attempts to relate the study to the rhythm of public life in that country and the potential for change within the current regime. Before embarking on the study itself, however, a brief description of the organization and function of CONASUPO will provide a necessary orientation for the ensuing discussion.

The Organization

Article 28 of the Mexican Constitution of 1917 prohibits monopolies. It singles out as illegal all combines, concentrations or hoarding of basic commodities, especially if this is done for the purpose of raising consumer prices. This article also confers upon the federal executive the right to create whatever agencies or control bodies are necessary to protect the consumer and regulate the staple products market. Currently, CONASUPO is the organization charged with fulfilling these tasks.[14] As presently constituted, the organization has two principal functions. First,

14. CONASUPO is a decentralized federal agency. "Decentralized" refers to a measure of financial and administrative autonomy from the central government and the laws which regulate the activities of regular ministries of state and their employees, rather than to internal organizational dispersal of authority or responsibility. Thus, for example, a decentralized agency need not acquire the approval of Congress to establish new programs, organizational units or activities, nor need it conform strictly to the law regulating the employment standards of federal employees. Moreover, a decentralized agency is free from annual budgetary review by the Congress and has the right to determine the use of the income generated by its activities. Internally, however, a

it is responsible for the administration of a price support program for agricultural products considered to be of importance to the nation. Second, it is responsible for stabilizing consumer prices of these and other products by stimulating the processing or marketing of the products it handles. In 1972, these two functions were codified by the management of CONASUPO into three operating objectives to permit more effective budgetary planning. The objectives specified and the proportion of the agency's annual budget destined for each are presented in Table 1.

The activities of CONASUPO to fulfill its functions are extensive and touch upon all phases of production and marketing processes of basic agricultural and consumer commodities. In terms of stimulating agricultural production, the agency advises the Ministry of Industry and Commerce on the establishment of official support prices for products such as corn, wheat, milk, beans, and rice and, subsequently, administers the guaranteed price program by purchasing crops directly from the farmer. Table 2 indicates the magnitude of the company's direct purchases of a number of agricultural products in recent years. The agency provides farmers with access to farm tools, fertilizers, insecticides, improved seeds, and bank credit as well as facilitating the marketing of their products through the operation of a network of rural receiving centers. These warehouses frequently provide auxiliary services such as corn shellers, gunny sacks, and local transportation for the products. In addition, CONASUPO engages in rural education programs directed at increasing the political, economic, and marketing skills of peasants. The primary target of its rural activities are farmers, especially *ejidatarios*, whose annual incomes are less than 12,000 pesos ($960).[15] Approximately

decentralized agency may be highly centralized administratively. For an interesting study of policy making and decentralized agencies in Colombia, see Bailey (1975). For a general perspective on government enterprises and economic development, see Baer (1974) and Sherwood (1970).

Most Latin American countries have marketing agencies which fulfill functions similar to those of CONASUPO. In Brazil, the National Supply Agency (SUNAB) sets retail food prices and attempts to coordinate a more effective national marketing system (see Schuh, 1970). The Ministry of Food and EPSA in Peru are responsible for functions similar to those of CONASUPO. In Chile, the Agricultural Market Industry (ECA) resembles CONASUPO in its functions and operations (see Bennett, 1968). The Institute for Agricultural Marketing (IDEMA) in Colombia and several divisions of the Ministry of Industry and Commerce in Bolivia are charged with marketing and price control functions for staple products (see Bailey, 1975; Thirsk, 1973; Wennergren and Whitaker, 1975). Venezuela maintains a national storage and supply agency (ADA) similar to ANDSA in Mexico. Jones (1972) provides comparative material on Africa.

15. *Ejidatarios* are the legally recognized beneficiaries of the right to farm lands belonging to an *ejido*, a corporately organized community of peasants. Most *ejidos*, based on indigenous pre-hispanic models, were organized during the Cárdenas administration (1934–1940). While *ejido* lands cannot be sold, rented, or mortgaged by individuals, plots of land are generally cultivated individually. About 48 percent of Mexican cropland is organized into *ejidos*, supplying about 35 percent of total agricultural output. Eighty-five percent of the *ejidos* are oriented to subsistence farming. Over 80 percent of *ejido* plots are under ten hectares in size (Hansen, 1971: 61–62, 79; see also Carlos, 1974; Chevalier, 1967; Stavenhagen, 1970).

TABLE 1.

Objectives of CONASUPO's Activities

Objective	% of Annual Budget
Regulate the basic commodities market	33.77
Assure the supply and reduce or stabilize prices, if necessary, of the national wholesale commodity market	20.22
Assure the supply and reduce or stabilize prices, if necessary, of the national retail commodity market	13.55
Increase the income of poor farmers	13.67
Raise the level of production of basic commodities produced	6.89
Raise the commercial value per unit of commodities produced	6.62
Raise the profit margins of producers and better their social conditions	0.16
Increase the ability of low income consumers to acquire basic commodities	25.89
Assure the physical supply of basic commodities to the low income population	11.87
Offer basic commodities at retail prices which correspond to the economic capacity of low income consumers	14.02
(Other budgetary expenditures, administration, financial reserves, investments, etc.)	26.67
Total	100.00

Source: CONASUPO, "El presupuesto por funciones en CONASUPO." Unpublished manuscript, 1974.

94 percent of those who derive their incomes from agricultural pursuits fall into this economic category.

CONASUPO is also involved in the processing of a number of items considered to be of prime importance to the country. It owns and operates milk, corn meal, and wheat flour processing plants. In its milk plants, the company reconstitutes powdered milk and produces several types of enriched, special formula lactic products for children and mothers. Wheat flour is marketed under CONASUPO's own label, and the

TABLE 2.

Direct Purchases of Agricultural Products by CONASUPO, 1969–1974

	% of Total Annual Production Purchased					
Product	1969	1970	1971	1972	1973	1974
Corn	17.8	13.8	16.3	15.1	8.3	13.8
Wheat	62.5	53.3	32.0	45.3	38.3	79.3
Beans	7.5	3.5	16.1	14.2	0.4	13.9
Sorghum	4.1	6.9	0.0	2.3	1.2	1.5
Rice	0.0	0.1	4.1	5.0	9.6	10.3

Source: CONASUPO, Gerencia Técnica.

agency operates bakeries which produce bread and rolls for consumers in low income areas of large cities and for wards of government institutions. Corn meal also bears a CONASUPO label in local markets, and tortilla dough made from it is produced and provided to tortilla bakeries. In 1975, it purchased a large company which produced much of Mexico's cooking oil and pasta products. Control over this company is expected to increase significantly CONASUPO's influence on consumer prices. In addition, the agency signs contracts with various industries, requiring them to purchase products regulated by the agency at official prices in return for a guaranteed supply of the commodity. On a limited scale, the agency helps finance small construction materials industries and sells the output to other government agencies.

Finally, CONASUPO maintains a distribution network of various kinds of stores—ranging from tiny rural supply stations to large urban supermarkets—to bring low cost foodstuffs, clothing, and other articles to rural and urban consumers. In 1975, there were over 2,800 retail sales outlets supplied and operated by CONASUPO in Mexico and another 2,200 run by other agencies but supplied by the company. The most publicized of its retail outlets are its mobile units, large trailer trucks which visit low income urban neighborhoods periodically to discourage local merchants from charging high prices and to provide consumers with greater access to basic commodities. The agency also maintains wholesale outlets for small private merchants to enable them to acquire lower cost goods. Additionally, it enters into contracts with private commercial establishments for the sale of commodities at regulated prices. The consumers toward which CONASUPO directs its activities are those with incomes of less than 2,000 pesos a month ($160), approximately 90 percent of the economically active population.

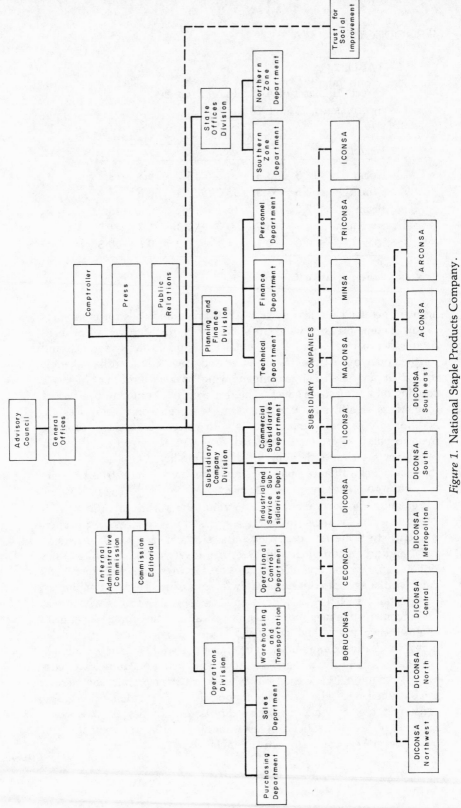

Figure 1. National Staple Products Company.

To accomplish its overall objective of market regulation, the agency establishes and maintains regulatory reserves of grains and seeds, and it has exclusive authority to import and export products such as corn and wheat. The products which CONASUPO is most interested in regulating are corn, beans, wheat, sorghum, rice, barley, edible oils, and powdered milk, although it also deals in a large number of other basic consumer goods, including clothes, shoes, construction materials, farm implements, household utensils, and school supplies.

To carry out these various programs, CONASUPO is organized into a parent company with sixteen subsidiary companies, shown in the organization chart in Figure 1. An Advisory Council, formed of various ministers of state and directors and subdirectors of agencies whose functions are related to CONASUPO, provides overall policy direction to the agency. The make-up of the council has changed somewhat over the years but is currently composed of the Minister of Finance (*Hacienda y Crédito Público*) who is its president, the Ministers and Subministers of Industry and Commerce and Agriculture, the Subminister and Credit Director of Finance, in addition to the Director General of CONASUPO. This council is expected to convene once a month to oversee the company's activities.

In reality, the marketing agency enjoys a considerable amount of freedom in establishing its own policies and programs. Its relative autonomy is due to several factors. Council meetings are in fact infrequently held; there are a great number of other demands on the members' time; they frequently lack practical knowledge about the company's operations and organization; and they may be less politically influential than the agency's general director. On several occasions, however, the council has exercised veto power over projects and programs it deemed politically unwise. Moreover, some of its most politically powerful members are presidential confidants and can be valuable allies to the agency when they act as conduits to the President of agency plans and problems. Within the agency itself, plans, programs, and policies are always considered confidential and preliminary until they are formally ratified by the Advisory Council, even if the approval is pro forma.

The parent company is composed of a General Office, responsible for overall coordination and control, and four subdirections or divisions, each charged with a major functional responsibility for the system as a whole. The Operations Division, for example, has staff responsibility for organizing all buying, selling, transportation, storage, conservation, distribution, importation, and exportation of agricultural products necessary for market regulation. The Planning and Finance Division provides short, medium, and long range planning in addition to overseeing financial and personnel administration of the company and, if requested to do so, providing technical advice to the subsidiary companies. The Subsidiary Company Division has authority to oversee the coordination and function of these organizations, although in fact they enjoy considerable autonomy. Finally, the State Offices Division is responsible for managing the thirty-one state level offices of CONASUPO dispersed throughout the country.

The subsidiary companies of CONASUPO were established to carry out the operative phases of the agency's activities. Currently, there are sixteen subsidiaries, twelve of which have been created since 1970. In 1973, eight of the companies were consolidated into a distributing system under the general management of one company, forming the DICONSA system. There is also a trust for social services operated by CONASUPO which is in many ways similar to the subsidiary companies but which has more financial autonomy. The subsidiaries have their own budgets and resources and the authority to use the income derived from their own activities. They may also solicit outside financing. The subsidiary companies are functionally divided into three main areas of activity: industrial, commercial, and service. Table 3 describes briefly the official functions of the parent company and each of the subsidiary organizations, the date of their creation, their operating capital, personnel employed, and units operated.[16]

Some measure of policy and operative control over the sixteen subsidiaries is achieved through four organizational devices. First, the general director and the four division managers of the parent company sit on the Advisory Council of each subsidiary, the general director acting as its president. Second, the Subsidiary Company Division of the parent company provides some oversight and feedback to the central organization. The Operations Division of the parent establishes the norms and quantities of farm products to be bought, sold, and transported by the subsidiary most involved in this regulatory process. Finally, the State Offices Division reports on problems involving subsidiary activities in the field and has some authority to correct these problems locally. External evaluation of the agency's programs is provided by two ministries of state which are responsible for overseeing and controlling the financial operations of the decentralized agency. The Ministry of National Resources has the responsibility of assessing the use made of CONASUPO's physical property, and the Ministry of the Presidency has charge of conducting external audits of its financial affairs.

16. Data in the chart should be considered approximate due to the rapid expansion of the agency and its subsidiaries. A number of different documentary sources, all internal CONASUPO reports, were used for obtaining the information, in addition to interview material. In each case, I have attempted to use the most recent and reliable information available. A glossary of acronyms appears at the beginning of this study for reference.

TABLE 3.

CONASUPO and Its Subsidiary Companies

Company	Principal Functions	Date Established	Income	Number of Personnel	Operating Units
Parent CONASUPO (National Staple Products Co.)	Policy and administrative direction of system responsible for: 1. Regulating the basic commodity market 2. Increasing the income of poor farmers 3. Increasing the ability of low income consumers to acquire basic commodities	Important antecedents in 1937, 1948, 1961; in present form, April 1965	Total for entire system: 18.3 billion pesos	Parent only, August 1974: 1,283	
Subsidiary (Industrial Activities) ICONSA (CONASUPO Industries Co.)	Produce and distribute pasta products and edible oils	1975	N.A.*	N.A.*	N.A.*
LICONSA (CONASUPO Processed Milk Co.)	Regulation and modernization of milk product market through 1. Reconstituting and selling milk and other dairy products to low income consumers in the Federal District 2. Producing and selling evaporated milk and infant formulas 3. Contracting with commercial milk producers to supply low cost milk products 4. Distributing butter, cheese, cream, eggs, and chicken for commercial sale	March 1961; in present form, 1965	Estimated 1974: 510 million pesos	April 1975: 650	2 Production 365 Sales

TABLE 3 (Continued)

Company	Principal Functions	Date Established	Income	Number of Personnel	Operating Units
MICONSA (CONASUPO Processed Corn Co.)	Regulation and modernization of corn and tortilla markets by 1. Producing corn flour and cereals 2. Producing corn dough and distributing it to tortilla processing plants	March 1950; acquired by CONASUPO SA, April 1961; in present form, 1965	Estimated 1973: 120 million pesos	June 1973: 242	1 Production
TRICONSA (CONASUPO Processed Wheat Co.)	Regulation and modernization of wheat products market by 1. Producing and selling bread to low income consumers, industries, and governmental institutions such as hospitals and schools 2. Producing and selling wheat flour to individuals and industries	June 1968; in present form, 1972	Estimated 1973: 31 million pesos	June 1973: 164	1 Production
Subsidiary (Commercial Activities)					
DICONSA (CONASUPO Distributing Co.)	Regulation and modernization of retail market system by establishing, running, and supplying retail outlets for basic commodities through various distribution systems (i.e., its own stores, supermarkets, mobile units, concessionary stores, rural cooperatives, and stores run by other government agencies) in both urban and rural areas	April 1961; in present form, 1965	Total for entire DICONSA system: 3 billion pesos	Nov. 1974: 5,716 (Entire DICONSA system)	5,000 Retail Outlets (2,800 of its own stores and 2,200 stores run by other government agencies)

Company	Principal Functions	Date Established	Income	Number of Personnel	Operating Units
(DICONSA General now oversees the activities of 8 subsidiary companies of the CONASUPO system:)	(Staff functions of 8 subsidiaries)				
DICONSA Central	DICONSA functions in 8 of the states of central Mexico	Nov. 1973	Estimated 1974: 400 million pesos	Oct. 1974: 618	577 Sales Outlets
DICONSA Metropolitan	DICONSA functions in Federal District and 2 nearby states	Nov. 1973	Estimated 1974: 1.06 billion pesos	Oct. 1974: 2,846	434 Sales Outlets
DICONSA Northwest	DICONSA functions in 5 northwestern states in Mexico	Nov. 1973	Estimated 1974: 300 million pesos	Oct. 1974: 299	219 Sales Outlets
DICONSA North	DICONSA functions in 6 northern states of Mexico	Nov. 1973	Estimated 1974: 460 million pesos	Oct. 1974: 483	368 Sales Outlets
DICONSA South	DICONSA functions in 6 southern states of Mexico	Nov. 1973	Estimated 1974: 430 million pesos	Oct. 1974: 497	439 Sales Outlets
DICONSA Southeast	DICONSA functions in 5 southeastern states of Mexico	Nov. 1973	Estimated 1974: 350 million pesos	Oct. 1974: 530	394 Sales Outlets
ACONSA (CONASUPO Provision Co.)	Regulation and modernization of perishable food market through retail sale of fruits and vegetables to low income population of the Federal District	July 1973	1973: 23 million pesos	Oct. 1973: 93	20 Sales Outlets
ARCONSA (CONASUPO Clothing and Shoe Stores)	Regulation and modernization of clothing market through retail sale of clothing and shoes to low income population in urban and rural areas	Feb. 1973	1973: 83 million pesos	Oct. 1973: 200	52 Sales Outlets

TABLE 3 (Continued)

Company	Principal Functions	Date Established	Income	Number of Personnel	Operating Units
MACONSA (CONASUPO Construction Materials Co.)	Regulation and modernization of construction materials markets by 1. Promoting and creating factories making construction materials, run by low income peasants and providing technical aid to rural construction materials industries 2. Selling construction materials to public sector dependencies 3. Providing construction materials to areas hit by natural disasters	June 1973	Estimated 1974: 72 million pesos	Nov. 1974: 100	
Subsidiary (Service Activities)					
BORUCONSA (CONASUPO Rural Warehouse Co.)	Aid peasants in marketing crops by 1. Aiding in reception, storing, conserving, distribution, and sale of their farm products through maintenance of network of rural warehouses 2. Providing farm tools and materials to improve production (seeds, fertilizers, insecticides) 3. Providing communication and education resources to low income farmers	Aug. 1971	1973: 26 million pesos	1974: 500	1,250 Rural Warehouses
CECONCA (CONASUPO Peasant Training Centers)	Train and educate *ejidatarios* and other low income rural inhabitants by offering extension courses on agricultural, commercial, and social subjects	May 1972		1974: 200(?)	20 Capacitation Centers

Company	Principal Functions	Date Established	Income	Number of Personnel	Operating Units
Subsidiary (Trust for Social Service) conasupo Trust for the Promotion of Social Improvement (known as Promotion Commission)	Promote rural organization and development through the establishment of rural industries and auxiliary social services	1966; became a trust in August 1973		1974: 200	

* N.A. = Data not available.

Its resources come from a number of sources which are relatively assured, allowing the agency a stable base from which to plan and program its various activities. Table 4 presents the proportional sources of the projected income budget for 1974. Table 5 shows the principal projected expenditures for the same year. Part of its income derives from an endowment of 4 billion pesos ($320 million) conferred upon the agency by the government. It receives an income from its own operations each year and also acquires an annual subsidy from the federal government. Finally, it receives operating money from outside financing. CONASUPO's total annual budget in 1970 was about 5 billion pesos ($400 million). In 1973 it was about 8.5 billion pesos, and by 1974, because of the agency's importance to the government's anti-inflation policy, it had a budget of 18.3 billion pesos ($1,464 million). In 1975, the agency was scheduled to receive far more money than any other federal organization within the agricultural sector (see Table 6). Its projected budget for 1976 was 35 billion pesos ($2,800 million).

It is clear from this overview that CONASUPO is a large and complex federal agency in Mexico. Within the framework of the formal organization just described it participates in a variety of activities and distributes a multitude of public resources to various clientele groups. As with all organizations, however, more than its formal structure is required to explain its operations. Important aspects of its informal structure such as its system of incentives and unwritten norms are discussed in the following chapter.

TABLE 4.

Sources of CONASUPO's Income for 1974*

Source	% of Total Income
CONASUPO resources	
Operations	71.80
Income from endowment	1.04
External resources	
Federal government subsidy	7.50
Loans	18.39
Other	1.27

Source: CONASUPO, "El presupuesto por funciones en CONASUPO." Unpublished manuscript, 1974.

*Preliminary

TABLE 5.

Sources of CONASUPO's Expenditures for 1974*

Source		% of Total Expenditures
Operations		
Commercial purchases	64.52%	
Production and service costs	0.97	
Marketing costs	7.85	73.34
Administration		3.36
Debt retirement and interest		18.53
Reserves		0.60
Other		0.34
Capital expenditures		3.83

Source: CONASUPO, "El presupuesto por funciones en CONASUPO." Unpublished manuscript, 1974.

*Preliminary

TABLE 6.

The Agricultural Sector in the 1975 Federal Budget

Organization	Federal Primary Sector Budget (%)	% of Total Federal Budget
CONASUPO	26.9	5.38
Ministry of Water Resources	18.5	3.70
Mexican Fish Products Co.	7.1	1.42
Ministry of Agriculture	5.5	1.10
Mexican Coffee Institute	3.6	0.72
Ministry of Agrarian Reform	1.5	0.30
Mexican Forest Products Co.	0.4	0.80
Other agencies, industries and trusts	36.5	7.30
Totals	100.0	20.72

Source: CONASUPO, *Gaceta*, No. 16 (January 15, 1975).

2

Organizational Alliances: A Theoretical Perspective

Exchanges in Organizations

> A lot depends on the personality of the person heading up the local office of CONASUPO.

> What we have to make the peasants realize is that CONASUPO is a *system* and they must work within this system. There are certain procedures which have to be followed.

> Very often we are limited in the reforms we can make by outside constraints.[1]

Organizations are composed of individuals who have values, expectations, and patterns of behavior, who communicate with others, and who attempt to realize a variety of personal goals. At the same time, however, organizations have stable and enduring structures which determine formal authority rankings, hinder or encourage coordination and the accomplishment of responsibilities, and generally influence the extent to which members are free to behave in accordance with their own values or expectations or to interact with other individuals. In a broader sense, the organization is influenced by the history, the culture, and the political and economic conditions of the society in which it functions. In turn, the organization may have an impact on the wider social, political, or economic environment. Therefore, individual, organizational, and environmental factors may all influence the behavior of people in organizations such as public bureaucracies. Consequently, a theoretical perspective which provides a framework to evaluate these diverse elements is essential for a satisfactory analysis of policy making and administration in a bureaucratic agency.[2]

---

1. These epigraphs and other quotations are from interviews conducted in Mexico in 1974 and 1975, unless otherwise attributed.
2. A helpful critique of major traditions in organizational research is found in Mouzelis (1967; see also Blau and Scott, 1962). A persistent difficulty in both classical bureaucracy theory (Weber, Marx, Michels) and organization theory (Taylor, Fayol, Gulick, Urwick, Roethlisberger and Dickson, Mayo, Simon) has been to integrate these three levels of variables into a general theory of organizational behavior. For a variety of examples of factors which influence bureaucratic behavior, see Anderson and Anderson (1970).

One such framework is exchange theory. This perspective focuses on the processes by which actors enter into alliances with others in the pursuit of certain goals. Interpersonal alliances based on exchange relationships link organizational members to each other and to others in the environment. They tend to develop into networks which influence the behavior of individuals and of the organization as a whole.[3] Either formally constituted or informally evolved, the networks process information, coercion, control, legitimacy, authority, compliance, and performance, directly affecting the nature of organizational output and directly influenced by the structural characteristics of the institution.

In general terms, exchange theory posits that rewards, either expected or experienced, motivate human interaction.[4] Exchange has been broadly defined to include any voluntary association of mutual influence between individuals in face-to-face encounter (see Blau, 1964; Homans, 1961). Exchange theorists such as Blau and Homans use small group research to demonstrate that individuals in social interaction are motivated by expectations of reward and calculations of cost. In their work, these theorists consciously introduce economic perspectives to the analysis of social interaction, using such concepts as cost, benefit, marginal utility, supply and demand, resources, investment, and credit. These are extrapolated to social environments where they are broadened to include, not rewards and costs calculated as money, but benefits and punishments such as approval, esteem, prestige, legitimacy, power, coercion, and control.

While Blau and others deal principally within the broad context of social life, some modifications can be introduced to make exchange theory useful for analyzing organizations.[5] For example, exchange processes in an organization may be much more consciously entered into and manipulated than in society in general. In the work of Blau and Homans, exchange is considered to be initially motivated by primitive (given) psychological or social needs. According to Blau, for instance, human beings are motivated to seek social acceptance and approval for a variety of psychological reasons; they are willing to offer inducements in the form of certain kinds of behavior in order to be rewarded with the approval of others (1964: Chap. 2).

3. Bensman and Vidich (1962), Blau (1955), and Dalton (1959) are examples of studies which analyze interpersonal networks and their effects on organizational behavior.

4. Important contributions to the development of exchange theory in sociology are Adams (1965), Blau (1957, 1964), Homans (1958, 1961), Thibaut and Kelley (1959). Useful reviews and critiques of exchange theory are found in Heath (1971) and Waldman (1972).

5. Variations of the basic propositions of exchange theory have been applied to organizations in some previous work. See especially Blau (1955) and Whyte (1969). Most recently, exchange processes have proved useful in analyzing specifically political organizations (see Cleaves, 1974; Ilchman and Uphoff, 1969).

Organizations, however, are more deliberately designed than society as a whole; they have specific purposes, certain tasks are assigned to given roles within them, and the individuals who assume these positions are expected to accomplish—or at least attempt to accomplish—the assigned tasks. Moreover, because individuals elect to become part of an organization, the reasons for deciding to join are likely to be more conscious than an ephemeral search for esteem, prestige, or the approval of one's fellows. Therefore, the conscious goal seeking of individual actors in an organization becomes more central to the discussion than when speaking of society-wide processes in which the desire for acceptance, approval, esteem, and status may be more subliminal motivations to behavior.

In addition, the range of resources useful as rewards and punishments in exchange relationships in organizations may be different from that in general social exchange. In an organizational setting, specifically institutional resources such as material and financial goods, as well as formal role resources like authority, access, and decision making responsibility, may all become subject to exchange processes. Of course, the social resources of status, obligation, friendship, and esteem remain important in linking individuals within the organization and others in the environment. Political resources such as influence, support, votes, patronage, power, and coercion are also valuable to organization members engaging in internal and external exchanges.

With these modifications, a theory of organizational behavior based on exchange processes may be briefly outlined. To begin with, organizations offer incentives to individuals in exchange for contributions which advance the interests of the organization or its leadership. In order to acquire the incentives offered them, actors must accomplish certain explicit tasks in their roles as organization members.[6] However, resources, which are controlled by other organization members or by individuals outside the organization, are necessary to accomplish these tasks. To acquire them with efficiency and regularity, organization members may enter into exchange relationships with others inside and outside the organization. They reciprocate by furnishing to others the resources they have under their command. The structure of formal

6. The concept of incentives in organizational behavior was first explored by Barnard in *The Functions of the Executive* (1938) and was later used as a basis for differentiating types of organizations in an influential essay by Clark and Wilson (1961; see also Simon, 1957). It is important to note that some behavior in organizations is motivated by things other than the inducements offered by the organizational leadership. For example, efficient performance might be motivated by professional ideals, political convictions, or psychological needs which do not figure in the incentive system of the organization. However, such motivations tend to be individual aberrations; in general, organization-relevant performance is maintained through organizationally provided incentives.

organizations means that control over resources is usually distributed hierarchically; internal exchanges therefore generally flow vertically between superior and subordinate rather than horizontally among peers. Exchanges in the external environment tend to be both vertical and horizontal.

In the pursuit of various goals, bureaucrats use the resources they control as tools for bargaining to elicit the behavior they desire from others. The resources needed to accomplish their goals are varied. Generally, they can be divided according to whether they are directly or indirectly instrumental to the achievement of specific tasks or goals. In the first category are resources such as financial and material support, information, authority, and decision making responsibility. Indirect resources are goods and services which can be manipulated to acquire other resources which are necessary to the individual in his assigned role. The bureaucrat may seek to acquire access to influential individuals, status, the obligation of his superiors and subordinates, and political support, all of which can be "cashed in" at an opportune moment to achieve job-related functions and goals.

Exchanges vary depending upon what goods and services are perceived appropriate for bargaining. In an organization, there is a virtually unlimited supply of potential goods and services available for exchange. Even formally constituted rules and regulations may be the objects of bargaining between superiors and subordinates (see Blau, 1955: 169–170). It is apparent, however, that in different situations or cultural and political settings, some resources are implicitly or explicitly excluded from bargaining and exchanges. For example, in a bureaucratic system in which jobs are strictly distributed through a civil service system which regulates hiring, promotion, and firing, jobs are generally not available as resources in a bargaining situation between superior and subordinate (see, for example, Crozier, 1964: 46–50, 70–71). In Mexico, on the other hand, where most white collar bureaucratic positions are classified as "confidence" posts at the disposal of bureaucratic chiefs, the job is an important resource which the superior has to offer to the subordinate in exchange for his diligent work, his loyalty, or his information. The goods and services available for exchange may also vary over time within the same environment.

Additionally, exchanges vary because of differences in the value accorded to goods and services. Resources may be more or less scarce or difficult to acquire because of the hierarchical position of the individual, the responsibilities of the organization, the structure of the external environment, or the cultural milieu in which the organization exists. Access to influential superiors, for instance, may be more important to a low level administrator who lacks authority to act on any important matter than to a higher level bureaucrat who has been assigned some formal decision making power. Members of an organization responsible for a rapidly expanding construction program will probably value material resources more than would officials in an organization with only clerical responsibilities. In a highly centralized system like the Mexican bureaucracy, authority may be more valued than in decentralized ones. In some cultural milieus, information may be regarded as a resource to be hoarded rather than shared or the status related to hierarchical authority may be more highly valued than in other environments. Therefore, in the bargaining which occurs over the acquisition of valued resources, some will demand a higher price than others.

In bureaucratic organizations in Mexico, the exchange relationships entered into by high and middle level officials tend to be based upon enduring personal bonds between individuals. Most commonly, the resultant alliance structures are between those in superior and subordinate positions. Fundamentally oriented toward the goal of career mobility, these alliances are based upon informal norms of reciprocity and personal loyalty. The bonds are thus conceptually similar to a specific type of interpersonal exchange alliance which has been termed a patron-client relationship in the literature of anthropology and political science. The patron-client concept therefore provides a convenient model for understanding elite politico-administrative behavior in Mexico.

The Patron-Client Model

The patron-client relationship, as it has been conceptualized by anthropologists and political scientists, is an enduring dyadic bond based upon informally arranged personal exchanges of resources between actors of unequal status. The objective of each actor is to achieve certain goals by offering the resources he controls or has access to in exchange for resources he does not control.[7] Thus, the identifying characteristics of the patron-client linkage are that it is (1) an informal or nonlegally binding and (2) personal or face-to-face relationship (3) involving an exchange of valued resources (4) between actors of unequal status which (5) persists through time. Individual alliances become pyramidal as patrons in turn become clients to more powerful individuals in order to gain access to resources they do not directly control.

The concept of the patron-client linkage was developed in anthropological field research in small, traditional, often isolated and closed communities. The prototypical example of local-level patron-client ties is that often encountered between the peasant and his landlord in remote

7. Flynn (1974), Foster (1967a, 1967b), Kaufman (1972), Landé (1973), Powell (1970), and Scott (1972) all present very useful treatments of the patron-client concept. Two general anthologies of studies on patron-client relationships are Schmidt, Scott, Gausti, and Landé (1976), and Strickon and Greenfield (1972). The first presents studies by political scientists, the second works by anthropologists.

communities (see Cotler, 1970: 536–538; Wolf, 1959: 202–211). Due to the vicissitudes of nature, the predatoriness of neighbors, the lack of communication ties to the larger society, and the unbridled power of local elites, the peasant may be dependent upon the local landlord for land, credit, subsistence, and protection. At the same time, the landlord wishes to obtain obedience, loyalty, information, superior service, gratitude, and deference from some of his peasants. A means of acquiring these goods and services on a relatively stable basis is to establish a patron-client dependency relationship.

The relationship is entered into and sustained because each actor values things which the other provides and which he cannot provide for himself. The exchange is usually not simultaneous; the relationship is understood to be an ongoing one in which the favor of one binds the other in obligation until a future situation provides the opportunity to reciprocate. In addition, the exchange typically involves many aspects of the lives of the actors; it is a multifunctional relationship in which the actors call upon each other for a wide variety of favors affecting all aspects of their lives. The linkage between exchange partners is frequently "institutionalized" through ritual coparenthood, godfathership, or *compadrazgo*.[8]

It is apparent that each actor is in a position to influence the behavior of the others. The patron obviously has great ability to elicit compliance from the client; no less important, however, is the ability of the subordinate to exert influence on the behavior of the superior because of his control over valued resources. The relative degree of dependence one actor has on the other may vary, and these imbalances are what determine the power relation between the actors. The more resources the superior controls which the subordinate needs, the greater will be his ability to elicit compliance. Conversely, the more valued and unique are the resources of the subordinate actor, the more power he will have. Generally, however, an imbalance in dependence benefits the patron, for he is by definition the superior partner in status and as such most often controls or has access to resources urgently needed by the client.

These general parameters of the concept were well established in early anthropological research. A conceptual advance was made when it was observed that in the local community, village authorities were often sought out as patrons because they had achieved and maintained extralocal ties. In the 1950s and 1960s, anthropologists contributed to a growing empirical literature which identified the role of the local authority as a personal intermediary or broker.[9] A broker does not directly command the resources relevant to an exchange but instead maintains a

8. See, for example, Boissevain (1966: 21), Campbell (1964: 217–224), Foster (1967c), Hollnsteiner (1967), Mintz and Wolf (1950), Pitt-Rivers (1954).
9. Anthropological perspectives on the personal broker are found in Betley (1971), Geertz (1960), Silverman (1967), Wolf (1965).

personal relationship both with an actor who does control the needed goods and services and with one who desires to acquire them.

The broker is of significant interest because of his role in linking the local community to the larger society. Brokers, it was discovered, "stand guard over the crucial junctures or synapses of relationships which connect the local system to the larger whole" (Wolf, 1965: 97). It has frequently been demonstrated that as central or regional governmental agencies control or effect more and more aspects of daily life, for example, the patron landlord will be used increasingly as an intermediary to represent local individuals or interests. The patron then becomes valuable to his clients to the degree to which he has contacts and patrons in the bureaucracy, political party, or military. He serves his clients as "a short cut through the maze of authority" in their dealings with regional or national authorities (Kenny, 1961: 135). The relationship of the broker to his superior is therefore crucial, for he must be able to gain some of the rewards desired by his dependents or they may seek an alternate patron.[10]

Similar triadic dependency interactions have been observed in low income urban neighborhoods where a local level boss mediates between community dwellers and urban or national authorities.[11] At this level of analysis, the individual patron-client bond is necessarily extended to the concept of a network of such relationships (see especially Powell, 1970). Where patrons function as intermediaries or brokers, it is worthy of note that each client is linked directly to the individual above him in a hierarchical system and has no direct linkage with individuals above his own superior. The conventional schematization of such networks is in the form of a pyramid, as shown in Figure 2.

The patron is limited in the number of clients under his influence due to his inability to interact personally and individually with large numbers of subordinates (Scott, 1972: 94–95). He is, however, able to enter into more of these relationships than the client because of his superior command over resources. This allows the patron to establish a personal following. Each subordinate is linked individually and vertically to the patron; most often he is not linked in any way with the other dependents of the same patron. In fact, the clients may actually be competing with each other for access to the resources controlled by the superior. Competition in vertical networks, except at the very top and very bottom, is two-directional; peers tend to compete with each other for the allegiance of followers while at the same time vying for the attention of those in directly superior positions.

10. See, for example, Boissevain (1974), Campbell (1964: 260–261), Silverman (1967), Singelmann (1974), Wolf (1965: 97–98).

11. Urban based brokers or intermediaries are analyzed in Cornelius (1975: Chap. 6), Lomnitz (1974), Ray (1969: Chap. 4).

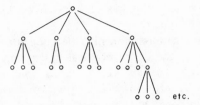

Figure 2. The Patron-Client Network.

A more recent advance in the use of the concept has been the demonstration that various kinds of political organizations, even those which
are nominally "democratic," may be pervaded by patron-client networks. Political parties, labor unions, and peasant syndicates may
demonstrate factionalism, personalism, and a lack of ideological commitment, all of which are indicators of the existence of patron-client
networks within an organization. Powell (1970, 1971), for example, has
described the rural organizational structure of the Acción Democrática
Party in Venezuela in terms of clientele linkages. Schmidt (1974) demonstrates that the Liberal and Conservative parties in Colombia have
persisted virtually unchallenged until recently because they are built
upon such networks. In Italy, the institutionalized factionalism of the
Christian Democratic party has been traced to similar mechanisms
(Zuckerman, 1971), while in China, ideological shifts of the regime have
been described as resulting from clientele relationships in the Communist
party (Nathan, 1973). Similarly, parties in Paraguay are shown to have
been formed and to have persisted on the basis of patron-client networks
(Hicks, 1971; see also Bailey, 1963; Landé, 1973).

These linkages existing within organizations have been of special
interest to political scientists because they imply that participation,
mobilization, and competition are channeled through and managed by
individual ties between leader and follower. Organizations integrated
through extensive patron-client networks present an alternative to
organizational alliances built on the shared recognition of class, eth-
nicity, religion, common interests, or commitment to ideology.[12] The
political consequences of clientele networks pervading political organizations have almost universally been described as factionalism, competition
between peers, vertical alliances maintained at the expense of horizontal
ones, lack of ideological or programmatic commitment, intense personalism, incomplete integration, and the fragmentation of demands on
government.[13] The political "payoffs" or exchanges which encourage

12. Patron-client linkages as an alternative to class and other alliances are discussed
in Landé (1973), Sandbrook (1972), Scott (1972), Zuckerman (1971). For an analysis of
clientelist linkages as a mechanism of class dominance, see Flynn (1974).

13. See Campbell (1964: 260–261), Graziano (1973), Ike (1972), Landé (1973), Leff
(1968: 126), Lemarchand and Legg (1972), Nathan (1973), Powell (1970), Scott (1972),
Tarrow (1967), Zuckerman (1971).

participation or mobilization in such a system are likely to be small scale, individualized, and material.

When patron-client relationships pervade most political organizations in a country, the entire political system may be described as a clientele system. Japan has been called a "patron-client democracy" (Ike, 1972); and Venezuelan society, politics, and policy making processes are described as being permeated by patron-clientelism (Blank, 1973). In Brazil, politicians act as brokers between the entire governmental apparatus and mass followings of clients, making demands upon the bureaucratic system for accommodations of general policy through individual decisions (Leff, 1968). Jaquette (1972) considers social and political relations in Peru to derive from clientelist patterns. A significant body of literature on corporatism also employs the patron-client model to explain political phenomena on a system-wide basis (see Pike and Stritch, 1974; Roett, 1972; Wiarda, 1974a). Given the extent and variety of environments in which patron-client networks have been observed, it is not surprising that they have been discovered in bureaucratic organizations also.[14]

Exchange Alliances in the Mexican Bureaucracy

> I would say that the trust between high level functionaries is extremely important in achieving intersectoral coordination and planning. . . . X, Y, and Z have a very close relationship. They all started their careers together, you know, and the fact that they have a certain amount of understanding among themselves is very important for how the organizations behave. Where no trust exists, on the other hand, there is little possibility for the organizations to work together. But, of course, you understand that trust can be created; it doesn't have to exist from a time prior to assuming a high level office.

> Now this team which has come in with this administration is special in that we are all very good friends and we almost all knew each other before we came here—some from as far back as ten years ago.

> The President's power to gain compliance with his policies from the various dependencies of the government resides in the very instru-

14. In the examples of patron-client linkages and networks considered above, the basic dyadic bond described always exists between identifiable individuals in face-to-face interaction. In some discussions of bureaucracy, however, clientelism has been considered to be a relationship between groups or institutions rather than between individuals. For instance, LaPalombara describes *parentela* and *clientela* as relationships between specific government agencies and political parties or organized pressure groups (1964; 262, 306; see also Carlos and Brokensha, 1972; Poitras, 1973; Poitras and Denton, 1971). Conventional usage has tended to apply this meaning to clientage when reference is made to bureaucracy. This kind of bureaucratic clientelism, however, is not an intended focus of this analysis. The conceptualization of patron-client linkages used here refers specifically to individuals interacting on a face-to-face and informal basis.

ments available to him through the political system. That is, they comply because of possibilities of upward political mobility within the system or because of fear of falling in political disfavor.

The networks and alliances which exist within Mexican public bureaucratic institutions differ in several ways from those described in most previous literature. First and perhaps most interestingly, the alliances to be described in the Mexican case study are intra-elite relationships. In the anthropological and political science investigations which have provided the conceptual framework of patron-client ties, the linkage itself is considered a mechanism which relates nonelites at the village level or nonelites in traditional or transitional environments to more modernized elites. When viewed as nonelite/elite linkages they are generally described as relationships which are consciously used by the modernized or modernizing sector to manipulate, mobilize, or control their less modern clients.[15] In the Mexican bureaucracy, however, vertical alliance networks are composed of highly sophisticated, urban, and educated individuals, many of whom are directly responsible for governmental policy making and implementation.

A second and equally important difference between the alliances in the public bureaucracy in Mexico and the patron-client relationships described by investigators in local communities is that bureaucratic networks are fundamentally organized to achieve or protect a particular goal: career advancement. In anthropological work, in contrast, the principal goals pursued by peasants, traditional villagers, and destitute city dwellers are protection and subsistence. In much political science research, the chief goal of clientele networks is considered to be the political power of the superior, achieved through the exchange of votes for material goods and services. For middle and high level bureaucrats, however, building a career is a long term investment which encourages superiors to offer resources such as access, authority, and budgetary support in exchange for performance, information, problem solving, discretion, and loyalty from their subordinates (see Greenfield, 1972; Leeds, 1965).

Another way in which the exchange networks in Mexican bureaucracy differ from those observed in other sociopolitical contexts is that they frequently coincide with and reinforce formal-legal hierarchical levels. In the village studies cited earlier, little formal-legal structure intervenes in the formation and maintenance of clientele bonds, social structure being by far more determinative of the resources to be exchanged. Similarities to the bureaucratic case, however, are found in examples of local level authorities who are sought out as potential patrons because of their office-related control over resources. Indeed,

15. Nonelite/elite bonds, frequently of an exploitive nature, are analyzed in Flynn (1974), Leff (1968), Pollock (1974), Powell (1970), Roett (1972), Scott (1972).

in the more extended form of clientelism discussed by political scientists, it has been demonstrated that loss of formal-legal status may mean a consequent loss of protectors and followers because of the withdrawal of office-related resources to exchange (Scott, 1972: 98).

The bureaucracy is an extreme example of a situation in which formal-legal structures delimit, often in detail, the resources which the superior or subordinate has to offer. It is important to note, however, that while formal-legal structures allocate institutional resources to certain positions, they often do not regulate their subsequent distribution. Thus, for example, a department chief may be granted the formal authority to hire and fire subordinates, but how he exercises this authority may not be regulated, and he is therefore provided with a resource which is useful to him to exchange for other resources such as loyalty, the provision of information, or on-the-job performance.

A related and final distinction is that alliance networks within the bureaucracy tend to concentrate power in the hands of a relatively few individuals at the top of the formal bureaucratic hierarchy. In anthropological studies, in contrast, the number of varied networks in the local community is limited only by the status differential of available actors, the control over resources to be distributed, and the quantity of resources available. Likewise, political scientists have tended to identify multiple and unrelated networks within the systems they have studied. In a bureaucratic organization, however, the pyramidal structure of control over resources is formalized and preexisting; moreover, the formal-legal organization of the entity means that authority is exercised from the top and channeled through hierarchical levels of command. Competing alliances and networks within bureaucratic units may in fact exist, but they tend to be constrained by chains of formal authority and responsibility.

Explanations of Patron-Client Networks

What causes patron-client exchange relationships to develop and persist? In the literature, several different answers to this question can be distinguished.[16] Some scholars, for example, have cited cultural phenomena as impetus to the emergence of patron-client linkages within the society. In brief, culturally determined values or behavioral expectations, often linked to religious belief, personalism or paternalism, lead to the formation and continued vitality of patron-client linkages.[17] In Mexico,

16. Various perspectives in the literature as to why patron-client relationships develop, persist, and change are not mutually exclusive, and, indeed, some commentators rely upon the convergence of multiple causal factors to explain the relationships (see, for example, Boissevain, 1966: 30–31).

17. Cultural perspectives on clientele bonds are found in Boissevain (1965), Kenny (1961: 135–136), Scott (1974).

for example, one observer has noted a fundamental cultural orientation toward personalism which has led to the emergence of such relationships.

> This dependency relationship among individuals is basic to Mexican politics. It means that most Mexicans tend to be submissive to authority and so insecure personally that they seek a reciprocal submissive-dominant relationship with some other person. One consequence of this sense of dependency . . . is the *patrón*-client relationship. Another consequence is that most Mexicans do not relate easily to abstract or impersonal organizations but only to the individual who leads the movement (Scott, 1974: 381).

An exclusive reliance on culture to explain clientelism, however, has proved inadequate for many scholars. Forms of clientele bonds, it has been pointed out, are found in nearly all societies, in widely different cultural milieus, from those in Southeast Asia and the Middle East to modern university settings in the United States. A general cultural explanation, moreover, does not easily explain instances within the same society in which the linkages are not operative. A more specific political culture explanation would deal with variation among different sectors of the society by categorizing individuals as "parochials," "subjects," and "participants," suggesting that patron-client ties are more often encountered among parochials and subjects than among participants or are manipulated by participants in the control of other subcultures (see Scott, 1974). Unfortunately, this analysis does not explain why the relationships permeate elite levels of the political system in Mexico, linking participant to participant.

Other scholars have used a developmental perspective related to tradition, transition, and modernity, as a point of departure for understanding the conditions giving rise to patron-client linkages.[18] Stressed in this explanation is the gradual emergence through historical phases or stages of national integration of formal, impersonal mechanisms which ensure individual and kin security.[19] Central to this explanation is the expectation of the eventual disappearance of clientelism as societies become increasingly modern.

This perspective is particularly inadequate to explain exchange relationships in the Mexican bureaucracy. The bureaucrats in question are all part of a highly modern elite group. They are university educated

18. Levels of political and social development are used as explanatory variables in Lemarchand and Legg (1972: 154), Scott (1969), Silverman (1967: 289), Stuart (1972: 39–40), Tarrow (1967: 74).

19. One aspect of the development or evolution of patron-client relationships which has been documented is that as national penetration or integration has proceeded and as central organizations have become more complex, single all-purpose patron-client pyramids are increasingly replaced by multiple and specialized networks (Heath, 1972; Powell, 1970).

and generally from urban and industrial areas of the country. They are often widely traveled and have been exposed to a broad range of experiences and opportunities. The organizations they belong to may be formally constructed according to rational, hierarchical principles. Moreover, the primary purpose of the networks bureaucrats participate in is not to mobilize or manipulate more traditional or transitional social classes. Nor is it apparent that these alliance structures are gradually disappearing in Mexican public life; they continue to be actively sought out in the accomplishment of a wide variety of tasks in highly modern contexts.

A third perspective is that patron-client linkages are brought into existence by a basic environmental condition of resource scarcity. This is perhaps the explanation most often favored by anthropologists who have been impressed by the precarious nature of existence in many peasant communities.[20] Foster, for example, explains patronage linkages as a means to ensure a minimal amount of resource availability in an environment in which nature is capricious and human relationships are treacherous. The "image of the limited good" is based upon the perception that goods and services are available in limited quantity; equal distribution of them would leave all with insufficient amounts. As all individuals are equally in need of the limited resources, this "zero-sum" or "constant pie" perception of the world means that anything gained by another necessarily diminishes one's own share (Foster, 1967b; Scott, 1972: 102). Patron-client linkages provide a relatively efficient means for acquiring access to the limited goods necessary for survival. It follows from the zero-sum nature of social, political, and economic resource distribution that each individual will attempt to protect the resources he already has and will not openly engage in competition beyond that needed to acquire a minimally acceptable quantity of desired goods and services. In the peasant community, therefore, a static and fiercely protective overall distribution of resources results, and risk is actively avoided (Foster, 1967b; see Erasmus, 1968; Strickon and Greenfield, 1972: 11–12).

This environmental explanation, especially as it stresses structural conditions, is perhaps most appropriate in the Mexican case. Insecurity is, in fact, an objective condition of life within the bureaucracy. The actors involved in the linkages are often subject to great risk in the pursuit of their careers and their job related functions; the wrong move might easily mean at least temporary loss of influence, prestige, and economic reward. In contrast to low status groups, however, middle

20. Wolf identifies patron-client linkages as a viable coping mechanism in environments in which "the formal institutional structure of society is weak and unable to deliver a sufficiently steady supply of goods and services, especially to the terminal levels of the social order" (1966: 17–18; see also Boissevain, 1966: 30; Kaufman, 1974: 286).

and upper level bureaucrats are very aware of their elite status and of the education and social background characteristics which open up a wide range of alternatives for them should their positions in the bureaucracy be threatened. Therefore, they may be more likely to take risks than individuals whose very survival may be endangered by a change in the status quo. Moreover, the involvement in vertical exchange alliances does not rest fundamentally upon a perception of a zero-sum environment. Rather, goods and services are required for the active pursuit of a goal which has little to do with maximizing a static sense of security.

In the bureaucracy, informal exchange networks develop because there are few structures which adequately regulate the allocation of goods and services on an impersonal basis. Under these conditions, enduring alliances are an efficient and effective means of ensuring the steady and regular flow of resources needed for the achievement of specific goals. This is not meant to imply that in the Mexican case, historical or cultural variables are not important in engendering or supporting clientele networks. A variety of factors may well be important in encouraging the development of the linkages. However, the most decisive reason why bureaucrats, and indeed peasants, urban squatters, and businessmen in Mexico seek to establish and maintain these relationships is that conditions make such strategies both rational and efficient. Under some environmental conditions, individual actors cannot, or perceive they cannot, demand as formal and impersonal rights what is necessary to them to achieve their goals. Consequently, they must arrange informal exchange relationships which assure them of the availability of the needed resources. Such a situation may be found in organizations considered to be highly modern or in much more traditional settings.

It is interesting to note that conditions may be consciously designed within a political system which encourage personal and informal exchange relationships. A recent study contrasting government-business relationships between the United States and Mexico points out that the Mexican government has preferred to regulate business through direct and disaggregated methods such as individually assigned quotas and licenses. This encourages the businessman to develop an informal exchange relationship with a government bureaucrat in order to achieve his individual needs such as an import quota, a license, or a tax exemption. Such a strategy is a rational means for him to pursue his interests. In contrast, the United States businessman participates in a legal and policy framework which more impersonally regulates resource distribution through tariffs, taxes, and the availability of money and credit and encourages the development of interest associations to pressure government (Purcell and Purcell, 1976). In this context, then, the businessman

has no long term need to seek out special personal relationships with
bureaucratic officials.

Similarly, where governments fail to establish or pursue explicit
policies or plans for the allocation of resources, citizen demands on the
bureaucratic apparatus for goods and services may be pursued through
personal exchange relationships. These may enable individuals to
achieve solution to their problems more rapidly and effectively than
if they were to press their claims through class or interest group activity
(see Cornelius, 1974, 1975). In an organization in which salaries are
strictly regulated through formal procedures of seniority and union
bargaining, informal alliances are less likely to be encouraged than where
personal relationships significantly influence raises, promotions, and
hiring practices.

In the Mexican bureaucracy, informal exchange networks develop
because they are perceived to be, and are in fact, an efficient and effective
means of goal attainment. They are sought out, in short, as a calculated
and rational response to a structural environment which severely limits
access to career mobility by other means. In Mexico, exchange relationships bind public officials from various institutions together for the
pursuit of policy goals; they serve to connect individuals within one
agency for defense against the functional encroachments of another;
they tie the bureaucratic elite to the political chiefs and make possible
intragovernmental problem solving; and the manner in which they link
the nationally oriented regional elite to the bureaucratic center is useful
in understanding problems of policy implementation. Environmental
conditions which structure the career mobility system are therefore of
fundamental importance in explaining the behavior of bureaucratic
officials in both policy formulation and policy implementation roles.
The following chapter describes these conditions.

3

The *Sexenio* and Public Careers in Mexico

The *Sexenio* and Mobility in Mexico

As you know, we have an institution called the *sexenio* when everything changes.

And we're here now for six years. You know how we all come in and get thrown out at the *sexenio*.

The Mexican system offers great opportunities for individual advancement, mobility. Anyone can advance himself through this system. I began by selling newspapers in the streets and worked my way up to be a director in three government companies. Then I lost out and was reduced to being a mere department chief . . . then a subdirector and now I have risen to being a director again. There is what you might call a great deal of capillary action in Mexico.

I expect that our program, too, will disappear in two more years, at the change of *sexenio*.

Political time in Mexico is measured by the six-year incumbencies of successive presidents. Each change of administration is marked by a massive turnover of personnel within the government at the national and state levels, echoed at the municipal level every three years.[1] The turnover is complete among occupants of elective positions who, like the President, cannot succeed themselves. Party officials also abandon their previous responsibilities, some to be appointed to bureaucratic positions and others to assume elected posts while many take up other functions in the party. Bureaucrats in turn are initiated into new appointed or elective offices. Cabinet members and heads of government agencies, commissions, trusts, and industries are appointed by the incumbent President; they are permitted a free hand in selecting their own subordinate nonunionized employees, subject only to the political suggestions of the President and the party.

The magnitude of the periodic personnel disruption was indicated by Brandenburg a decade ago.

1. Elections for state governors do not always coincide with presidential elections or with one another.

41

From the presidential office down to municipal government organs, from giant state industries to small regulatory agencies, from the official party to captive opposition parties, every six-year administration witnesses a turnover of approximately 18,000 elective offices and 25,000 appointive posts[2] (1964: 157).

Much of the turnover in political and bureaucratic offices occurs through interpositional change as when a senator takes up a bureaucratic position or when an administrator moves from a job in a federal agency to one in a regular ministry of state. In this respect, the six-year procession often resembles a national game of musical chairs in which the same actors may reappear in different positions; new players are freely admitted, however, and the number of chairs may be enlarged to accommodate some of them. Those who fail to find a chair and must leave the game do so knowing they have the possibility of reentering it at a later date.

Many of the positions which become available at the *sexenio* are poorly remunerated, particularly low level elective offices and the appointive jobs found in the party; frequently they are only part time posts.[3] These and other positions, however, are widely aspired to and actively sought. This is so in part because of limited employment possibilities in the private sector. In rural regions agriculture has been decreasingly rewarding since the 1940s while in urban areas natural population growth and migration have far exceeded the capacity of industrial and commercial enterprises to provide employment. In addition, occupying any public position, even at a low level, offers the possibility of making contacts which can be manipulated for advancement to more important and remunerative positions. Jobs within the public administration are particularly attractive because salaries are generally good—often competitive with the private sector—and a bureaucreatic position carries with it more prestige than does a strictly political post. As a government employee, the bureaucrat also enjoys innumerable official fringe benefits such as access to low cost housing; free medical care and drugs; subsidized food, vacations, and clothing; periodic pay bonuses which fluctuate between four and a half and five and a half months pay annually; free child care; and a forty-hour work week.

2. The impact of the personnel change in the bureaucracy is greater than actual numbers would suggest, however, because *all* upper middle, and top level officials (e.g., all those in decision making capacity) are replaced. Turnover always affects administrators to the level of office chief and generally extends further down the hierarchy through group leaders and supervisors. It is particularly marked among those who hold staff rather than line positions. For data on public careers in Mexico, see Camp (1974, 1975), Cochrane (1967), Conklin (1973), Gruber (1971), Smith (1974).

3. Party positions, while not legally recognized as public employment, can be considered so for the purpose of career analysis. The dominant party, the PRI, is largely supported by public funds, and official public personages such as the President, the governors, municipal presidents, congressional figures, and cabinet chiefs determine the selection of party office holders.

Within the administrative apparatus, it is the "confidence" or white collar workers who are the most subject to appointment and dismissal when each new administration takes office.[4] Lower level bureaucrats generally have job security protected by union contracts and law, largely insulating them from removal when the administration changes hands. The vast majority of the open bureaucratic positions are therefore at middle and high levels and are posts which often pay handsome salaries, provide generous fringe benefits, and may bring the bureaucrat into contact with the top political elite in Mexico. Moreover, for high level officials and many upward-aspiring middle level administrators, government employment is important as a means to acquire power, influence over policy making, or contacts which can be used for personal economic benefit. Because the government plays such a central role in the society and economy, its leading public administrators are correspondingly influential in determining the course of much of the nation's life. In addition, young, middle level officials are given the opportunity to help seek solutions to pressing national problems. This was particularly true during the Echeverría administration, and the influence of a new generation of public officials is likely to continue to be important under his successor, López Portillo. Positions within the government may also lead to contacts with politicians and individuals in the private sector who can offer important economic rewards. It is not unusual for high and middle level bureaucrats to be involved in outside business ventures, for example. Finally, undoubtedly for some, public employment offers opportunities for feathering one's nest, through semilegal and illegal uses of information and authority.[5]

4. Employees in Mexican public administrative organizations are divided into two categories, base and confidence (trust) workers. Base workers may unionize and are somewhat protected from arbitrary dismissal or chastisement. Maintenance and service personnel are base workers, as are employees such as mailmen, messengers, semiskilled workers, and clerks. Confidence personnel are directly dependent upon their hierarchical superiors for continued employment although their salaries are now generally set by statute or regulation. A chief who wishes to dismiss a confidence worker simply informs him "you have lost my confidence," and, after receiving indemnification, the employee must seek another job. At the change of administration, many confidence workers follow their chiefs to new appointments.

5. See Brandenburg (1964: 160–162), Castellanos *et al.* (1969), Saldaña Harlow (1974: 73–78, 85–86), *New York Times* (June 29, 1976: 2), Wilkie (1967: 8–9). Frequent job rotation perhaps inevitably means that many individuals in public office in Mexico will view the opportunities provided by their present positions as insurance against future unemployment. The individual bureaucrat or politician, through his discretion as mediator or rule applicator, is able to use the rewards at his disposal to increase his wealth and to assert power over the supplicants who come to him for services. Short tenure means that the bureaucrat or politician can move on to another position or out of public life altogether before his venality is exposed, or if irregularities come to light, he can always accuse his predecessors of misconduct (Ugalde, 1970: 98). In many cases, the rewards of office are consciously used to expand or fortify the circle of influential contacts available to the bureaucrat or the politician (see Saldaña Harlow,1974: 73–78).

Popular commentary on venality in public office in Mexico is almost mythical in extent and is the most frequent charge hurled against the government by individuals in

Given that public employment is attractive and sought after, what does the high turnover of official positions mean for government in Mexico? It means, above all, that political mobility is high. Aspirants to public office have a multitude of opportunities available to them at regular intervals at all levels of government. While high level positions are preponderantly available only to those advantaged individuals who are males from urban areas with the economic and social backing necessary to obtain a university education, at lower levels of government, selection criteria for official posts are much less stringent. At the municipal level, for example, Ugalde offers this description of the individuals who take up bureaucratic tasks.

A large percentage of the municipal jobs is distributed every three years by the newly elected Municipal Council. These employees can hardly be considered civil servants. . . . They are recruited mostly from the lower socioeconomic groups and are laborers and peasants. . . . These temporary bureaucrats have no training for the white collar or administrative occupations given them at City Hall, and their performance is very low (1970: 88).

In the national bureaucracy and in the PRI and elective offices, there are numerous jobs at middle and lower levels for individuals who do not possess the social characteristics of the top elite. Many of the middle level positions requiring specialized training are distributed to young university graduates who have the opportunity to move upward in future *sexenios*. Moreover, important for the process of government in Mexico is the public perception that high mobility exists. The counterparts of the American adages "from rags to riches" and "from a log cabin to the White House" clearly encourage many Mexican youths to consider that they too can make it in the system. Indeed, even among low income urban dwellers, those whom journalists and academics in the past have described as the hopeless, anomic, or revolution-prone inhabitants of squatter settlements, the vast majority in Mexico are confident of mobility opportunities for themselves and/or for their children in the future (Cornelius, 1975: 230). Some of this optimism is due to the ability of the government apparatus to absorb aspiring job seekers (see Hansen, 1971: 178–179).

A number of consequences of the high level and high perception of mobility within the political system are of fundamental importance for understanding the impressive regime stability Mexico has enjoyed since

---

the private sector who resent the intervention of the state in free enterprise. A story is told of a municipal president who spent the major portion of the municipal (county) budget for luxuriously refurbishing the town jail, rather than fixing up the local school as many good citizens thought he ought. When finally approached by a group of inhabitants wanting to know why the funds were not being spent on the school, the municipal president replied that he didn't imagine he'd ever be going back to school.

the 1940s. First, movement within the political system is based upon *individual* mobility. Those who aspire to political influence do so through competition for successively more important political or administrative positions. Within the party apparatus and within the bureaucracy, politics consists of jockeying for a favorable position and building hypothetical futures on calculated guesses about the selection of the next, as yet undisclosed, candidate for President. Because the outcome will likely determine the individual's position, his rank, income, and influence and because the rewards of office are distributed through appointment rather than election, there is little incentive for group cohesion or collaboration in pursuing common political goals. Moreover, competition for positions takes place within the confines of the dominant party and the government bureaucracy.[6] As a result, there is little public debate around which collective political pressure can coalesce. Finally, those who are "losers" when positions are distributed know that a new *sexenio* will provide them with another opportunity.[7] The search for political mobility is, above all, personal and publicly disclaimed, and it is the individual who is rewarded for his activity and patience (Hansen, 1971: 200–202).

Second, political stability is enhanced by the opportunity which exists for the systematic cooptation of dissidents. The Mexican regime is sophisticated in its use of cooptive mechanisms such as the timely distribution of government jobs in order to ameliorate potential or actual opposition.[8] If in a rare case leadership cannot be coopted, the rewards and sanctions which are available to the government make coopting and dispersing the followership an easy task. So successfully does the regime control the resources of political and economic life that open political dissidence is in fact rarely encountered (see Fagen and Tuohy, 1972). Where opposition does develop, the distribution of public office in addition to repressive measures and some substantive policy changes are used to thwart confrontations (see especially Stevens, 1974). Indeed, the current government of Luís Echeverría has, as a deliberate policy, provided middle and high level positions to young professionals and intellectuals who were disaffected by the rightist policies and political repression of the administration of Díaz Ordaz (1964–1970). Through the manipulation of available positions and other resources, the regime has, in the past thirty-five years, successfully discouraged the formation of large scale, cohesive opposition movements.[9]

6. The selection of official candidates and the competition surrounding this practice is discussed in Brandenburg (1964), Camp (1974), and Hansen (1971).

7. See Brandenburg (1964: 159), Johnson (1971: 77–80), Smith (1974: 27–29).

8. See, for example, Adie (1970), Anderson and Cockroft (1966), Hansen (1971: Chap. 7), Johnson (1971: 80–84), Reyna (1974), Tuohy (1973).

9. An example of the regime's ability to use the rewards of office and public resources, as well as its repressive capabilities, to ameliorate threats to its continued elite-dominated

A further underpinning of political stability is the contribution of high turnover to the maintenance of diffuse regime support among the population.[10] Few members of the middle class, for example, have not held a political or governmental office at one time in their lives or else have not had a relative or *compadre* involved. Moreover, many may have the opportunity to participate in the government in the future. For ambitious individuals among the lower socioeconomic groups, the same possibility also exists. In the federal bureaucracy alone, a recent administrative census indicated that over 900,000 individuals are employed by the government (*Excelsior,* April 2, 1975).[11] One of the costs exacted by the political elite for office holding is explicit and public loyalty and support for the regime, even if privately not deeply felt. In the nineteenth century in the United States and Great Britain and currently in countries such as Colombia and Venezuela, the distribution of public office is dependent upon which of the competing political parties is triumphant in elections. Loyalty is therefore directed primarily to the party rather than to the regime. In Mexico, however, identification with the dominant party is synonymous with commitment to the government. The large pool of actual or potential beneficiaries of public office helps substantially to maintain support for the political system and its goals.

Another consequence of rotation in office is the intertwining of political (party and elective) positions and bureaucratic posts. As noted earlier, with the turnover of public office every three and six years, political personnel move into administrative positions, and bureaucrats assume "elected" positions within the party or the government. In addition, public functionaries may hold an administrative sinecure at

---

rule, is the history of the cci (*Central Campesina Independiente*) in the early 1960s. This peasant organization, led by former PRI members, began to demand that the government revise its agricultural policies and fulfill its promises to the peasants. The movement, functioning outside the official peasant sector of the PRI, grew in strength in the first years of the 1960s, particularly in the northwestern sections of the country. Three tactics were followed by the political regime in controlling this threat. First, the leaders of the movement were encouraged to see the advantages of collaboration with the PRI when their attempts to run for public office in 1964 were thwarted. Second, when cci members demonstrated to publicize their demands, repression was swift and harsh. Third, the regime acted to alleviate some of the peasants' grievances. These tactics made reconciliation with the PRI an attractive possibility. A wing of the cci which did not welcome collaboration with the party was repressed and its leadership imprisoned. Currently, the cci holds the position of an officially sanctioned "dissident" group within the dominant party (see Adie, 1970; Anderson and Cockcroft, 1966, for details).

10. For survey data on attitudes of the Mexican population toward the political regime, see Almond and Verba (1963), Cornelius (1975), Davis and Coleman (1974), Fagen and Tuohy (1972), Kahl (1968).

11. The 1970 census, however, categorizes only 406,607 individuals employed in government in 1969. This figure excludes almost 370,000 teachers and doctors and employees of state industries. Scott (1974: 372) states, "In all, including government bureaucrats and school teachers, the number of people on one or another government payroll totals over 1,150,000, nearly 9 percent of all economically active Mexicans."

the same time that they are actively engaged in technically nonremunerative party work. Many of the top level bureaucrats are publicly recognized as the spokesmen for influential sectors of the party. At all levels of public administration, but particularly at high ones, political criteria are considered in recruitment. As a result, few bureaucrats are insensitive to, or lack understanding of, the party apparatus, and few party politicians are unable to visualize themselves occupying some important administrative post in the future. This engenders a high degree of at least public cohesion among elite actors who control access, participation, and policy making.[12] There is not, then, a gap between a political and an administrative elite as has been observed in Third World countries where a professionalized civil service was consciously created by colonial powers.[13] Nor is there a meaningful distinction among office holders at municipal, state, and federal levels as there was under the spoils system in the United States where independent machines controlled patronage at each level. In Mexico, there is considerable mobility from one level to another, indicative of a high degree of elite interaction.

The party and the administrative organs of the Mexican government are in fact used to somewhat distinct ends. The party is principally a mechanism for support building, electoral mobilization, political communication, and control which is manipulated by the political elite to maintain its ascendance.[14] To the extent that the party represents the interests of its membership, it often does so as a broker, pressing individual grievances on the appropriate bureaucratic agency (see, for example, Cornelius, 1974; Ugalde, 1970: 148). While the administrative apparatus of the government is also involved in support building and mobilization, its primary function is in policy formulation and implementation and the processing of claims made upon the government (see Purcell, 1973; Tuohy, 1973). In spite of this division of labor, the important point is that individuals who occupy or aspire to governmental or political positions and influence make their ascent through the party and through the administrative apparatus, often interchangeably. Indeed, the government and the party are generally perceived as a single structure in terms of the pursuit of regime goals and the public pronouncements of elite actors.

This is not meant to imply that conflict does not occur in the Mexican political system.[15] Within the party, for example, differences of interests

12. The public stance of brotherhood and continuity in the pursuit of regime goals among political and administrative actors is so impressive that Brandenburg (1964) christened the top political elite a "Revolutionary Family"; Hansen (1971) refers to it as a "Revolutionary Coalition."

13. See, for example, Berger (1957), Heeger (1973), Pye (1962), Riggs (1964).

14. For more extensive discussions of the nature of the PRI, see Anderson and Cockroft (1966), Brandenburg (1964), Hansen (1971: Chap. 5), Needleman and Needleman (1969), Padgett (1966).

15. Reyna (1974) and Stevens (1974) are two recent studies dealing extensively with the topics of conflict, cooptation, and repression in Mexico.

do exist between the constituent groups of peasants, workers, and middle class syndicates, differences which have been accentuated as inflation has threatened the economic position of the sectors in recent years. State governors have been known to impede the progress of national programs supported by the President if these are detrimental to their interests. At high levels, conflicts are often the result of covert and competing factions within the party or administration, usually resulting from attempts to influence the presidential succession; the incidence of such events increases during each *sexenio* as the moment for unveiling the new candidate approaches. Moreover, guerrillas have operated in the hills of the state of Guerrero, and groups of university and preparatory school students continue to meet to discuss opposition tactics and to paint epithets about the government on fences and the walls of buildings. Occasionally, their activities break the surface of official calm; the student strikes and resultant repressions of 1968 and 1971 and the national attention focused on the hunt for guerrilla leader Lucio Cabañas in Guerrero are cases in point. In addition, the business sector, especially that part which is known as the Monterrey Group, is hostile to the current regime and has been implicated in acts of civil violence. Other attacks on the regime have been traced to urban guerrilla groups.

What is significant, however, is the degree to which these conflicts are resolved, or at least kept below the boiling point, within the government and party apparatus. In part, it is the opportunity structure of the Mexican regime which keeps conflict and competition from escalating into threats to the regime itself. The consequences of the system of open opportunity within the regime have been summarized by one observer.

> Whether under Díaz or under the regime of the PRI, loyalties have been given to individuals, not ideas; and they have been given on the clear understanding that the reward for loyalty is personal advancement. What actually holds the present regime together is not a set of uncoordinated policies that pleases all sectors and paralyzes the government, but rather a system of mobility that attracts the personal allegiance of spokesmen for all the PRI sectors from the bottom to the top of the party hierarchy. And the strength which that structure of personal loyalties has given the Revolutionary Coalition has allowed it . . . to suppress discontent and opposition in some instance and disregard them in others (Hansen, 1971: 220).

Building a Career in Mexico

> One thing you Americans don't understand, I think, is the need in Mexico to be involved in two or three things at once. For example, what if the general director should get "sick" and have to leave CONA-SUPO? I have to think of that eventuality and be prepared for it.

If someone has a chief who is capable and has the prospects for a good future, then that person will probably think, "Perhaps I can go with him at the *sexenio*"; and it happens in reverse, too, if someone has a chief who is not particularly capable but who has influential friends, some will want to follow him. There are a lot of changes and it affects our program, especially when people stop working to pursue their futures.

No one has a political future in this country. There is no such thing as a political career here. Someone can be strong and have lots of power and the next day he's out in the street; they sack him.

The risk comes when everyone is trying to guess who the next choice for President will be and trying to attach himself to that person. This is when there are lots of divisions and factions in the government.

The organization of public life in Mexico has observable consequences for the performance of individuals who seek to achieve or maintain a political or bureaucratic position. Every middle and upper level bureaucrat knows that chances are very good that he will not continue in his present position after the next national elections; politicians are certain of their impending unemployment. Thus, an ever-present concern for the individual involved in government is to ensure that he has access to other employment opportunities after the change of administrations. For many, this means keeping a hand in activity in the private sector, perhaps in a family business. For most, however, attempts to plan for the future involve seeking alternative prospects in the public sector. Because all bureaucratic positions which become available depend upon personal appointments, usually made by high level administrators in each ministry or agency, and because elective positions are carefully doled out by appointment as official candidates in the PRI, future employment possibilities depend upon the cultivation of personal and political ties to individuals who *might* be influential in the future.

While many bureaucrats have scarce skills, knowledge, and training which make them valuable to the government and thus almost assure them of a position somewhere within the public sector, individuals who hope to *improve* their income and status must make contacts and alliances with individuals perceived to be more influential than themselves. In the PRI, similarly, the methods by which the party councils determine the appointment of the candidates (who are virtually assured of winning), places a premium on the establishment and timely mobilization of personal contacts, friendships, and coalitions (see Brandenberg, 1964: Chap. 6; Hansen, 1971: 200–202). The ambitious and the insecure in both politics and bureaucracy, therefore, tend to seek personal vertical attachments, for it is on individuals, not policy, ideology, or party loyalty, that their futures depend.

In contrast to the distribution of public office under the spoils system in the United States, in Mexico the criterion for an official position is not one's ability to "get out the vote" (see Hoogenboom, 1961). Rather, the promise of personal loyalty is the most important qualification an individual can provide a potential employer. As demonstrated by the classification of many bureaucratic positions as confidence jobs, the ability to trust one's subordinates is extremely important in Mexico. If the superior in a bureaucratic position feels that he is intimately acquainted with those who work for him and if he has confidence in their motivations, he can be more certain that the directives he gives will be faithfully executed and the information he needs will be conscientiously provided. Moreover, the personal loyalty of subordinates ensures that official business will be accomplished discretely, with a minimum of public disturbance which might endanger the position of the superior with his own chief. Similarly, active and public obedience is an important qualification for an official position. This often manifests itself in the failure or reluctance to question and criticize superiors or sponsors, but it also means being continually "on call" to the chief, even if he works twelve or fifteen hours a day.

Some have noted that the demonstration of personal loyalty and obedience results in conservatism and a lack of initiative. The bureaucrat, for example,

> serves his jefe and contributes to the latter's career not only in personalistic and private ways, but also by not letting potentially embarrassing political situations get out of hand. . . . He is rewarded not for his innovativeness, initiative, or positive accomplishments in the making or implementing of public policy, but rather for his capacity to facilitate the functioning of the apparatus through the balancing of interests, the distribution of benefits, and the control of potentially disruptive and disequilibrating forces. . . . Conformity and conservatism are the inevitable consequences (Fagen and Tuohy, 1972: 27; see also Greenberg, 1970: 115–118).

Loyalty and obedience do indeed contribute to great centralization of decision making, reluctance to delegate responsibility, and attempts to avoid public disturbances, all of which are important ingredients of bureaucratic rigidity and sloth.

However, it is wrong to assume that there is little pressure on the individual to perform satisfactorily the responsibilities assigned to him. Active and effective job performance is often the third type of behavior which the bureaucrat or politician in Mexico offers his chief in the expectation of future mobility. Within the bureaucracy, there is frequently great pressure on confidence workers to achieve the performance goals of successively higher levels of chiefs, ultimately determined by the President and his close advisors. Most middle and high level officials will be found in their offices, long after the work day has officially ended, concentrating on the tasks they have been assigned. The administration of Luís Echeverría placed great emphasis on the solution of a number of major national problems such as inflation, external economic dependence, and politically threatening maldistribution of wealth and even identified the regime's survival with the handling of these issues. Consequently, there was considerable pressure on bureaucratic chiefs, and therefore on their subordinates, to seek meaningful and long range solutions and to make use of what decision making power was dispersed to achieve resolution of problems. Successful job performance, implying expertise, innovativeness, and efficiency, does indeed play an important part in ensuring one of a brighter future within the government.

Obedience, loyalty, and job performance in the pursuit of career mobility tie individuals into extended vertical coalitions and pyramidal alliance structures within the government. Such networks are not entirely stable or durable, however. The individual's future may depend not upon cashing in on the obligations of a single influential person but on the ability to call upon a wide range of contacts and alliances, "on having a variety of contingency plans should the sponsors fall from favor" (Fagen and Tuohy, 1972: 25). This was explained more fully by one informant, a *técnico* working for CONASUPO.

> Well, of course, one would like to stay working with Y and Z if they end up doing something really useful and innovative in the next administration—something not bureaucratized and which would allow one to go on developing one's own potential. But if that doesn't work out, it's necessary to keep open certain contacts with other people and other organizations just in case.

Because of the wide variety of jobs available, the involvement in vertical alliance structures, and the fact that alliances are open and shifting, a career in Mexico is far more than simply filling a succession of jobs. Also, career patterns are widely variable and dependent on a range of circumstances and conditions. Statistical analysis of the career patterns of high level officials in Mexico led one scholar to conclude:

> In general, however, the possession of one office does very little to determine what the next office will be. . . . from almost any location in the political system, one could reasonably hope to move to almost any other location (Smith, 1974: 18, 23).

The public career in Mexico is therefore highly varied and frought with uncertainty. Once an individual has entered public life at the national level, there are a diversity of means by which he may achieve membership in the top political elite. Arrival depends upon the aggregate of resources and alliances he controls or has access to. Certain prerequisites to a successful career in the governmental apparatus can be identified, however. Especially for those who aspire to middle and top level bureaucratic positions, it is virtually essential in present-day Mexico to have a university education (Smith, 1974: 27–28). This is not only important to gain a prestigious professional title (*licenciado, ingeniero, arquitecto, doctor*) but also to make the initial connections which will be used later to obtain employment. Those who have graduated from UNAM (the National Autonomous University of Mexico) have a greater chance for mobility within the government than those from less prestigious institutions (see Camp, 1974). Graduate degrees are also increasingly important, and those who have acquired one from a famous foreign or a prestigious national university have a significant advantage in seeking middle and high level appointments. A university education in Mexico today is a public symbol of middle or upper class social background and an indication that one is qualified intellectually for high government appointment.

An important prerequisite for high level appointments is party activity. One need not necessarily have held or have run for elective office, nor is constant activity on behalf of the PRI important. Rather, it is necessary sooner or later to be identified with the party as a symbol of one's public commitment to the masses and to the ideals of the Revolution. Individuals who have spent their entire careers in the public bureaucracy will also have collaborated with party activists in their spare time, engaging in such activities as running campaigns for PRI candidates, organizing youth affiliates, or sitting on committees to offer special "technical" advice. This does not mean putting oneself at the disposal of the party or its leadership. Instead, party activity has become more of a tool to be manipulated for personal advantage than activity which will lead to the achievement of party or party sector goals. Middle level administrators who have specialized training need not always be members of the party unless they wish to achieve entrance into the upper levels of the administration. Party membership and activity are best understood as means to broaden the circle of one's contacts and to acquire the necessary marks of a qualified candidate for high office.

Another qualification for movement into the upper ranges of the government is familiarity with politics and political personages in the national capital. An informant explained the relative advantages of working in Mexico City.

> Surely there exist fewer opportunities in the field than in the capital for someone who wants to move upward in the bureaucracy. It's

necessary to be in the capital to foment the kind of personal relations
necessary to get ahead and to keep an eye out for openings.

In the capital, of course, competition is greater. "It's a bloody battle,
a constant fight of one against the other to get ahead," commented
another respondent. Most upwardly mobile careerists spend some time
in the provinces, however, either in elective or bureaucratic posts, and
many maintain strong ties to state level political factions and machines.
But provincial appointments, to be helpful in a career, should ideally
be infrequent and preceded and followed by assignments in the capital
city. Otherwise, a field position may be a form of political exile or an
indication that one has been "burned" at the national level (see Greenberg, 1970). Even when posted away from the capital, bureaucrats and
politicians may spend a large portion of their official time in Mexico
City (see Ugalde, 1970).

Some indication of how a career is managed can be obtained from a
brief summary of anthropologist Anthony Leeds' work on Brazil. In that
country, Leeds discovered in the informal, nonwritten discourse of daily
life a lexicon which is used to describe career advancement. The career
begins with a *trampolim* which launches the aspiring individual; this
springboard can be found in such activities as involvement in student
politics, journalism, opposition movements, sports, politics, or an
opportune marriage, or by soliciting help from family, godparents, and
influential acquaintances (1965: 387). These various activities are not
sought as ends in themselves, nor as ultimate careers. Rather, for the
Brazilian careerist, they are engaged in for the purpose of establishing
a name for oneself (*nome*) and projecting the image that one is on the
way up. It is important, after acquiring an initial *trampolim*, to seek out
and accept a series of jobs, each of which can be used to make new
contacts and form new alliances. Several activities may be pursued
simultaneously; a number of full time jobs may even be held at the same
time, a practice reflected in the Brazilian term *cabide de emprego*, or
coathanger of jobs (1965: 382–383; see also Greenfield, 1972).

Once a career is launched, according to Leeds, the Brazilian careerist
must constantly emit information about himself and be aware of the
cues others are transmitting about themselves so as to be available and
knowledgeable about who is involved in what activities. Information
to this end is exchanged through the newspapers, in cafés and social
clubs, and through communications on radio and television. The
emission and reception of cues leads to the initiation of a series of
contacts between individuals who perceive a mutual benefit from their
association. Gradually, individuals who emit positive cues may build
up a following of supporters called an *ingrejinha* (little church) or
rotary. Supporters are tied to the careerist through his aid to them as a

trampolim for their own careers; in return they publicize the availability of their benefactor.

If and when the circle of supporters has achieved sufficient size or influence, the leader will be asked to join a *panelinha* (little saucepan). The *panelinha* is deliberately but informally selected among actors who have control of resources useful to the other members of the group. Thus, a banker, a politician, a bureaucrat, a lawyer, and a businessman might collaborate in a *panelinha*, each offering the services at his disposal to aid the other members in their pursuits in return for reciprocal aid from them. Involvement in one *panelinha* is not an end goal, however. Other, more influential, alliances beckon.

> Ideally, [the career] should pass through a hierarchy of *panelinhas*, mainly identified with the *município*, state, and federal political levels. As a man grows in connections, activities, experience, and wealth and contracts more vertical relationships upward and more supporters behind him, his career tends to reach into the next higher level *panelinha*. From the career point of view, he gradually universalizes or nationalizes himself . . . (Leeds, 1965: 396).

Panelinhas pervade Brazilian society, each possibly tied to a more powerful one, eventually linked to the highest governmental authorities. *Panelinhas*, linking economic, political, and bureaucratic elites and relying upon the clientelistic support of the lower classes, are what successfully maintain the structure of society divided into "masses" and "classes" while permitting individual mobility from one group to the other (Leeds, 1965: 384).

The career in Brazil, as described by Leeds, is similar to that encountered in Mexico, including a special vocabulary of terms to describe the public careerist and his following.[16] Individual careerists seek to acquire a *palanca* (lever), *apoyo* (push), or *trampolín* to initiate them into public life, to gain entrance into specific political arenas, or to solve problems; high level bureaucrats use their appointive powers to build loyal and efficient *equipos* (teams); a job is frequently referred to as a *chamba* (piece of good luck), and one gained for purely political reasons may be called a *huesito* (little bone); *camarillas* (cliques) are the extended alliance networks which compete for the prize of Mexican politics, the presidency; those whose upward mobility is stymied, often through their own indiscretion or wrong guesses, are *quemado* (burned). These characteristics were all evident in CONASUPO, where they were observed to have an effect not only on the behavior of individuals but also on the achievement of organizational goals.

---

16. Careers in the private sector are similarly based on personal ties (see Davis, 1968). However, for simplicity and relevance the discussion here is limited to public office holders. It is important to remember, however, that public office holding often implies ties to powerful private economic and social actors.

Building an Organization: Careers in CONASUPO

> How did I come to CONASUPO? Well, you see, I'm from Chiapas and the director is from Chiapas and we've been friends since childhood and when he became director of CONASUPO he asked me to take charge of this. . . . No, I'm not nervous about the *sexenio*. I have some business that the family is taking care of for me. I don't know what will happen to the director in the future, whether he will go on to other government business or will leave. If he stays in government, I'll probably follow him.

> I'm here because one belongs to certain political groups, you know, and when "X" asked me to come here, even though it was for much less money than I was making and even though it meant working in an office which I don't like to do—when one is asked, one more or less has to do it for political reasons. I have known "X" for years.

> Don Roberto and I are *compadres*. We have been friends ever since preparatory school days—we really got to know each other at the university. We worked together in the PRI, and then Don Roberto asked me to collaborate with him . . . here.

> How did I get here? Through an ad in the newspapers, just like everyone else!

In CONASUPO, personnel turnover is high and is highest among middle and upper level confidence workers. In the agency 30.5 percent of the 1,283 individuals employed in the parent organization are officially recognized as confidence workers, and another 10.5 percent are "free professionals" who, contracted by the day, week, or month, can be considered to share the same employment status.[17] Seventy-three percent of the total number of employees in the parent company has less than five years experience in an agency whose roots can be traced back thirty-seven years; this proportion includes almost the entire cadre of confidence personnel.

When the administration of Luís Echeverría took over command of the government in December 1970, a new director, Jorge de la Vega Domínguez, was appointed to head CONASUPO. In the following few months, he selected twenty high level subordinates.[18] These recently

17. This proportion is much smaller in the subsidiary companies which are responsible for the physical operations of the system. For example, of the 5,500 employees of the DICONSA system (DICONSA General and six regional subsidiaries) only 14.5 percent are confidence workers while 85.5 percent are base employees. Greenberg (1970: 112) notes that at least 75 percent of the employees of the Water Resources Ministry are confidence personnel.

18. In CONASUPO, the majority of appointments among the respondents occurred immediately after the new administration took over, that is, in December 1970 (nineteen appointments) and in the first six months of 1971 (twenty-two appointments). Thirty-seven of the respondents were appointed after mid-1971, largely in response to the creation of new offices or departments.

installed division managers, subsidiary company heads, and department managers then selected their immediate subordinates—submanagers and directors who often in turn had discretion to assemble their own underlings. That they used this discretion liberally is attested by the fact that of seventy-eight middle and high level bureaucrats interviewed, only twelve had worked in CONASUPO immediately prior to December 1970, and none of these occupied the same position before and after the start of the new administration. Ostensibly, the hiring of new employees was strictly regulated by a position roster; no new employees could be hired until a vacancy in the roster appeared or a new position was created. However, as CONASUPO was a rapidly expanding agency, new positions were frequently created. The sixteen subsidiary companies were also available for placing individuals for whom no positions existed in the parent organization. Middle and high level positions could also be added through the appointment of "assessors" or free professionals hired for a stipulated amount of time.[19] Between 1971 and 1974, the number of employees in the parent company increased by 69 percent. All additions to the roster had to be made through the authorization of the agency director, who signed the agency's contract with each new employee. These formal responsibilities gave De la Vega great control over personnel expansion.

Holding a position in CONASUPO did not limit an individual from holding posts in other government agencies or in private business. Ten of the CONASUPO administrators interviewed had part time teaching positions at UNAM. In Mexico, teaching is engaged in partly for the extra income it affords, partly for its prestige value, and partly for the future elite contacts it makes available. Those who teach in the university are regularly called upon to serve in various capacities in the government. Other individuals in CONASUPO had interests in private businesses which provided them with extra income and a fallback position should they find themselves out of a job in the public sector. Among those interviewed were officials who also owned large farms, car dealerships, trucking firms, and private schools, for example. Still others among high level personnel served on the boards of directors of various federal agencies and private companies. One high level official, for instance, served on the boards of three government industries and one private company.

For many administrators in the past, CONASUPO has been a stepping stone toward other public positions. Several former directors of the agency moved on to other high level posts, two to become Ministers

---

19. Thus, there is always the possibility of obliging an outside recommender, in making a position available for the protégé should the recommender be of sufficiently high political status to merit attention. If, on the other hand, the recommender is not influential or properly connected, the full employment roster is used to excuse the agency politely because there simply are no positions available.

of Agriculture, one to become Governor of the state of Mexico, and another to become Secretary to the President. A director of an important commission of CONASUPO became Minister of Health and Welfare and then Governor of the state of Mexico while another was Minister of Industry and Commerce before becoming Governor of the state of Michoacán. An interim director of CONASUPO left to head up an urban development program in the state of Mexico. Jorge de la Vega, the director under Echeverría, became Governor of the state of Chiapas.

These characteristics of the agency and its middle and high level officials, however, reveal very little about how careers and alliances are managed and how they affect the pursuit of organizational goals. Of fundamental importance to the operation of CONASUPO, and the basis upon which alliances are formed, is *confianza*, the interpersonal trust which ideally exists between superior and subordinate. Given the importance of personal ties to career advancement in Mexico, of particular significance to the organization and its leadership are patterns by which individuals are recruited into the agency and the use made of the *palanca*. Moreover, within any given department or section of the agency, personal ties determining loyalty, obligation, and job performance can be instrumental in building an effective and innovative corps of subordinates, an *equipo*. Finally, because of the significance of the general director to the success of the agency in achieving its goals, it is important to consider the position of this individual within the national political elite and the integration of a *camarilla*. Therefore, to understand more completely the career system as it affects CONASUPO, it is necessary to consider the importance of *confianza* (trust), the *palanca* (lever), the *equipo* (team), and the *camarilla* (clique).

Confianza and Sexennial Reorganizations

A number of the characteristics of the Mexican political system already discussed made *confianza* an extremely important concern of officials in CONASUPO. First, frequent turnover of high and middle level personnel means that officials are often placed in charge of organizations and programs they know little about. They may have no professional or experiential background to aid them in administering programs. Unprepared for their responsibilities, they are nevertheless expected to take charge quickly, to plan new activities for the unit under their command, to revise operating procedures, and to implement rapidly the directives of their superiors. These conditions place a premium on the availability of trustworthy subordinates.

Furthermore, knowledge of their short term of office makes all high level and most middle level officials in the organization aware that the results they seek must be achieved rapidly. The leadership of the agency in the Echeverría administration was determined to bring about fundamental changes in its objectives and to transform the previously lax and inadequate organization into an effective and efficient one. Middle and high level officials were aware that they were being evaluated on the basis of their capacity to carry out adequately, diligently, discretely, and promptly the tasks they had been assigned. The overriding concern expressed by program, department, and office heads in CONASUPO was to get a program going before they moved on to other posts. In effect, the CONASUPO officials sought to institutionalize their efforts to such an extent that they became routine and therefore more difficult to change by the next person to take charge of the program. This explains, for example, the concern of the administrator who stated, "We want to do away with programs which are subject to the *sexenio*," and another who was determined to "set this program in motion before the next *sexenio* so that it will really be carried out." In early 1975, an office chief admitted, "We're in a race against time to get this program moving because the presidential campaign is getting closer and closer." Each official, knowing his term is limited, is aware that opportunities for carrying out his responsibilities and performing them well are also limited.

Other characteristics of the system which make *confianza* important are the inadequacies of the administrative, control, and information systems for overseeing the activities of subordinates. For example, although operating and procedure manuals abounded in CONASUPO and its subsidiary companies, officials were not generally knowledgeable about their contents. The manuals themselves frequently outlined extensive and complicated steps for requesting, submitting, or storing information, generally involving multiple copies, signatures, and archival depositories. In reality, most internal affairs of the agency were conducted over the telephone or in personal encounters; the paperwork often followed upon the transcurrence of business rather than being instrumental to it. Generally, this handling of affairs facilitated and encouraged prompt action on official matters. It also made control tenuous as an official at any one moment might have only a vague idea of what his subordinates were doing. This problem was particularly acute in CONASUPO because its personnel were dispersed over the entire country, and field offices were responsible for vital aspects of the company's activities.

Officials in CONASUPO were also aware that mistakes made by them or their subordinates could be extremely detrimental to their careers. Frequently dependent upon superiors for future career advancement and employed in an agency stressing performance and productivity, administrators were sensitive to the risks involved in making the wrong decision at the wrong moment.[20] Moreover, many handled large

20. One respondent indicated his awareness of the risks of indiscretion in public positions under Echeverría. "There is a Law of Responsibility of Public Officials which we are all aware can be applied. Clearly it isn't applied very rigidly now, but I think in this *sexenio* the President has made very clear to what point he is willing to tolerate

amounts of money or were responsible for the transferrence, storage, or sale of huge quantities of grain, foodstuffs, and other products. Careless or indiscrete handling of these could bring scandal or disgrace on both the individual immediately responsible and on his superiors, seriously damaging the career chances of all. Many officials interviewed alluded to predecessors or officials they knew who had been quietly but suddenly removed from their positions for unspecified misconduct and "problems." Mistakes made in the fulfillment of responsibilities have serious personal ramifications and are not contemplated lightly.

Finally, for officials at all levels, competition for advancement is often intense. At the same time, because of the emphasis on performance, decisions must be made and action must be taken, regardless of the risk involved and in spite of an information system which is frequently inadequate for making sound decisions. To one administrator, the two most important rules to follow if one wishes to get ahead are, "Do things fast" and "Don't make mistakes," axioms which underscore the risk and pressure on middle and high level bureaucrats.

All of these characteristics—short term in office, pressures to perform, inadequate administrative controls, the damage mistakes can mean for career advancement, and the risk of taking any action at all—make it imperative to surround oneself with subordinates one can trust, in whom one has *confianza*. From the point of view of the individual administrator, this is the most efficient way to ensure that orders are executed, that mistakes are avoided or covered up discretely if made, that activities are justified as rational by all who take part, and that subordinates fulfill their responsibilities, even when not directly supervised. The fundamental importance of *confianza* to administrators was summed up by an official engaged in personnel administration in the CONASUPO system.

> The administration of personnel here in Mexico is almost necessarily more subjective than in other countries. There are two reasons for this. First, it's often necessary, for "public relations" reasons, to hire certain people who come recommended by influential people. Public relations, in terms of political support and image, is very important to CONASUPO. The second reason is that because of the *sexenio* change, because individuals are called to positions they often have no training or experience for, because they must often build programs practically overnight, and because if they make mistakes it can have grave consequences, it's extremely important for people to have under them those they trust, *personal de confianza*. The word *confianza* is a perfect term for it; it means someone I trust personally.

---

deviant or dishonest behavior from public officials, and when anyone steps over this line, he is *out*, even to levels of subministers of state! It may not be through the application of the Law of Responsibility, but they are out nevertheless."

The most effective way to surround oneself with this type of subordinate is to recruit and hire individuals one knows personally or who come recommended by people one knows and trusts. The *palanca* therefore serves to ensure *confianza* between superior and subordinate.

The *Palanca* and Recruitment in CONASUPO

> Recommendations are used a great deal in applying for jobs . . . it depends on the recommendation how much weight it carries—the level and importance of the recommender. Why, just three days ago I received a recommendation from the party leader of the Chamber of Deputies. You can bet I will attend to it—it is in my interest to do so!

All but eight of the seventy-eight individuals interviewed in CONASUPO mobilized personal ties to acquire jobs in the agency, including all of those who formed part of the highly qualified technical corps of the agency. A position was most frequently acquired through the use of a personal introduction, often referred to as a *palanca*.[21] Recommendations from influential figures were an important means of entering CONASUPO at all levels and for all types of jobs (see Greenberg, 1970: 100). When a recommendation came from the agency director, any of his immediate subordinates, or any of the subsidiary company managers, hiring by the personnel department was automatic; in other cases, the political or bureaucratic status of the recommender was evaluated carefully. If a recommendation came from someone outside the agency and if this individual was of importance, the recommendation was sent to the director for decision. Consequently, he was in a position to do a personal favor for the recommender, a favor which could be exchanged for support of the agency or himself at a later time.

Three significant recruitment patterns using different kinds of *palancas* were observed in CONASUPO: (1) recruitment through direct ties to individuals in the agency, (2) recruitment mediated by another individual in the agency, and (3) externally mediated recruitment. In the first two cases, the loyalty and performance which were offered in return for a job served to strengthen the organization internally and to reinforce hierarchical command structures. In the third case, organization leaders had the opportunity to mobilize external support for the agency; at the same time, however, loyalties and obligations were dispersed to actors outside the organization. This could be dangerous for CONASUPO, for when certain key posts were distributed through this kind of external mediation, overall agency performance could be affected.

21. The term *palanca* (lever) is used to refer both to individuals and to attributes of individuals. Thus, for example, someone might say, "He is my *palanca*" or "He has *palanca* (leverage)." (See Carlos, 1974: 70; Foster, 1976b: 229.)

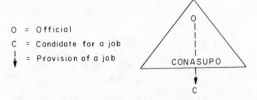

O = Official
C = Candidate for a job
↓ = Provision of a job

Figure 3. Direct Recruitment Pattern. Note: In this and other diagrams to follow, an attempt has been made to indicate the vertical or horizontal status positions of the actors and to suggest the hierarchical position of the officials within the agency's pyramidal structure.

The simplest type of recruitment to CONASUPO occurred when an official in the agency directly appointed his own underlings. This was the case, for example, when Jorge de la Vega appointed many of his immediate subordinates at the beginning of the *sexenio*. This direct means of obtaining a position is illustrated in Figure 3. Interestingly, in CONASUPO this pattern was most evident in cases in which an individual was appointed to a relatively high level position and was able to bring a number of his subordinates from his previous post to work for him in his new capacity. In this case, the recruitment pattern looked like that in Figure 4.

A second frequently encountered pattern was one which was mediated internally by an official of the agency acting as a broker. In this case, the official did not directly control the provision of a job, but he could introduce the job seeker to some higher level administrator who did. Two variations of this pattern were observed; one utilized vertical relationships between superior and subordinate exclusively whereas the other pattern mobilized peer or horizontal alliances also. In the first, an actor wishing a job was approached by or sought out a previous

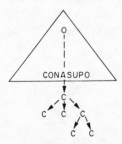

Figure 4. Direct Recruitment Pattern, Extended Hierarchically.

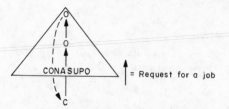

Figure 5. Internally Mediated Recruitment Pattern, Vertical Alliance Only.

acquaintance who was his status superior and who was already employed by the agency; the official then recommended the job hunter to his superior. The higher level official might then provide the job directly to the supplicant. This pattern is diagrammed in Figure 5.

In the second variation of internally mediated recruitment, a job seeker might contact an official within the agency who was his status equal—a peer from school, for example—and would attempt to arrange an introduction to his superior. The job would be provided directly by the superior. This kind of recruitment tended to strengthen the formal hierarchical organization and to contribute to overall agency performance and success. Occasionally, however, it meant that loyalty and performance obligations would skip a hierarchical level, the new recruit owing more to his chief's chief than to his direct superior.

A third pattern was more complicated as it involved figures such as party leaders, governors, and state senators. In externally mediated recruitment, high level officials, especially the agency director, used the provision of a job as a means to gain support for the agency or himself at a later time; in effect, the director could "cash in" on the obligations incurred through job patronage. Among those directly responsible for personnel administration, this was termed "public relations" hiring when it involved middle and lower level officials; if a high level appointment were made in this manner, it was widely recognized as a "political" appointment. An individual wishing a job would contact an influential person outside the agency with whom he had a special acquaintance. This person might then communicate with his high level friends in the

Figure 6. Internally Mediated Recruitment Pattern, Horizontal Alliance.

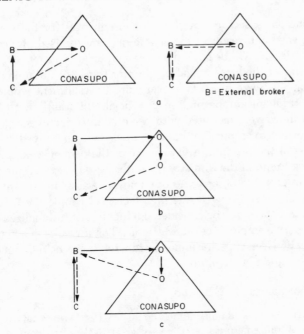

Figure 7. Externally Mediated Recruitment Patterns.

agency or use his political prestige to inquire whether a position existed for the job seeker. The CONASUPO official might provide the job directly, or he might offer it to the political figure who then would dispense it to his supporter, as indicated in Figure 7a. At times more than one high level official would be involved in satisfying the job request of an external broker. For example, a federal senator of some reputation accompanied one young aspirant to the office of the director in order to facilitate a personal introduction. The young man was subsequently sent to a subsidiary company manager who installed him in a middle level position. The director was thus able to incur the obligation of the senator, the senator demonstrated his influence to his protégé, and the young man became obligated to all three of his benefactors. This example is diagrammed in Figure 7b; another variation of external mediation involving multiple actors appears in Figure 7c.

Often, the external broker might represent political alliances or groups whose support was essential to the agency or who had more political power than CONASUPO. However, this might mean that part of the organization would pursue goals not condoned by agency leaders or not conforming to current policies. This happened because the person heading that part of the agency owed first allegiance not to the agency director but to someone outside the agency. Loyalty and job performance owed to political figures such as state governors or the leader of one of the party sectors could have consequences for the performance of the agency and result in the erratic or compromised implementation of its policies, as will be seen in a later chapter.

In terms of the hierarchical position of the actor obtaining a job, all three channels were used. However, direct recruitment would seem to be more frequent among high level officials. In addition, all high level administrators were recruited with personal introductions (see Table 7). It is important to emphasize that the *palanca* was employed in CONASUPO regardless of the training or experience of the person seeking a job. As Greenberg found in the Ministry of Water Resources, it seems also to be the case in CONASUPO that "who one knows" was as important as "what one knows," even for well qualified technical people (1970: Chap. 7). The *palanca*, then, can be considered a highly institutionalized means of securing public employment in Mexico. When it results in a high level of *confianza* between superior and subordinate, it can be the foundation of an effective and loyal *equipo*.

The Formation of an *Equipo*

> During this administration, CONASUPO has become an effective and well-run enterprise, and a very great deal of credit must go to the director. . . . He has put together a fine team of individuals.

> This is an *equipo* here—we work together.

In any given department, division, or office, an *equipo* or team is made up of the confidence employees who are tied to the highest ranking official in that part of the agency and who rely upon him for future career advancement.[22] Program directors, office chiefs, and managers in CONASUPO were aware of the importance of employing competent and trustworthy subordinates for their work and for their careers. A high level official in one of the subsidiary companies commented, for example,

> When I took charge of this position, I found that although I had many friends, there were few I trusted enough to invite them to help me. There are three people I brought here whom I trust blindly. . . . I trust them with my prestige, with my signature, and with my honor. . . . This is my *equipo*.

The means used to recruit a loyal *equipo* is demonstrated by the Field Coordination Program in CONASUPO. This program was designed to help coordinate the extensive activities of the agency at the grass-roots

22. Involvement in vertical dependency relationships was operationally defined by four measures: (1) face-to-face interaction between individuals, (2) unequal *organizational* status, (3) personal protestations of loyalty, respect, deference, obligation, and observation of obedience and job performance, and (4) parallel or dependent career trajectories, perhaps the most important and indicative measure.

TABLE 7.

Recruitment Patterns for High and Middle Level Officials

Recruitment Channel	High Level (%) (N=37)	Middle Level (%) (N=41)
Direct	40.6	26.8
Internally mediated	24.3	24.4
Externally mediated	35.1	29.3
Open recruitment	0.0	19.5
Totals	100.0	100.0

level by stimulating community involvement in the agency's programs. Outside the capital city, communication, chains of command, and personal loyalties often meant that the various divisions and subsidiary companies of the agency pursued conflicting goals and hindered the successful and rapid solution of local problems. The Field Coordination Program required a group of employees who would be actively and personally involved in achieving overall coordination while at the same time minimizing tensions and jealousies among local level officials and encouraging them to accept and pursue new work habits. It was imperative that they not be available for cooptation by local interests and that they deal effectively but discretely with the problems arising at this level, avoiding the antagonism of officials over whom they had no functional authority. Thus, the program manager required an *equipo* of individuals whose behaviors and motives he could trust and who would continue to perform their tasks diligently when they were not being directly supervised.

He used a number of methods to put together this special *equipo*. Before he assumed the leadership of the program, the administrator had served as the manager of CONASUPO's planning department. While in this position he had recruited a number of young university graduates to work for him in designing and planning an integrated set of agency programs to serve rural communities. He had met many of these individuals through the university courses he taught, through positions he had previously held in the government, and through participation in government study groups. When he became Field Coordination manager, some of his subordinates followed him to form the basis of his new team. These were the individuals in whom he had most *confianza* in terms of ability, preparation, and dedication. Then, as coordination manager, he recruited a number of new subordinates, frequently making use of the peer alliances of his underlings. The result of the recruitment of this *equipo* was a group of individuals actively engaged in achieving the goals of the coordination program and deeply convinced of the correctness of the manager's approach to local level problem solving.

At the agency level, Jorge de la Vega attempted to build an effective and dedicated *equipo* in the same fashion. He needed a team which would be committed to achieving the overall policy goals of the agency and which would support him in conflicts with other governmental agencies and in the mobilization of support for his policies. In fact, a number of his appointments achieved just this result. Many individuals were recruited because of preexisting personal ties to him. Others, however, were appointed by the director as payment for past political obligations or in an attempt to tie the agency to the party elite or to the President. Therefore, he sacrificed some of his control over agency activity and saw some of the agency's economic resources utilized in questionable or unproductive activities.

In many cases, high level officials attempted to use their authority and prestige to extend their *equipos* throughout the organization under their command. They did this by influencing the appointment of individuals to certain key posts, seeking to insure that people in these positions were personally loyal to them rather than to their direct superiors. This was the way the subsidiary, DICONSA, sought to ensure honest and responsible performance in its field operations. A high level official in the subsidiary explained how the process worked.

> Effectively, I have complete power to select the regional sales managers. The subsidiary head has given me a free hand in that matter. What usually happens is that he calls me up and asks me to suggest someone, and I take a few days to think of it and hopefully can give him the name of someone honest and good for the position. Then he calls up the regional manager and very politely suggests this person and says he's sending him up. This is a political management of the control problem we have.

It was expected that a team put together in this fashion could be relied upon for effective performance.

The General Directors: *Camarillas* and the Party-Bureaucracy Interface

> You will find the explanation of a great deal of Mexican politics and of many things which occur in the political system in the ties of friendship and loyalties between people.

> If you would look at my professional *curriculum vitae,* you would find little reason for me to be here. But if you were to look at my

political *curriculum,* you would see much more clearly why I occupy this position. What kind of politics? Well, party politics doesn't really matter all that much since it's effectively a one-party system. What counts is group politics and the politics of personal relations.

As may be clear by now, recruitment to official positions in Mexico serves two interrelated functions. Selecting a suitable cadre of subordinates is extremely important to the bureaucratic chief who wishes to direct an effective and efficient organization. Performance goals may be influential criteria for recruitment for reasons such as ideological or professional goals but also because career advancement opportunities may be more abundant if an official is known to be capable of directing a well-run agency or program. Making a name for oneself as an efficient administrator is therefore important in present-day Mexico. The second function is more overtly political. Recruitment can be used as a means to enhance a political career by strengthening ties to important political actors. This is particularly true at high levels of the organization where officials are generally members of political factions, or *camarillas.*

The *camarilla* is formed of actors who have established politically significant followings. The power and influence of these followings may be pooled to achieve the goals of all members of the clique, and implicit understandings of mutual advantage bind the membership together. *Camarillas* are built through the mobilization of both vertical and horizontal alliances; the horizontal alliances frequently place actors in a near-equal bargaining relationship. This makes *camarillas* more fluid and shifting than the smaller scale *equipos* in which personal loyalty and dependence are stronger.

Through a number of high level appointments, the director of CONASUPO made friends among the leadership of the peasant and middle class sectors of the party, obliged a number of state governors, developed a following among university students, and established friendships with officials in key government agencies. The extent of the political support he accumulated in this manner made him a valuable member of a political faction whose importance increased as it attempted to influence the selection of the presidential candidate for 1976. Success would enhance the director's eligibility to be a close collaborator of the new President. His subordinates were aware of the advantages of "winning" for their own careers. "If De la Vega becomes a minister," commented one respondent, "then his entire *equipito* will follow him, and we'll all have positions in the ministry."

Camarillas not only advance the careers of their members; they also may be important for expediting official business. The director under Echeverría, for example, was often able to deal effectively with the heads of other government agencies because of the understanding of

mutual benefit which existed among them. This in turn had an important effect on his ability to have access to the President and to influence
him in supporting CONASUPO's claims for a greater role in market
regulation and agricultural policy development.

The career of Jorge de la Vega Domínguez is instructive of the way
in which individuals ascend in the politico-administrative apparatus
and become eligible for membership in a *camarilla* in Mexico. Although
born in the provinces, he attended the prestigious National Preparatory
School in Mexico City and then entered the National School of Economics at the National Autonomous University (UNAM). His political
life began in secondary school and continued in the preparatory school
and then in the university where he held important positions in student
politics. Even before finishing studies at the university, he began working
in the bureaucracy in various positions in the Ministry of Economics in
the early 1950s. In the last years of the Ruiz Cortínez administration
(1952–1958), he occupied positions as manager and subdirector of a
government bank and as professor of economic theory in a technical
institute in a provincial capital. The initiation of the López Mateos
administration in late 1958 brought him back to the capital city where
he taught at the National Polytechnic Institute, was subdirector of a
small federal agency and then of a bank, in addition to becoming the
president of the prestigious College of Economists of Mexico. While con-
tinuing to head the economists' association, a politically influential group
of intellectuals, he accepted a position in the newly formed Ministry
of the Presidency and became director of the Graduate School of
Economics at the National Polytechnic Institute. At the same time, he
worked for the PRI's Political, Economic, and Social Studies Institute in
the presidential campaign of 1963–1964 and ran for election as a federal
deputy from the state of Chiapas in 1964.

In January 1965 De la Vega was appointed manager of the Sales
Department in CONASUPO, a key position in the overall performance of
the agency. He maintained his position in the National Chamber of
Deputies and traveled on several congressional missions to other countries. In 1968 he left CONASUPO and became the general director of the
Political, Economic, and Social Studies Institute of the PRI for the
duration of the campaign of Luís Echeverría (1968–1970). In this position
he built up a national network of over 300 Political, Economic, and
Social Studies centers, which served as a basis for political mobilization
during the campaign. When Echeverría assumed office in 1970, he immediately appointed De la Vega to head CONASUPO, reflecting the President's desire to integrate an active, well-educated, and forceful new
generation of administrators into the government. Until February 1976,
the director sat on the boards of its sixteen subsidiary companies, along
with the boards of several other federal trusts and agencies, formed part

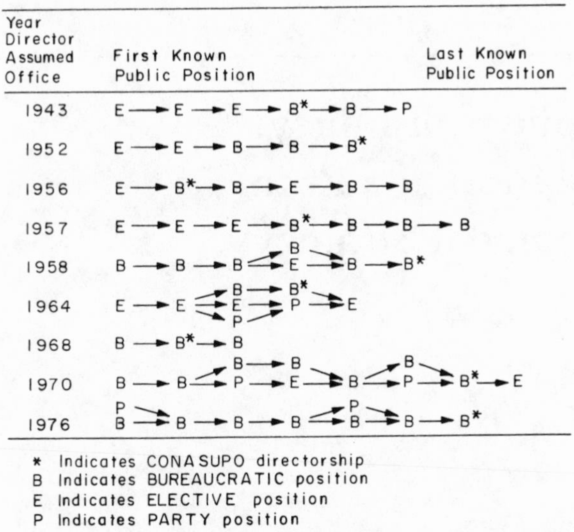

Year Director Assumed Office	First Known Public Position	Last Known Public Position
1943	E → E → E → B* → B → P	
1952	E → E → B → B → B*	
1956	E → B* → B → E → B → B	
1957	E → E → E → B* → B → B → B	
1958	B → B → B ⇄ E ⇒ B → B* (B above)	
1964	E → E ⇄ E ⇒ P → E (B → B* above, P below)	
1968	B → B* → B	
1970	B → B ⇄ P → E → B ← P → B* → E (B above, B above)	
1976	B ⇒ B → B → B ⇄ B → B → B* (P above, P middle)	

* Indicates CONASUPO directorship
B Indicates BUREAUCRATIC position
E Indicates ELECTIVE position
P Indicates PARTY position

Figure 8. Career Trajectories of Directors of CONASUPO.

of a high level agricultural policy committee, and continued his involvement in the College of Economists. He was then appointed to be the official candidate for the governorship of the state of Chiapas.

This example demonstrates how an individual may shift between bureaucratic, party, and elective positions and how several posts may be held at once. It is corroborated by data on other past directors of the agency, most of whom were involved, often simultaneously, in party, elective, and bureaucratic positions. In the history of the company, there have been twelve directors. Immediately prior to being appointed to the CONASUPO directorship, one director held an appointive party position, four held elective positions, and four served in federal agencies (information is not available on three former directors). Their career trajectories over time are schematized in Figure 8, demonstrating the party-bureaucracy interface of careers in Mexico.

The various trajectories of the directors have all been determined by the *palancas*, the *equipos*, and the *camarillas* they formed or mobilized. Their careers have been built upon the exchanges of loyalty, obedience, and job performance which cement vertical alliances in Mexican public life. These relationships are of fundamental importance in ensuring and maintaining elite cohesion in the political system. Careers and the consequences of the personnel turnover which accompanies the *sexenio* are also important in understanding the manner in which public policy is formulated and support for it is mobilized in Mexico. In CONASUPO, these factors were certainly important in the formulation of the agency's rural development policy and the way in which the management sought to ensure support for the policy, as will be seen in the following chapter.

4

The Politics of Policy: Formulation of a Rural Development Strategy

The initiation of a new *sexenio* is characterized by widespread reorganization within the bureaucratic apparatus in Mexico. In each ministry and agency, the newly assembled *equipos* embark upon studies of the administrative organization they have acquired, its budget, its past programs, and the consequences of its previous policies. Undoubtedly, some of the activity is spurred by the desire of the new team to appropriate the organization for six years, to erase from it the imprint of the last *sexenio*, and to remold it in the image of its new masters. Much, however, can be ascribed to the need to establish policies and programs which reflect the concerns and ideas of the incumbent President. Moreover, the reorganizations and policy revisions provide an opportunity for enthusiastic neophytes to test theories and to demonstrate the importance of their particular agency and themselves to the solution of Mexico's economic, social, and political problems.

CONASUPO was no exception to this practice in 1971. In August of that year, the director of the agency reported to its Advisory Council:

> The new economic and social policies of the present government and the complexity of the problems which confront CONASUPO necessitate a general and complete analysis of its past activities and policies.

Predictably, De la Vega affirmed that CONASUPO was instrumental in achieving the principal public goals of the Echeverría administration:

> The regulation of the staple products market has a direct relationship to income distribution, efficient production, effective use of labor, social solidarity, and improved returns on public investments. As an instrument of the federal government, CONASUPO has numerous capabilities to achieve these new national policies. It is, without a doubt, one of the most effective short term means to benefit the low income population.

However, the report continued, the past activities of the agency were not without their faults:

> The efficiency of many methods used is low: There are losses, thefts, and other illicit practices, failures in organization, operation, and control. The objectives [of the company] can be achieved at lower cost.

Reflecting this concern of the management for efficient and effective operation, it was proposed that the company

> Subject all operations . . . to a precise quantification of their effects, including all financial, economic, and social aspects, permitting a systematic and on-going evaluation of the priorities among objectives and the goals and amount of resources which should be assigned to each program (CONASUPO, 1971a).

Such an analysis was in fact carried out. It resulted in the programming of agency activities in terms of the objectives specified in Table 1 and the statement of budgetary priorities among them. With objectives and subobjectives firmly stated, CONASUPO's leadership thought it would be possible to reorient the agency's activities and to provide the policy direction badly needed by the company. Specifically, it was hoped that CONASUPO could achieve its dual goal of benefiting both urban and rural low income populations in a more balanced way. Important in the new approach of CONASUPO's management was a conviction that the transformation of the subsistence farming sector was essential for agricultural development in Mexico. During the first eighteen months of the Echeverría administration, a comprehensive policy for rural development was designed by CONASUPO officials. The policy was based on a theory about the dynamics of development and CONASUPO's role as a change agent in that process. Much of the agency's subsequent efforts were directed toward achieving the objectives of the policy.

The Roots of Interest in Rural Development

The interest of CONASUPO administrators in new policy objectives can be traced to three circumstances which they faced in 1971 and 1972. To begin with, the new directorship inherited an inefficient and directionless apparatus—a hodgepodge of programs, a defective infrastructure of warehouses and stores, and widespread skepticism about the agency and its personnel—which needed to be reformed if it was to become a respected and influential organization within the government. In addition, the Echeverría administration intended to diverge from past policies which stimulated industrial development and economic growth at the expense of agricultural production and an equitable distribution of income. Throughout his campaign, the President had stressed the importance of the rural regions of Mexico to national economic development and internal peace; CONASUPO's leadership was sensitive to his concerns. Third, the team of individuals installed in CONASUPO was aware of a critique of economic development policies pursued by national decision makers since the 1940s, an analysis which had been widely discussed among intellectuals during the 1960s but which was generally unacknowledged in high level official circles prior to 1971. A closer look at these three sources of policy change will provide understanding of why the rural development policy itself was attractive to CONASUPO officials.

CONASUPO in 1971

> At the time I took over, there were a number of problems we faced. First, there was a complete lack of confidence in our program—from the peasants, all through CONASUPO and from other agencies of the government. . . . [Another] problem we faced was the definition of programs. In 1970 and 1971 we didn't know where we were going. We had to find the road, decide on the best ways of following it and then evaluate.

The condition of CONASUPO in December 1970, when the new administration took office, invited reorganization and reform. During its thirty-three-year history, the agency had acquired an array of programs with multiple objectives and beneficiaries. Its price supports for agricultural products had grown and diversified in response to crisis situations rather than through systematic diagnosis of needs and projection of agricultural productivity and capabilities.[1] Because of convenience, cost efficiencies, and political pressures, purchases of crops were generally made from large commercial farmers in highly developed agricultural zones. Each of the purchasing and selling programs had engendered a group of beneficiaries reluctant to see changes in CONASUPO's activities which might be harmful to its interests. Moreover, all of the programs

---

1. An analysis of CONASUPO's guarantee price programs during the early years of the agency is found in Fernández y Fernández and Acosta (1961).

of the agency—its purchasing programs, retail outlets, rural warehouses, and commercial supply programs—had frequently been appropriated by politicians, economic influentials, and local level *caciques* for less than altruistic ends.

The particularistic use of CONASUPO's resources was noticeable during the presidency of Díaz Ordaz (1964–1970). An expansion of its activities in the 1960s made the agency of considerable value to the regime for its role in support building among the low income sectors of the population and for its ability to dispense resources as political rewards. The *Graneros del Pueblo*, a program of rapid expansion in rural areas begun in 1966, provides an example of the consequences for the agency when its activities were directed to purely political objectives. The program was ostensibly designed to resolve one of the most persistent problems of the agency and one for which it was frequently criticized: its failure to ensure the poorest farmers and *ejidatarios* of a timely and effective support price for their products. In the past, collusion of CONASUPO employees with exploitive middlemen, inadequate and expensive transportation, the concentration of agency programs in zones of high productivity, and a lack of local storage facilities had often meant that the small scale farmer was unable to acquire the benefits publicly promised by the company.[2]

The solution to this problem was announced to be the construction of a series of local level warehouses throughout the country which would serve as reception centers for corn, beans, wheat, and other agricultural products. At the same time, the cone-shaped granaries were highly visible evidence of the federal government's concern for its rural population and therefore were considered valuable for increasing political support in these areas. A massive program of promotion and construction was initiated throughout the country. *Ejidatarios* and small farmers were organized to build their own community granaries and by the end of 1970 there were 3,558 *Graneros* in 1,109 localities. The fanfare, publicity, and presence of beneficently smiling local officials which accompanied the building and inauguration of the granaries indicated the relationship of the program to the presidential campaign of 1969–1970.

Unfortunately, the speed with which the local warehouse reception centers were constructed and the political impulse behind their promotion resulted in defective construction, in dishonest handling of the grain

2. Most CONASUPO crop purchases were made through large ANDSA (Almacenes Nacionales de Depósito, S.A.) warehouses. These reception centers were generally located near zones of high population density rather than in rural areas. This location favored large commercial farmers who were able to pay the cost of transporting their crops to the warehouses. Many small farmers, lacking means to transport their crops, sold them to intermediaries at low prices. The middlemen then sold the crops to CONASUPO at a profit.

that was stored, and in the poor location of the granaries. So great were their deficiencies that the majority of the warehouses had to be closed or used for other purposes. In 1971, only 15 percent of them were operating and "none of these efficiently or with adequate controls," the agency reported to its board (CONASUPO, 1971a; *El Universal*, April 11, 1971). Moreover, only 13 percent of CONASUPO's total purchases of agricultural products was being made through the *Graneros*.

The new *equipo*, therefore, inherited a network of inserviceable storage centers. "In 1971, the *Graneros* Program was a white elephant," was the opinion of officials who were assigned operational responsibility for the warehouses in the Echeverría administration.[3] Moreover, they also confronted the distrust of the farmers and *ejidatarios* who had believed the rhetoric that the *Graneros* would open up new economic possibilities for them. The peasants communicated to CONASUPO officials and others their feeling that they had been defrauded by the government and more specifically, by CONASUPO, when the promised changes failed to occur. The new leadership realized that something had to be done about the peasants' cynicism and disillusion or they would resist selling their harvests to the agency in the future. The *Graneros* program was thought to be based on a sound analysis of the problems faced by the agency; it had failed because it had not been adequately tested and because it had been poorly promoted and improperly administered (CONASUPO, 1971a). To salvage as much as possible from the four-year program, CONASUPO officials proposed that the *Graneros* be turned to other uses: as storage centers for products other than grains, as sites for small community industries, or as local social and educational centers.

At the same time as the rural network of CONASUPO was expanding through the *Graneros del Pueblo* Program, its retail program was also being expanded and used for political support building. CONASUPO's mobile retail units were increasingly seen in low income urban neighborhoods during the presidential campaign, and a number of rural outlets for CONASUPO products were also opened. In these and other stores, school supplies, uniforms, Christmas toys, and kitchen utensils were sold in addition to the clothes, shoes, foodstuffs, and medicines previously handled. By the time of the election, CONASUPO operated 1,735 stores of various types and supplied them with 3,500 different articles.

3. In 1971, CONASUPO publicly acknowledged the failure of its *Graneros del Pueblo* program and admitted the poor location and management of its installations (see CONASUPO, 1971a; *El Universal*, April 11, 1971). Public acknowledgment of failure of government programs, even those promoted by previous administrations, is infrequently encountered in Mexico. However, the Díaz Ordaz administration had been unusually repressive in its handling of student disturbances in 1968 and its public support was low. The Echeverría administration found it politically wise to break with the past administration, even to the extent of publicly repudiating some of its programs and policies and criticizing their consequences.

In 1970 the retail network reported an annual loss of 38 million pesos—3.04 million dollars (CONASUPO, 1971a). Many of the stores were franchises whose operations it was physically impossible to oversee with the personnel at CONASUPO's disposal. A number of the outlets had been placed in politically useful locations even when these were not economically or socially desirable sites. The number of stores had expanded so rapidly and anarchically that supplying them was a major problem; some closed or went bankrupt because the company could not give them proper attention. Moreover, industries which supplied many of the products sold through CONASUPO outlets frequently delivered inferior or damaged goods, a practice made possible through collusion with the company's employees. This tended to exacerbate CONASUPO's already significant image problem.

Finally, in addition to the deficient infrastructure inherited by the new managers, there existed the problem which had plagued the regulatory activity since its inception in 1937: how to benefit both the low income consumer and producer. In fact, CONASUPO's commitment to *ejidatarios* and small farmers had always been tenuous. The government's policy for several decades had been to subsidize growth in the urban and industrial sector through the exploitation of agriculture.[4] Agency rhetoric about raising the profit margin of the most economically disadvantaged peasants had not been achieved in practice. As an example of its urban consumer bias, guarantee prices remained fixed at 1963 levels throughout the Díaz Ordaz administration. The skewed impact of the agency's past performance was frankly admitted by its officials in 1974. As one administrator explained,

> The traditional role of CONASUPO until this administration has been to protect consumers. The government's economic policy was to keep prices stable, especially in the urban areas, keeping salaries low and stimulating industry. That is why DICONSA has grown so greatly in urban areas and why corn was bought in the areas of highest production with little thought to the protection of producers.

4. The policy of subsidizing the urban consumer began in the late 1940s and early 1950s under CONASUPO's progenitor, the Mexican Import and Export Company (CEIMSA). The company's activities in this period were primarily directed toward stimulating industrialization by providing a large and subsidized urban work force. The company set and maintained guaranteed prices for the production of corn, beans, eggs, wheat, and other products which were below the potential free market value of these products; and, in order to meet the demand for consumer items in the rapidly expanding metropolitan areas, it used a variety of mechanisms to coerce producers of corn to sell only to the company (Fernández y Fernández and Acosta, 1961: 202–203). The company imported, at a loss, the commodities it needed to insure that tortillas, bread, beans, and other products were available to the working class population, principally that of the Federal District, at a low and stable price. In addition, subsidies were established on corn flour and dough for the tortilla industry, and the price of beans in the capital city was maintained at a lower level than in the rest of the country.

The government's previous agricultural policies also indicated the need for reforming CONASUPO. Public resources destined for investment in agriculture had been concentrated in zones which promised high returns on export crops such as coffee, sugar, cotton, wheat, fruit, and vegetables (see Barkin, 1970; Carlos, 1974). Commercially oriented farming for domestic markets was consequently partly abandoned in favor of crops which could be sold internationally, principally to the United States. The consuming population increased through urban in-migration and population growth, and domestic crop production failed to increase at an adequate rate. As a result, in 1970 Mexico was forced to import corn for the first time since 1964. CONASUPO was implicated in the failure to stimulate greater production and in the economic consequences of the need to import the grain.

Presidential Concern for Agriculture

> The President, when he was Minister of the Interior, must have seen a great many things which made him realize that the lid was not on so tight and that the apparent peace, especially in rural areas, was not so deep as many believed. He seemed to realize that the very stability of the country depended on some redistribution of welfare and resources.

In addition to the internal problems caused by its past activities, CONASUPO's leadership was stimulated to seek new policy goals by the publicly expressed concern of President Echeverría for agricultural production and for the inhabitants of rural Mexico. Throughout his presidential campaign, he stressed the need to increase agricultural production by stimulating more rural-directed investment from both the private and the public sectors and to institute policies and programs which would achieve a more equitable distribution of income. Stressing that the "first phase" of the Agrarian Reform was at an end, the presidential candidate reiterated on numerous occasions that this should serve as a stimulus to government activity in order to raise productivity and to improve the conditions of rural life and allow the peasant "an increased capacity to acquire Mexican products."[5]

According to my informants, several perceptions lay behind the President's concern with agricultural and rural areas. First was the officially expressed awareness that agricultural production was failing to grow in comparison with other sectors of the economy (see Banco Nacional de Comercio Exterior, 1971: 35). Between 1940 and 1970, for

5. Campaign speech, October 23, 1969. Echeverría reiterated his views on Mexican agriculture in a speech on January 18, 1970. See also Banco Nacional de Comercio Exterior (1970).

TABLE 8.

Average Annual Growth Rates, Mexico, 1940-1970

	1940–1950 (%)	1950–1960 (%)	1960–1970 (%)	1965–1970 (%)
Gross domestic product	6.7	5.8	7.1	7.1
Population	2.8	3.1	3.5	3.5
Per capita product	3.9	2.7	3.6	3.6
Agricultural production	8.2	4.3	3.6	2.2
Manufacturing production	8.1	7.3	8.9	9.0

Source: Banco Nacional de Comercio Exterior, *La política económica del nuevo gobierno* (Mexico, 1971), p. 35; Hansen, *The Politics of Mexican Development* (Baltimore: Johns Hopkins, 1971), p. 42.

example, growth in the industrial sector rose by 8.1 percent per year; in agriculture, the rate was 5.4 percent. More importantly, the agricultural growth had declined from 8.2 percent annually in the 1940–1950 decade to 3.6 percent in the 1960s. In the same ten-year period, industrial growth climbed to an annual 8.9 percent. The growth rate in the primary sector had declined especially rapidly during the second half of the decade of the 1960s, as is indicated in Table 8. In 1960, agricultural activities accounted for about 16 percent of the gross domestic product in Mexico; in 1970, the percentage had declined to 11.5 (see Table 9).

The failure of agricultural growth to keep pace with the rest of the economy meant that the country was becoming more dependent on imports to feed its burgeoning population. Previously self-sufficient in basic foodstuffs, between 1965 and 1971 Mexico became increasingly a net importer of important staple products. This trend of lagging domestic market production, indicated in Table 10, were clear to Echeverría and his advisors, even allowing for poor agricultural cycles. Moreover, much of the export-oriented commercial agriculture was in the hands of transnational companies. In 1970, Mexican leaders saw these conditions as proof of the country's growing economic dependence and its increasing imbalance of trade in the international market.

This undesirable state of affairs, considered to amount to a development crisis by government officials, was thought to be the result of the country's past "developmentalist" policy. Beginning in the 1940s, Mexican decision makers, like those in a number of other Latin American countries, accepted and pursued a policy of import substituting industrialization (ISI), relying on the agricultural sector to provide the foreign exchange needed to finance further industrialization. A critique of ISI

TABLE 9.

Industrial Origin of Gross Domestic Product, Mexico, 1960–1973
(Constant 1960 Prices)

	1960 (%)	1970 (%)	1973* (%)
Agriculture, forestry, fishing, hunting	15.9	11.5	10.6
Mining and quarrying	1.5	1.0	0.9
Petroleum and basic petrochemicals	3.4	4.2	4.2
Manufacturing	19.2	22.4	23.1
Construction	4.1	4.6	5.0
Electricity, gas, and water	1.0	1.9	2.0
Transportation, storage, and communication	3.3	3.1	3.5
Wholesale and retail trade	31.2	32.7	31.7
Public administration and defense	4.9	5.7	6.2
Other services	15.5	12.9	12.8
Totals	100.0	100.0	100.0
Gross Domestic Product	150.2	300.8	354.2

Source: Economist Intelligence Unit, *Mexico, Annual Supplement*, various years.
*Estimated.

Table 10.

Net Exports of Basic Agricultural Commodities,
Mexico, 1965–1971 (Tons)

	Corn	Wheat	Beans	Rice	Milk
1965	1,469,377	751,369	17,960	(−15,703)	(−17,132)
1966	932,902	51,494	111,968	(−12,667)	(−18,975)
1967	1,374,006	233,633	61,660	(−36)	(−26,186)
1968	895,770	(−225)	77,621	14,603	(−34,256)
1969	779,861	247,310	53,118	(−4,945)	(−41,542)
1970	(−760,758)	29,810	2,469	(−16,388)	(−48,979)
1971	285,429	(−167,496)	(−499)	(−881)	(−51,944)

Source: 1965–1970, computed from Banco Nacional de Comercio Exterior, *Anuario estadístico*; 1971, calculated from Secretaría de Industria y Comercio, *Anuario estadístico*.

Note: Negative figures denote net imports.

TABLE 11.

Foreign Trade Balance, Mexico, 1964–1974
(Millions of Dollars)

Year	Exports	Imports	Balance of Trade	Exports as % of Imports
1964	1,023.9	1,475.9	−457.0	69.4
1965	1,113.9	1,559.6	−445.7	70.8
1966	1,185.6	1,608.6	−423.0	73.7
1967	1,103.8	1,745.8	−642.0	63.2
1968	1,180.7	1,960.1	−779.4	60.2
1969	1,285.0	2,078.0	−693.0	66.6
1970	1,372.9	2,460.8	−1,087.9	57.0
1971	1,474.5	2,407.3	−932.8	61.2
1972	1,813.7	2,936.8	−1,124.5	61.7
1973	2,452.0	4,145.8	−1,693.8	59.1
1974	3,409.4	6,516.3	−3,106.9	52.3

Source: Economist Intelligence Unit: *Mexico, Annual Supplement*, various issues.

was increasingly accepted by high level officials in the early 1970s and began to be reflected in economic decision making.[6] The critique challenged the capacity of an import substitution policy to foster development and stressed the dangers of economic dependency and inequitable distribution of wealth for Mexico's growth in the future. Continued economic development, it was postulated, would be stifled by balance of payments problems and the small size of the internal consumer market (see Reyes Osorio and Eckstein, 1971). One means by which the government hoped to overcome these problems was to stimulate the production of domestic foodstuffs to reachieve self-sufficiency (Banco Nacional de Comercio Exterior, 1971).

A growing awareness among high level politicians and administrators of the anomalies in the distribution of wealth was also important in convincing President Echeverría of the need for greater government attention to rural areas. Although political rhetoric in Mexico since the 1930s has stressed the regime's commitment to redistributing personal income more equitably, government policies have in fact encouraged a greater concentration of wealth.[7] Since 1940, income distribution in Mexico has

6. Discussions of the effects of Mexico's ISI policies can be found in Banco Nacional de Comercio Exterior (1975), Felix (1968), Pellicer de Brody (1974), Solís (1971), Wionczek (1973).

7. Navarrete (1970), Prieto (1969), and Tello (1971a, 1971b) analyze data on income distribution in Mexico.

TABLE 12.

Economically Active Population,* by Sectors,
Mexico

	1940 (%)	1950 (%)	1960 (%)	1970 (%)
Agriculture	65.4	58.3	54.2	39.5
Industry	12.7	16.0	19.0	23.0
Services	21.9	25.7	26.8	37.5

Source: Mexico, *Noveno censo general de población*, 1970.
*Twelve years of age and older.

been characterized by increasing inequality between the poorest half of
the population and the rest of the society. In 1950, for example, the lower
50 percent of the population shared 19.1 percent of the total personal
income in Mexico. By 1968, this amount had dropped to 18.3 percent
(Banco de México, 1971; Hansen, 1971: 75).

Income inequality was most marked in rural zones, where 42.3
percent of the population lived in 1970. While the percentage of the
population employed in agriculture has dropped steadily since 1940,
nevertheless, in 1970, a sizable proportion of the economically active
still derived its income from agriculture. In that year, more than five
million Mexicans were employed in agricultural pursuits, nearly 40
percent of the economically active population (see Table 12). Seventy-
seven percent of these agricultural workers had monthly incomes of less
than $40. In contrast, only 17.5 percent of workers in the industrial
sector and 30 percent in services earned so little (see Table 13). The
average monthly income in 1968 was 1,136 pesos for families engaged
in agriculture, compared to 2,731 pesos for nonagricultural families
(Banco de México, 1971).

According to my respondents, Echeverría was clearly conscious of
the potential for social unrest which increasing social and economic
inequality presented and of the impulse such inequities provided for
migration from rural to urban areas. As Minister of the Interior during
the previous administration, he was privy to closely guarded knowledge
about guerrilla activity and other threats to the country's much touted
peace and stability. Organized movements of peasants in a number of
states were of concern during the 1960s as were the burgeoning squatter
settlements in urban areas. Moreover, in perhaps the most extensive
presidential campaign since that of Cárdenas in 1933–1934, Echeverría
traveled to numerous remote and impoverished rural communities to
listen to the problems and aspirations of their inhabitants. He therefore

TABLE 13.

Average Monthly Income Distribution,* Mexico, 1970

Monthly Earnings	Agriculture (%)	Industry (%)	Services (%)
Less than 500 pesos ($40)	77.2	17.5	30.0
500–999 pesos ($40–$80)	16.8	44.7	29.7
1,000–1,499 pesos ($80–$120)	2.5	17.6	17.8
1,500–2,499 pesos ($120–$200)	1.5	10.9	11.9
2,500 pesos and more ($200)	2.0	9.3	10.6
Totals	100.0	100.0	100.0

Source: Calculated from Secretaría de Industria y Comercio, *Noveno censo general de población*, 1970.

*Economically Active Population, twelve years or older.

had substantial first-hand knowledge of the radical contrasts between wealthy and cosmopolitan sections of Mexico City and most of the rest of the country (see Turner, 1973: 153–154).

CONASUPO's leadership was eager to become involved in rural development efforts in response to the President's interest in the problem. Because of the great power of the President in Mexico, decision making elites are extremely sensitive to his policy initiatives. Indeed, the influence of the President in public affairs is frequently perceived to be boundless. As one respondent stated,

> There is a very important day in Mexico. That's the first of September of the very first year of the *sexenio* when the President tells the people what's going to happen for the next six years—tells them what to believe in and how to behave—even if things turn out completely opposite, at least they have this official line. Everyone is glued to the radio and TV that day—waiting to hear what the future will be for six years.

Given this perception of the President's power, in addition to his ability to support and advance the fortunes both of individuals and agencies, it was little wonder that for many newly installed officials, advocating the "official line" was good politics.

Diffusion of the Developmentalist Critique

> There is a tendency to identify development with indicators of productivity and, therefore, to think that development is occurring when actually it isn't. Increased production does not mean development when it occurs at the expense of an ever-increasing marginalization of certain sectors and an increasing rate of disequilibrium.

The rural development policy which emerged in CONASUPO in 1971 and 1972, however, was not simply the result of opportunistic officials jumping on the President's policy bandwagon. Significant in their decision to reorient the agency's activities was the gradual diffusion of the critical analysis of Mexico's past development strategy, especially as this concerned agriculture.

In 1970, it was becoming evident to government officials that stimulating the agricultural sector would be the key to further economic development in the country.[8] Committees of interested administrators, formed during the Díaz Ordaz administration, studied analyses of Mexico's development which were current in intellectual circles in the 1960s. The writings of Leopoldo Solís were particularly influential (see, for example, Solís, 1971). Among the middle and high level administrators recruited by the general director of CONASUPO were several individuals who had been involved in these efforts to understand the problems of national agriculture. Aware of the trends of sectoral disequilibrium which disturbed Echeverría and his advisors, these officials were becoming convinced that growth in agricultural production and rural development were not synonymous terms.

In addition, their concern with agriculture led them to read the studies of scholars at the Centro de Investigaciones Agrarias under the leadership of Salomón Eckstein and Sergio Reyes Osorio and works by Rodolfo Stavenhagen, Arturo Bonilla, Angel Palerm, Fernando Paz Sánchez, Edmundo Flores, and others.[9] These studies made clear that the consequence of government policies which encouraged only the production of export crops was the development of areas of technologically advanced commercial agriculture, principally in northwestern sections of the country, in conjunction with extreme backwardness in areas devoted to the production of domestic crops. In the backward regions, rural unemployment and underemployment were considered to be the source of the urban in-migration which was causing grave problems in Mexico City, Monterrey, Guadalajara, and other cities (see Reyes Osorio and Eckstein, 1971: 38–39).

8. This perspective is presented in Centro de Investigaciones Agrarias (1974), and Reyes Osorio and Eckstein (1971).

9. See for example, Centro de Investigaciones Agrarias (1974) for a complete description and analysis of the condition of Mexican agriculture during the 1960s. See also Durán (1967), Eckstein (1966, 1968), Flores (1961), Martínez Ríos (1972), Palerm (1968, 1972), Stavenhagen (n.d.), Stavenhagen, Paz Sánchez, Cárdenas, and Bonilla (1968). Alonso Aguilar and Roger Bartra were also influential intellectuals. See Aguilar Monteverde (1967) and Bartra (1974, 1975). For conditions of Latin American rural and agricultural problems in general, see Barraclough and Collarte (1973), Beltrán (1971), Smith (1969). Wharton (1969) includes a number of useful articles on subsistence agriculture. An overview and historical interpretation of the Mexican economy, 1900–1965, is found in Reynolds (1970). Appendix C provides recent statistical information on Mexican agriculture.

In addition, a number of individuals in CONASUPO's newly recruited *equipo* at middle levels had practical field experience in observing the failure of the traditional agricultural sector to develop as the commercial sector had. For example, a CONASUPO agronomist recalled,

> When I was working in the Yucatán for the Water Resources Ministry, there was a group of us who wanted to know why all the projects failed. There were economists, agronomists, and sociologists all observing that this great amount of money being poured into irrigation works was not producing any results. We saw tremendous resistance to changes in technology from among the peasants in spite of teaching them how to use it. We started to wonder why. . . . At times, not one-tenth of the results expected [from irrigation works] was being obtained.

The impact of the experiences and observations of these concerned officials was slight prior to 1971, however. Although they sometimes arrived at fruitful evaluations of the problems of agricultural underdevelopment, they had no operative authority and lacked high level direction or interest in their findings, in addition to functioning outside the regular ministries of government (see PIDER, 1973). "I suspect the President did not even know they existed," one official recalled about the study groups. The Ministry of Agriculture itself remained convinced that agriculture would progress through the introduction of more capital and better technology. In short, although technical evaluations of the problem of agricultural development existed before 1971, they had not influenced the thinking of high level policy makers. By 1971, however, interest in rural development was an idea whose time had come. One informant who was directly involved in agricultural sector planning summarized official attitudes in 1971 by pointing to the coincidence of both technical and environmental factors.

> I think the present government was almost forced, because of economic conditions, to take new postures toward agriculture. Above all it was the fact of having to import corn—corn is religion, it's culture, it's economics, it's life, it's art in Mexico—which really brought things to the attention of the President and others. Simultaneously, there was also a technical analysis which pointed up the problems of agriculture at the time; but technical dictates were not what *caused* the policy; circumstances did that. Before that, no one really paid any attention to the *técnicos* and their proposals.

The Evaluation, the Theory, and the Policy

> We have a complete new policy which is very much a part of CONASUPO. We are now convinced that problems of agriculture in the traditional sector are related to economic relations rather than to infrastructure and technology.

TABLE 14.

Production of Corn and Yield of Crops
by Agricultural Zones, Mexico

| | Corn Production as % of Total Area Harvested | | Yield |
Zone	Total	Irrigated	kg./ha.
Pacific north	5	17.6	1250
Gulf	11	0.9	950
Pacific south	19	4.1	830
Center	41	11.0	820
North	24	12.0	730

Source: Centro de Investigaciones Agrarias, *Estructura agraria y desarrollo agrícola en México* (Mexico: Fondo de Cultura Económica), p. 85, based on 1960 census data.

One of the first official actions of the new director general of CONASUPO was to create a department of technical management within the Planning and Finance Division of the agency and to appoint as its head a trusted and innovative administrator who had been active in studying Mexico's development problems during the previous administration. This new manager recruited a group of young economists and agronomists in whom he had *confianza* and directed them in an evaluation of the agency's impact on agricultural production. Subsequently, the group embarked on a full scale study of rural Mexico and the dynamics of agricultural development.

They began with the observation that there were, in fact, two kinds of agriculture in Mexico. Modern, or commercial agriculture was characterized by production responsive to the market economy, employment of more or less advanced technology, and receipt of the major portion of private and public investment in agriculture. The traditional agricultural sector, on the other hand, was characterized by production motivated by self-consumption, use of primitive technology, and the achievement of low yields per unit of land. The differences between the two types corresponded to geographical zones of the country, as is evident from the figures on productivity levels and use of technology in Tables 14 and 15.

According to a national survey of 3,670 peasants carried out by the group, only 17 percent of them had ever sold their crops to CONASUPO. Instead, the agency tended to contract with large commercial farmers to buy all or part of their crops at current support prices. Generally, the support prices offered more reasonable returns to technologically

TABLE 15.

Mechanization and Average Plot Size
by Agricultural Zones, Mexico

Zone	% of Agricultural Surface Exploited Without Aid of Machines	Average Plot Size (ha.)
Northwest	1.2	14.03
Center	29.2	2.69
South	39.0	3.72

Source: Musalem López, "La renta de la tierra, el
desarrollo agrícola y la migración rural." Paper presented
to the XLI Congreso Internacional de Americanistas,
Mexico, D.F., September 2–7, 1974, based on data for
1971–1972 agricultural cycle.

advanced agriculture because of lower per unit costs than in traditional
farming (CONASUPO, 1972b). Therefore, CONASUPO's protective activities
had benefited the more advanced agriculture, stimulating rapid increases
in production, impressive yields per unit cultivated, and a high rate of
capitalization. But the agency was dealing with only a small sector of
the agricultural population, and this was not the one with the greatest
need of its services (CONASUPO, 1971b).

The CONASUPO officials concentrated further study on an analysis of
the production of corn. Corn is the most important commodity that
CONASUPO is charged with regulating; annually it spends 63 percent of
its 80 million dollar subsidy from the government on the purchase and
sale of corn.[10] A study of its records demonstrated to the technical
department group that nearly 90 percent of the nation's corn crop comes
from the more agriculturally backward regions of the country, indicating
that the principal producers of corn were not the large scale commercial
farmers who exploit nearly all Mexico's irrigated land, but small farmers
and *ejidatarios* who have little land, little water, and little official or
private formal credit. In fact, they calculated, these traditional farmers

10. In April 1974, the subsidy was doubled to 160 million dollars to subsidize the
production of tortillas to offset the rise in guarantee prices. Almost half of the cultivated
area of Mexico is dedicated to growing corn; this crop represents 20 percent of the value
of all agricultural production; it is the basic staple of the Mexican diet, especially of the
least advantaged sectors. The technical group discovered that over 43 percent of the
nation's families spends between 18 and 25 percent of its annual food budgets on corn.
This product represents 12 percent of total food consumption in the country (CONASUPO,
1972b). While corn is not a highly remunerative crop for commercially oriented
agriculture, CONASUPO specialists considered that it was frequently grown by modern
producers because of soil conditions or high risks involved in changing to another crop
or because it had an assured market through CONASUPO (CONASUPO, 1972b).

were responsible for over 60 percent of the total amount of corn produced (CONASUPO, 1972b). This suggested to the study group that efforts
to stimulate increasing commercialization of this crop in response to the
government's self-sufficiency policy would be most effective if they
focused on this sector. They therefore decided to direct their efforts to
understanding better the dynamics of the traditional agricultural sector.

The study group subsequently affirmed that, in contradiction to all
official expectations that Mexico could engender its own class of small,
independent commercial farmers, the traditional agricultural sector was
increasingly turning to subsistence farming (Argaez *et al.*, n.d.). Because
of competition from commercial agriculture and the stable official
support prices offered by CONASUPO, the money received by the peasant
for his crops remained the same while the general cost of living increased
(see Table 16). In the absence of technological improvements to increase
production, the study group demonstrated that more and more agricultural work days were required for the peasant to generate the same
returns on his participation in the national economy. It therefore became
increasingly uneconomical for him to grow market crops to exchange
for the food, clothes, medicines, and other staple products and services
he needed to live. Simultaneously, it was increasingly rational for him
to retire from the production of crops for market and to grow only
enough food for his own consumption and that of his family. He could
then spend the remainder of his time in the labor market in nearby urban
areas, or he could even abandon agriculture altogether and migrate to
Mexico City, Guadalajara, Monterrey, or the United States. Migrating,
suggested one informant, the peasant

> becomes a market consumer of those goods which he formerly produced
> for himself outside the market. . . . Thus, the government is suddenly
> faced with an acute scarcity of food products, especially staple items
> like corn and beans.

By early 1972, the technical analysis group had developed a theoretical explanation for the growing marginalization of the subsistence
sector. They arrived at the conclusion that traditional agriculture was
not developing as expected because the peasant is a victim of unfavorable
economic relationships in the rural areas. Their argument began with
the assumption that in order for a traditional farmer to pass to the
modern agricultural sector, it is necessary for him to produce a surplus,
to retain the use of the surplus, and finally to invest it productively in
the improvement of his production. The problem is that any surplus
produced by the Mexican peasant is extracted by individuals and groups
who make their livings by exploiting him.

The explanation of this process of extraction began with the observation that even though most of his production is destined for self-
consumption, the subsistence farmer still maintains a relationship with

TABLE 16.

**Consumer and Corn Prices
in Mexico**

Year	Consumer Price Index 1963 = 100	Guaranteed Price of Corn Pesos/ton
1953	60	350
1958	90	550
1959	92	800
1960	97	800
1961	98	800
1962	99	800
1963	100	800
1964	102	940
1965	106	940
1966	110	940
1967	114	940
1968	116	940
1969	120	940
1970	126	940
1971	130	940
1972	138	940
1973		1200
1974		1500
1975		1750
1976		1900

Source: United Nations, *Statistical Yearbook*, 1972; CONASUPO, unpublished memoranda.

the money economy. This is true, for example, when he buys staple goods he cannot produce himself, when he purchases emergency services such as medical attention, when he rents out his labor, or when he sells his small agricultural surplus after a good harvest. Due to his low economic level, however, the peasant is often in a weak bargaining position when dealing with representatives of the national economy. Frequently, it is necessary for him to sell his crops before they are harvested in order to have enough money to meet his needs; he may be forced to apply for informal and usurious credit at the local store; he may not have enough money to buy sacks to transport his products to market nor sufficient capital for storage or transportation of his crops to obtain a better price. More often than not, therefore, the peasant must rely on middlemen who enable him to subsist from harvest to harvest but who take advantage of his weak bargaining position. The most general consequences of these economic relationships were posited to be the following:

1. The subsistence farmer receives inferior prices for his products.

2. He receives salaries which are less than the official minimum level.

3. He pays prices for goods and services (including credit) which are more than the national market price (CONASUPO, 1972c).

The basic problem then is that although he might produce a surplus through his labor, the peasant is incapable of retaining and investing it. Instead, the surplus is siphoned off by the economic intermediaries such as store owners, truckers, crop buyers, large landowners, and others who benefit from the peasant's lack of bargaining power. Moreover, the CONASUPO group stated, these same agents of the national economy attempt to stimulate the consumption level of the peasant when he does produce a surplus in a favorable agricultural cycle in order to inhibit his productive investment (CONASUPO, 1972b; 1972c).[11]

This analysis of the dynamics of agricultural development was a significant change over previously prevailing models. Agricultural development in Mexico had traditionally been defined as increased production. To stimulate production, the government invested in large infrastructure programs such as irrigation projects and transportation networks; it provided credits to efficient producers; it encouraged the use of advanced technology; it provided incentives for the growth of exportable market crops such as cotton, coffee, tomatoes, strawberries, and wheat; it focused development efforts on large regional river basin projects; and it concentrated its investments in regions with high output potential because of the availability of water or fertile soil.[12] The effects of this policy were summed up in a document written by members of the study group.

> Confusing an increase of productivity with economic development results in the concentration of production in a few hands, eliminating many more farmers from the market than those who result as beneficiaries of increased production locally, condemning subsistence agriculture to monoculture, and provoking a greater influx of peasants to the city; in effect accelerating enormously the process of proletarianization of the peasants (Argaez et al., n.d.).

11. The studies reported in Instituto de Investigaciones Sociales (1975) provide insight into local level politico-economic relationships.
12. Descriptions of Mexico's agricultural policies up to the initiation of the Echeverría administration are found in Barkin (1970, 1975), Carlos (1974), and Centro de Investigaciones Agrarias (1974).

Standard government policies of providing infrastructure and technology to increase production had failed, the analysis continued, because they did not substantially affect the bargaining position of the subsistence farmer. Instead, the peasant tended to resist initiatives to increase his productivity or his participation in the market because it was generally uneconomical for him to produce more than enough for self-sufficiency. Increased governmental aid in terms of infrastructure, technology, and credit did not achieve the desired goals because benefits tended to remain in the hands of the intermediary economic agents.

The solution to this problem was a simple one. It was proposed that a policy was needed which would allow the peasant both to retain his surplus and to invest it effectively. This meant breaking the hold of inter-mediaries on the peasant economy. In short, a new policy aimed at altering structural economic relationships in the rural areas was necessary if agricultural development was to occur. In early 1972, the technical department of CONASUPO produced a general policy statement and a program plan whose goal was the transformation of subsistence agri-culture in Mexico. The federal government, by means of deliberate and programmed activity, should intervene more decisively in rural areas to provide a change in the impact of market forces on the peasants, suggested the group.

Specifically, it was proposed that CONASUPO offer an integrated package of services which would replace the local economic agents or intermediaries with government programs. For its designers, the key word in this new policy proposal was "integrated"; only by offering all the services provided by the middleman or *coyote* could CONASUPO and other government agencies hope to free the peasant from exploitation. This meant that CONASUPO's programs should

1. Provide peasants with the goods and services they needed at real market prices. This would include items such as clothes, food, fertilizers, insecticides, improved seeds, agricultural tools, medicines, and medical care.

2. Buy their harvests directly from them at support prices correspond-ing to real market prices.

3. Provide them with preharvest consumer credit and basic harvest-related services such as corn shellers, gunny sacks, storage, and transport.

4. Assure them of the efficient marketing of their crops so they would acquire national market prices.

5. Encourage them to find productive uses for their additional income (CONASUPO, 1972c).

Each of these general goals was accompanied by a battery of pro-grams to be implemented. For example, to sell goods to the peasants at

real market prices, CONASUPO proposed establishing rural cooperative
stores; expanding its regular and mobile retail outlet channels in rural
areas and developing a program of consumer credit in these stores;
supplying rural warehouses with sacks, tools, fertilizers and improved
seeds, and corn shellers; renting or selling these to the peasants with the
aid of official credit; training local peasant groups to man the stores;
and constructing local level medical centers and pharmacies to provide
low cost care and medicines. To encourage the productive use of the
peasant's income, other programs would initiate training in horticulture,
bee keeping, animal husbandry, home economics, and agricultural
improvement; production cooperatives would be fomented; rural and
cottage industries would be stimulated; and farm machinery would be
made available for purchase by groups of farmers. The particular mix
of programs to be offered in any given community would be determined
by the criterion of breaking the exploitive relationships which prevented
development in that area.

The new policy of rural development meant a significant change in
CONASUPO's overall activities. It meant that support prices would have to
be set with the rural producer in mind rather than the urban consumer.
It meant that each CONASUPO program would have to be planned and
evaluated in terms of its impact on all other programs and of its overall
consequence for the peasant. It implied the need for a buildup of
CONASUPO's organization to fulfill adequately its new role. Consequently,
greater budgetary resources would be needed. Related to its new activities, more overall coordination of CONASUPO programs would be
required. Additionally, the new policy required the willing collaboration
of other governmental agencies involved in agricultural development
because often some of the requirements of a community—irrigation,
bank credit, roads, medical attention, or electrification, for example—
were outside CONASUPO's ability to supply. Therefore, mobilizing support
for the new policy, both within CONASUPO and without, was important
if the rural development scheme were to become a reality. While the
process of policy making was well underway by late 1971, the most
difficult task—that of mobilizing support for it—still had to be
addressed.

Mobilizing Support for the Policy

> We have to wait until just the right moment politically to line up
> support and disperse opposition. We need to have the President
> completely behind us.

Through 1971 and early 1972, the study of rural development problems
was confined to the *equipo* in the technical planning department. Those

involved shared a perception that they were seeking an answer to an important and potentially explosive problem. Moreover, they enjoyed the complete support of their superior, the technical manager, who in turn benefited from the *confianza* of the general director. This support encouraged high morale within the group and stimulated its members to work quickly to produce concrete outlines of what needed to be done. In February and March 1972, their propositions about subsistence agriculture and a preliminary package of CONASUPO activities to achieve a new impact in rural areas were summarized on paper and given to the manager of the technical department.

In a number of discussions with De la Vega in the early spring of 1972, the manager presented the conclusions reached by his *equipo*. The director had long been interested in the problems of rural and agricultural development and was easily convinced of the importance of an integrated rural development strategy for the objectives of CONASUPO. All informant reports indicate that at this time he became sincerely convinced of the intellectual integrity of the plan and its promise to resolve anomalies and inequities in Mexico's economic and social development. There were, however, additional reasons for him to become a fervent advocate of the policy.

Not unimportantly, pursuit of such a policy offered almost unlimited opportunities for the expansion of CONASUPO's activities. The new orientation included an elastic definition of staple goods: "Those consumer articles which are indispensable for nutrition, health and physical well-being" (CONASUPO, 1972a). Additionally, the theory indicated a broad range of ways in which the peasant was a prisoner of economic relationships. Therefore, CONASUPO had the rationale for providing such diverse goods and services as medicines, construction materials, consumer production credit, rural education, agricultural extension, community development assistance, seeds, fertilizers, food, and clothing—anything, in fact, which involved the peasant in economic relationships with other sectors of the society.

An expansion in the agency's activities implied a large increase in the amount of financial support it would need from the government. A higher budget, in turn, introduced the possibility of enhancing the impact of the agency's programs. Concomitantly, as its activities affected more people in a beneficial way, CONASUPO could expect to become increasingly important to the government, and the handling of more resources would give its leaders greater personal influence within the bureaucratic-political system. Acceptance of the new policy was also attractive because it might easily result in presidential support and lead to improved career opportunities for the agency's management. The President, in the early months of his administration, was interested in stimulating response to his own concern for agricultural development,

and the CONASUPO scheme provided a comprehensive and logical explanation of the failure of rural areas to develop and outlined clear guidelines
for subsequent policy and decision making. Consequently, once he
became an advocate of the comprehensive rural development policy,
De la Vega quickly set about gaining its acceptance.

Policy Support Within CONASUPO

First of all, it was important to acquire the support of the constituent
parts of CONASUPO itself. In response to the new policy, each division and
subsidiary company head would have to be prepared to make organizational changes and be ready to seek flexible and innovative solutions to
bureaucratic bottlenecks which might inhibit policy implementation.
Moreover, efficient cooperation among the various divisions and subsidiaries required that all high level officials share a dedication to the
new policy goals and a willingness to break with established routines
and resistance to open communication. Much, of course, had already
been done to ensure that a policy advocated by the general director
would be accepted by his subordinates. As described in Chapter 3, he
had appointed a number of subordinates he knew personally; *confianza*
and career aspirations cemented their working relationship. All high
level CONASUPO officials would find it to their personal advantage, aside
from any purely intellectual conviction, to exhibit the loyalty, support,
and flexible administrative outlook needed by the director to reorient
the agency's activities. However, willingness to support the policy was
more forthcoming from some high level officials than from others.

Differential response to the policy was observed among the divisions
of the parent company, for instance. At the time the policy was being
discussed among CONASUPO's high level officials, there were three of these
divisions: Operations, Planning and Finance, and Subsidiary Companies.
High level officials of these divisions were interviewed in 1974 and 1975,
and the statements they made in response to questions about their job
objectives provide an indicator of their support of the new policy.
Among division leadership, dedication to the rural development strategy
varied in relation to the dependence of each unit on the General Office of
the company for resource allocation. In cases where resource dependence
was less great, the bonds of loyalty and obligation between high level
CONASUPO officials were observed to be less strong. This tendency is
clear in a comparison of policy support in two of the divisions.

As will be remembered from the description of the agency presented
in Chapter 1, the Operations Division was directly responsible for
carrying out the traditional market regulatory programs of CONASUPO,
that is, the buying, transporting, and selling of agricultural products,
including importing and exporting them when necessary. Operations
had a specific job to accomplish: determine the quantity and quality

of crops to purchase and sell and issue directives about where, when, and how such purchases were to be made, using whatever means were within its powers to accomplish this. So important were its functions and its claim to most of the budget of the agency that Operations was the most powerful of the three divisions. Its support was needed in the implementation of the new rural development policy because special efforts were required to target crop purchasing programs for the small farmers and *ejidatarios* of the traditional sector.

At the outset of each agricultural cycle, the Operations Division collected information about projected production from their agents in the field, from the Ministry of Agriculture, and from the agricultural credit banks. On the basis of these data, the amount of each harvest CONASUPO would need to purchase in order to regulate the market was determined. The division was then appropriated sufficient funds by the Finance Ministry to accomplish its goals. When high level officials in the General Office were interviewed in 1974, the process of obtaining resources for Operations was considered to be automatic. It was denied that politics intervened in the budgetary process as far as this division was concerned.

> It is not a great problem to get more money because our operating needs are fixed, even though our financial needs change. That is to say, there is a given amount of commodities we must buy so we simply have to have the money. This is the policy of the federal government and as long as we are fulfilling it, we receive the money to carry out this task.

Thus, Operations had a fixed and secure source of financial support which was independent of the influence of the general director over budgetary allocations in the company. In order to accomplish its objectives, it made little difference to Operations that small farmers and *ejidatarios* were being bypassed when CONASUPO bought crops from commercial farmers, truckers, or intermediary agents. In fact, contracting with a large number of dispersed marginal farmers actually meant more work to achieve the same results for these officials. It is not surprising that the Operations Division leadership did not become wholehearted advocates of the "new line" of policy. Almost three years after the rural development policy went into effect, decision makers within the Operations Division defined their goals in the following manner.

> Our principal goal is to get the agricultural products in the best condition and at the best price we can in order to regulate the market.
>
> The objective I have is to try to get the best possible diagnosis of what the harvest will be, to create a functioning and reliable system of information to aid us in regulating the market.
>
> I consider it my main objective to head up a good crop buying program.

When the need to involve marginal farmers in purchasing programs was mentioned, it was emphasized that CONASUPO was offering services to them in order to "capture" as much of the harvest as possible because of national and international scarcities. The important thing, these officials stated, was to get the crops.

The ties of loyalty to De la Vega, noticeable in all other divisions, were weaker among the officials interviewed in the Operations Division. Among all respondents, it was only among Operations Division functionaries that even veiled criticism of the director was heard. Thus, for example, one high level Operations official complained,

> The real problem when the *sexenio* comes is not the change of personnel. The real problem is that each new director comes in with his own program, and that causes real disruption and a lack of continuity. I think that if a program is working well in one *sexenio*, it should be continued in the next one. But that's not always the way it works, unfortunately.

It was, of course, possible for De la Vega to dismiss those who did not become active adherents of his new policy. Because of the nature of the task performed by Operations, however, such action was risky. The estimations of crop production which Operations developed were the result of long practical experience in observing Mexican agriculture. In the absence of reliable figures from other agencies of government, Operations officials had become skilled in collecting and evaluating their own information and deriving from it reasonable predictive figures. This expertise was valued by CONASUPO's management; an indication of this is the fact that of the twelve respondents who served in CONASUPO prior to 1970, five had remained in the Operations Division. The technical expertise which these officials had acquired gave them some independence to remain aloof from the new policy.

Nevertheless, while enthusiastic support was not forthcoming, neither did Operations personnel openly oppose the director, attempt to sabotage the plan, or convince him of the inappropriateness of the policy for the agency's primary goals. Instead, they acquiesced to the new policy. Their behavior was related to the fact that there were, in fact, limits to what would be tolerated from subordinates, even those with valued expertise. Open opposition or policy disagreement undoubtedly would have resulted in the loss of their jobs.

While in the Operations Division the requirements of resource allocation and career mobility were in tension, they were mutually reinforcing influences on officials in the Planning and Finance Division, conditions which dictated strong adherence to the new rural development policy. A larger budget would give them more resources; it would, for example, allow them to administer a program of consumer credit in coordination with the agricultural banks. It would give the division greater opportunity to coordinate overall agency programs and the chance to plan and test new programs and ideas. In short, Planning and Finance Division's role would wax or wane in direct relation to the success of the director. High level administrators in this division indicated strong adherence to the overall policy goals and awareness of its implications for rural development when they were interviewed.

> We have become aware that it is not enough that the guarantee price reaches the producer. We know that this is not the only way he is tied to economic relationships in the country. He is not just tied by what he sells but also by what he buys.

> The quantity of crops purchased doesn't matter; what matters is the consequences of what has been bought and sold.

> This simply is not the same organization we encountered when we entered in 1971. . . . There has been a change in the idea of subsistence; it's not just food but whatever is needed to maintain an adequate level of living.

Similarly, different responses were evident among the subsidiary companies. The two which were to be most affected by the policy change were BORUCONSA, the rural warehouse company, and DICONSA, the retail outlet organization. To participate in the program and fulfill their assigned roles, BORUCONSA and DICONSA officials would have to be dynamic, innovative, and dedicated. In 1974 and 1975 most BORUCONSA officials interviewed were impressively devoted to the new policy. In DICONSA, on the other hand, officials evidenced a much more disparate range of objectives and criteria for making decisions. In one subsidiary, the entire organization chart was drawn to coincide with what was thought to be a rational pursuit of the rural development goals. In the other subsidiary, no new high level unit was created to handle specifically rural projects. This variation in support for the objectives sought by CONASUPO's director resulted from different degrees of dependence on the parent company for resources.

BORUCONSA, established in 1971 to salvage the *Graneros del Pueblo* program, was to be responsible for delivering the major portion of the programs included in the rural development policy package. Its expanded and improved network of rural warehouses was to be the nucleus of the integrated services offered to the peasants to liberate them from the vicious cycle of backwardness and dependency. The director of BORUCONSA was enthusiastic about the new policy and specifically mentioned its relation to CONASUPO's general director.

> The objective I have in BORUCONSA is that the *Granero* be the center, the hub of the infrastructure necessary for the development of the

community. . . . This requires an integral program. . . . This program
is our horizon; it is a horizon shown us by Jorge de la Vega Domínguez.

This statement was made by a man who, prior to coming to CONASUPO in
1971, had little experience in agriculture or rural development. He had
been trained as a civil engineer, and before heading up BORUCONSA his
responsibilities had included school administration and functions within
the Ministry of National Resources. His first appointment in CONASUPO
had been as head of the subsidiary responsible for processing wheat flour
and baking bread. Moreover, this official had been appointed through
the suggestion of the President; as a consequence, he had no a priori
obligation to exhibit loyalty to the general director. Why, then, did the
manager of BORUCONSA become such an avid defender of the rural
development policy? Ignoring for the moment the undeniable importance
of sincere intellectual conviction, an explanation can be found in the
exchange of policy support for the allocation of resources BORUCONSA
needed for its programs.

This newly created subsidiary was set up as a service organization.
Many of its activities did not generate an income for the company. In
effect, BORUCONSA had to be subsidized by the parent company. It also
needed to work in close collaboration with other agencies of the government: its warehouses and related medical facilities were to be built by
the Ministry of Public Works; fertilizer, improved seeds, and insecticides would come from the government industries producing these
goods; production and marketing credit would have to be coordinated
with the agricultural banks; agricultural extension, community organization support, and irrigation works would have to come from three other
institutions. Communication and cooperation with these agencies would
be markedly facilitated by the strong support of the agency director and
access to his network of contacts in other agencies. In fact, the subsidiary's fixed capital base grew from 4 million pesos in 1971 to 15 million
in 1973. By 1975, the subsidiary was in a position to absorb ANDSA, the
government warehousing company. This was proof that BORUCONSA
could gain both financial and political support through willing collaboration with the new policy.

The relation between resource allocation and policy support was less
strong in DICONSA, the subsidiary in charge of CONASUPO's retail outlets.
Wholehearted acceptance of the new policy meant that DICONSA would
have to shift its organization from an emphasis on urban areas to rural
ones. Instead of expanding its services in large urban centers by building
more supermarkets and medium sized stores which often earned a profit
on their sales and encouraged DICONSA administrators to think of themselves as part of the modern business sector, DICONSA would be expected
to organize and supply less remunerative and smaller rural outlets and

invest more heavily in mobile units to service remote areas. In short, the policy meant that DICONSA would be expected to devote a great deal of attention to stores whose impact on a profit and loss balance sheet was slight or negative.

DICONSA was established as a subsidiary with commercial objectives; it could not easily justify the need for subsidies on its operations as BORUCONSA was able to do. Its network of supermarkets and concessionary stores was largely self-financing. Moreover, the nature of its operations allowed it to seek outside financing independently. DICONSA also had a large number of attractive resources to distribute—stores and supply contracts, for instance—which allowed it to become a force to reckon with in the CONASUPO system.[13] In addition, collaboration with other government agencies was not as important to DICONSA as it was to BORUCONSA. The majority of its external contacts were with the private commercial and industrial sector which supplied it with merchandise for its stores. By and large, these relations were mutually beneficial to DICONSA and the private sector. The political support of the director was therefore not crucial to the subsidiary.

Because resource dependence on the parent company was not significant, the career aspirations of high level officials in DICONSA became more important to ensure at least partial support for the policy. According to informants, one director of the subsidiary, appointed under the auspices of the President, was suspected of using DICONSA to build an independent organization responding to his own political ambitions. When the general director became aware of this, he skillfully maneuvered the offending official into another high level position within the agency, one which provided fewer opportunities for empire building. He then replaced the leadership of DICONSA with individuals who were more personally loyal to him. To some degree, then, career ties compensated for the lack of resource dependency.

Gaining the compliance of his subordinates was only a first step for De la Vega in the process of mobilizing support for his policy, however. In fact, the willingness of his subordinates to accept his directives would be influenced by the extent to which he was able to acquire support for the new rural development policy outside the agency. External support, both in finances and politics, would serve as an indicator of the power and influence of the director among the bureaucratic-political elite and would figure in calculations about his future within the government. These calculations in turn would influence decisions about whether to identify one's own future with him or not. As would be expected in the

13. In addition, DICONSA had nearly three times the number of employees as the parent company, a correspondingly stronger labor union, large amounts of resources to distribute, and valuable ties to the private industrial sector.

centralized Mexican system, the support of the President was considered to be the keystone for ensuring that CONASUPO's financial resources would be enlarged, that political importance was given to the agency, and that other government agencies would be willing to cooperate with it.

Presidential Support

> Above all, [the director of CONASUPO] has been the key person in influencing the President on the change of agricultural policy. He went directly to the President and presented a well worked out and defined plan of what was needed. He has really been a forward impulse in this whole procedure of policy formulation. From the beginning, he has had a very clear idea of the problems and what was needed to solve them.

Whether in fact the President actually has the near-dictatorial authority frequently ascribed to him, it is consistently acknowledged in governmental circles that his backing is absolutely essential for the success of any program, plan, or policy. Presidential support was particularly crucial to CONASUPO in order to improve its financial situation, which in 1971 and 1972 indicated a lack of confidence in the agency (see Figure 9). Therefore, as soon as the theory and the plan were fully developed, the director sought to explain the new policy idea to the President. A series of contacts with him culminated in a full presentation of the plan by the planning department manager and the general director at a meeting in June 1972 (see CONASUPO, 1972d). According to informants, the President was impressed by the proposal and indicated willingness to support CONASUPO and its general director.

Important in convincing the President of the efficacy of CONASUPO's program were two of his closest advisors, the Minister of the Presidency, Hugo Cervantes del Río, and the Finance Minister, José López Portillo. Ties of friendship and *confianza* between high level CONASUPO administrators and the Finance Minister were forged when they had collaborated in groups studying Mexican development problems in the late 1960s. Moreover, the general director had become well acquainted with the Minister of the Presidency and with a number of politically important individuals who were close to him. These contacts were pursued and strengthened in the new administration. Additionally, López Portillo became head of the Advisory Council of CONASUPO. Cervantes del Río, a right-hand man to Echeverría, was himself convinced of the need for rural development and figured as an important source of support for CONASUPO. Informal communication among the high level officials of these agencies increased the chances that the President would come to

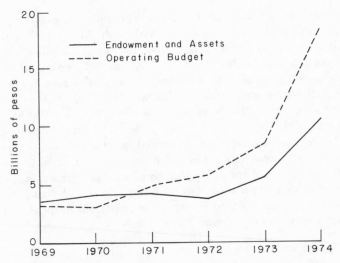

Figure 9. Financial Support and Budget Growth of CONA-
SUPO, 1969–1974. Source: 1969–1970, CONASUPO, Departa-
mento de Presupuestos; 1970–1974, CONASUPO, *Gaceta*,
No. 15 (January 1, 1975).

support CONASUPO and enable it to achieve greater importance in agricultural development.

An indication of the success in gaining presidential backing is seen
in the budgetary resources acquired by CONASUPO. Figure 10 indicates a
significant increase in federal financial support between 1972, when the
the program was presented to the President, and 1973. This increased
allowance enabled the company to grow from an organization with a
4.8 billion peso budget in 1971 to one with 18.3 billion pesos in financial
resources in 1974. A rapidly rising inflation rate in 1973 and 1974 was
helpful in demonstrating the need to increase CONASUPO's activities and
budget.[14] In April 1974, CONASUPO leaders and its Advisory Council
members emerged from a meeting with the President in his official
residence, Los Pinos, to declare,

> The federal government will provide CONASUPO with all help and
> financial resources it needs to consolidate its traditional programs,
> fortify its new programs, and extend its activities in every area it
> deems necessary . . . (Press Release, Mexico, D.F., April 20, 1974).

After this, government officials began to refer to CONASUPO as a
"regular ministry of state" because of its obvious political support and

14. In 1970, inflation in Mexico was officially reported to be 5.2 percent; in 1971,
5.7 percent; and in 1972, 5.1 percent. In 1973, however, it was 12.1 percent and in
1974, 23.3 percent (*Latin America*, May 30, 1975).

the growth of its financial resources. For 1975, its projected budget was almost five times that to be received by the Ministry of Agriculture and one and a half times larger than that of the Ministry of Water Resources. It would, therefore, account for 5.4 percent of the total federal government budget, far more than any other ministry or agency in the agricultural sector (*Gaceta*, January 16, 1975). By the time public interest was aroused in the presidential succession of 1976, Jorge de la Vega was "not often referred to as a presidential candidate himself, but was being attacked [by other hopefuls] because of doubts [about his aspirations] or because of his eventual declaration in favor of some candidate" (*Excelsior*, April 15, 1975). Thus, political interest in the power of the director was growing. His influence, along with that of the Ministers of the Presidency and Finance, was important in spearheading the initiative for sectoral planning in agriculture.

Support for Sectoral Planning

In addition to support from the President, the rural development strategy of CONASUPO implied the need for coordination of overall agricultural sector policy. Given the hypothesis of structural barriers to rural development, investment in the countryside had to be planned and coordinated among various agencies to provide, in any community, the total package of resources necessary for development. Otherwise, the balance of economic relationships affecting the peasant could not be altered. From the beginning of the planning process, agency officials recognized that "without the collaboration of other dependencies of government in current agricultural policy, CONASUPO could continue its own operations, but it would not achieve anything." CONASUPO's plans could, therefore, best be achieved by actively supporting a drive to coordinate agricultural sector policy.

However, coordination is a difficult goal to achieve in the Mexican bureaucracy. The dominant position of the President, the extreme fractionalization of responsibility among numerous agencies and programs, and the possibility of building career-oriented feudalities within each of them had caused a number of previous attempts at agricultural planning to fail. Past failures were also deeply rooted in earlier agricultural policies, as explained by one respondent.

> Policies have been a reaction to specific problems ever since the Revolution. Land distribution was carried out in accordance with specific climatic and local circumstances. Then the policy was to produce more so there was all sorts of activity directed at greater production—irrigation, insecticides, fertilizers, better seeds—and then the policy was to teach the peasant to produce more. In each case, government organizations had specific tasks assigned to them and they became completely committed to the fulfilling of that task without

seeing how it fit into overall agricultural policy. Means became con-
verted into ends and no one questioned why.

At the June 1972 meeting with the President, the general director
emphasized the importance of the sectoral planning required by
CONASUPO's new policy. His concerns were amply supported by the
Minister of the Presidency and the Minister of Finance. As a result, in
February 1973, the President decreed the establishment of the Agricultural Sector Planning Committee (COCOSA) to be chaired by the Minister
of the Presidency and to be made up of the heads of all agencies with
significant responsibilities in rural areas. Perceptions of the utility of
sectoral planning varied among the eighteen member agencies and their
willingness to collaborate in the effort was related to the ability of each
to acquire new financial resources and the consequences increased
coordination would have on the importance of the leaders of each
institution.

The key agencies whose support was needed were the Ministry of
Agriculture (SAG), the Water Resources Ministry (SRH), the Department
of Agrarian Affairs and Colonization (to become the Ministry of
Agrarian Reform in 1975—SRA), and the Ministries of the Presidency
and Finance. According to informants involved in the sectoral planning
effort, each of these organizations had its own perceptions about the
utility of collaborating with CONASUPO in overall agricultural planning.
SAG, for example, was an enormous and fragmented ministry whose
frequently inefficient performance had earned it a decreasing share of
annual budgetary allocations. Its leadership recognized that by supporting sectoral collaboration, it would be opening itself up to outside
scrutiny and criticism; its inefficiencies would be publicly revealed; its
claim to importance in agricultural policy making would be threatened;
and its budget perhaps further reduced in relation to other agencies. Nor
was the Minister of Agriculture, Oscar Brauer Herrera, regarded seriously as a presidential aspirant; performance in terms of presidential
criteria was, therefore, not as important to him as it was to other
ministers. In any event, only harm could come to the career expectations
of SAG officials if the performance level of the ministry became widely
known.

Congruent with SAG's understandable reluctance to cooperate on
purely pragmatic grounds was the official ideology of its agronomist
leadership. These officials believed strongly that the problems of
production and agricultural backwardness could be solved through the
introduction of more and better technology. Thus, in contrast to CONA-
SUPO's concern for structural factors, SAG's perception of the problem
did not require communication or coordination with other agencies.
Finally, SAG had long expressed the perspective that it should have

preeminence in decisions about the agricultural sector rather than the finance ministry or presidency. In short, SAG thought "other agencies were attempting to invade its territory" as one high level official explained. Ministry oficials, therefore, calculated that they had little to gain and much to lose through cooperation with CONASUPO and others.

SRH, on the other hand, enjoyed a reputation for being an efficient and technically competent ministry (see Greenberg, 1970). Because of this reputation, the ministry was wealthy in comparison with SAG and, should more money become available for rural development, SRH could expect to be an important recipient. Furthermore, its leadership was concerned with questions similar to those being asked by CONASUPO officials: why had the money SRH had channeled into the countryside failed to produce the expected results? The ministry was coming to the same conclusions about rural development as those reached by the regulatory agency. Finally, the Minister of SRH, Leandro Rovirosa Wade, was a very good friend of both the Minister of the Presidency and the President himself; all three had begun their careers together in the same ministry and had maintained close contact over the years. In fact, so intimate was their relationship that Rovirosa was publicly regarded as a spokesman of the President's viewpoint. The ministry was therefore inclined to support the initiative for sector-wide planning.

SRA was responsible for land distribution and the administration and promotion of the *ejido* communities. Although the organization was plagued by bureaucratic bottlenecks in dealing with *ejido* problems and had often been implicated in exploitive relationships with the peasants it was charged with aiding, its high level leadership was concerned with increasing the amount of resources flowing into the traditional agricultural sector. In spite of the risk that its inefficiencies or corruption would be revealed, it was expected that agricultural sector planning would result in greater resources for SRA. The Minister, Augusto Gómez Villanueva, was also a presidential aspirant. As a result, SRA was inclined to support the initiative for sectoral planning.

The most convinced ministries were Finance and the Presidency. Finance, for example, was mindful of the need to achieve greater returns on public investments. As explained by one observer, this meant much in terms of that ministry's support of sectoral planning.

> Some ministries are evaluated on the basis of efficiency. Finance is one of them and the minister knows it—other ministries like SAG are not evaluated on that basis. Performance on the basis of efficiency is a stimulant to integrated planning: he's going to be evaluated on what use was made of the resources he was given.

Mexico's central planning ministry, the Presidency, was similarly motivated. Moreover, both ministers were presidential aspirants, and their performance in achieving the public goals of the administration could be influential in the final evaluation made by Echeverría about his successor.

Once again, then, it can be suggested that careers and resources were both centrally important factors in influencing bureaucratic behavior. The support demonstrated for agricultural sector cooperation and coordination was a response to individual ministry perceptions of advantage. Eventual, if not always enthusiastic, cooperation from SAG, the most resistant ministry, gradually resulted from two circumstances. First, COCOSA and the other ministries were able to demonstrate their usefulness to SAG in achieving solutions to routine problems of limited scope which presented themselves at regional or local levels. Second, resource allocation mechanisms set up within Finance required inter-agency coordination before funds were disbursed. Because of CONASUPO's active promotion of sectoral planning in agriculture, its representatives to COCOSA were charged with drafting the first statement of overall agricultural policy which would be used as a basis for discussion and to guide the efforts of all agencies involved. The policy statement which they produced in 1973, "Agricultural Policy Guidelines," reflected CONASUPO's perspective on rural development (COCOSA, 1973).

Dealing with External Opposition

With the President's strong political support and with the acquiescence or active adherence of other governmental agencies to the policy of integrated rural development, CONASUPO officials considered themselves free to pursue their policy objectives with confidence in their ultimate success. In another setting, it might be expected that the proposed changes in the beneficiaries of agricultural investments would engender strong and vocal opposition from both bureaucratic and nongovernmental groups who perceived their interests to be threatened by the change. For instance, the histories of agrarian reform movements in Latin American countries such as Peru, Colombia and Chile in the 1960s indicate the ability of opposition groups to obstruct or significantly modify the design of new policies.[15] But in Mexico, little time was lost by CONASUPO policy makers in dealing with such impediments. Opposition to the policy of rural development did not coalesce because of efforts by the President and by CONASUPO itself to ameliorate hostility to the plan.[16]

For instance, the President and his advisors managed budgetary allocations among agencies and ministries so that increased investment

15. See, for example, Feder (1971) and Kaufman (1972).
16. Purcell (1975) describes the management of opposition to a policy of profit sharing and demonstrates the skill of Mexican presidents and administrators in dealing with potential conflict.

TABLE 17.

Average Public Sector Investment Percentages by Presidential Period, 1925–1974

Years	President	No. of Years in Average	Industry (%)	Communications/ Transport. (%)	Agriculture/ Forestry (%)	Social Welfare (%)
1925–1928	Calles	4	—*	79.1	15.1	5.8
1929	Portes Gil	1	—	73.5	10.2	16.3
1930–1932	Ortiz Rubio	3	—	76.6	11.5	11.9
1933–1934	Rodríguez	1	—	75.9	11.0	13.1
1935–1940	Cárdenas	6	5.1	66.3	18.1	9.6
1941–1946	Avila Camacho	6	10.6	59.1	16.9	11.6
1947–1952	Alemán	6	22.0	43.0	20.1	13.6
1953–1958	Ruiz Cortínez	6	32.4	37.2	14.9	13.8
1959–1964	López Mateos	6	34.6	29.9	9.8	22.4
1965–1970	Díaz Ordaz	6	40.3	22.4	10.5	24.7
1971–1974	Echeverría	4	35.5	24.1	15.4	25.0

Source: Banco Nacional de México, *Review of the Economic Situation of Mexico*, various issues; Wilkie, "Recentralization: The Budgetary Dilemma in the Economic Development of Mexico, Bolivia, and Costa Rica," in David J. Geithman (ed.), *Fiscal Policy for Industrialization and Development in Latin America* (Gainesville: University of Florida, 1974), p. 216.

*Zero or less than 0.5%.

Note: Where percentages add to less than 100, figures for administration and defense, usually amounting to 2 to 3 percent of the budget, have been omitted.

in agricultural development did not strongly jeopardize the positions of the other sectors. Therefore, opposition from agencies which had no direct input into rural or agricultural activities was kept at a minimum. Public sector investment in agriculture during the Echeverría administration is compared with previous *sexenios* in Table 17. Echeverría devoted a larger proportion of the total to agriculture than any President since the *sexenio* of Miguel Alemán, 1947–1952. Between 1971 and 1974, the proportion of federal investment funds destined for agriculture rose from 14.5 to 17.3 percent. In 1975, and again in 1976, it was scheduled to be 20 percent. But increased attention to agriculture did not result in absolute decreases in allocations to other sectors, except that destined to administration and defense, as is evident in Table 18. Thus, for example, although the proportion of money allocated to the industrial sector dropped by over 9 percent between 1971 and 1974, it increased absolutely by almost 12 billion pesos, more than enough to offset the effects of inflation.

The President was also instrumental in managing opposition to the agricultural policy from outside the government. Throughout his campaign, he had stressed that efforts to alleviate rural poverty and backwardness would not be accomplished through additional land distribution, the phantom which haunted Mexico's large landowners and its considerable commercial agricultural sector. This was the subtle meaning of Echeverría's emphasis that the "first phase" of the agrarian reform was over. Indeed, in the policy making which occurred within CONASUPO, no consideration was ever given to the need to distribute more land to subsistence farmers even though some middle level officials privately admitted that this should be a key element in the policy. Land distribution was clearly understood to be a "hands off" issue by all concerned.[17] If the plots of land cultivated by individual farmers were too small for productive output, the solution was declared to be in collectivization rather than increased area (see, for example, *Excelsior*, August 19, 1974). The private industrial and banking sectors were also reminded again and again of the need to expand the consumer market in order to achieve more industrial development.

In addition, the commercial producers of wheat and other products continued to receive special treatment and the agency maintained its traditional activities even while it was formulating new plans to benefit subsistence farmers. These activities were continued in order to avoid political problems.

There are political constraints which inhibit the modification of the major part of the traditional activities [of the agency]. The political

17. In fact, land distribution did occur during the Echeverría administration, but it was pursued quietly and with few official policy statements to herald it.

TABLE 18.

Federal Public Investment by Objective, 1970–1974 (Billions of Pesos)

Year	Total	% Increase	Agriculture		Industry		Social Welfare		Transportation/ Communication		Administration and Defense	
			Pesos	%	Pesos	%	Pesos	%	Pesos	%	Pesos	%
1970	29.2	—	3.9	13.4	11.1	38.0	7.7	27.1	5.8	19.9	0.5	1.6
1971	22.6	−22.8	3.3	14.5	9.3	41.3	5.1	22.5	4.6	20.3	0.3	1.4
1972	34.7	53.8	4.9	14.3	11.4	33.1	9.2	26.5	7.9	22.7	1.2	3.4
1973	49.8	43.6	7.0	14.2	16.2	32.5	13.1	26.2	12.7	25.4	1.6	1.7
1974*	66.4	—	11.5	17.3	21.2	31.9	14.8	22.3	17.4	26.3	1.4	2.2

Source: Banco Nacional de México, *Review of the Economic Situation of Mexico*, various issues.

*1974 reflects amounts authorized for spending. Generally, authorized funds in Mexico are 5 to 10 percent higher than amounts actually spent. See Wilkie, 1967.

importance that the activities of the agency have rob it of flexibility (CONASUPO, 1971b).

As long as the agency continued to buy large quantities of corn, wheat, rice, and other products from the commercial farmers and thus protect them from market price fluctuations, they did not organize to oppose the agency. Indeed, it is likely that the commercial farmers were unaware of the agency's long range intentions. Only within the confines of CONASUPO was there any discussion of a gradual phasing out of the traditional programs.

Other interests which were certain to be affected were those of the local merchants, middlemen, and economic bosses whose power the policy was intended to destroy. These individuals, living in rural areas far from Mexico City, were unaware of the new objectives. Widely dispersed and not in communication with each other, when they were eventually affected by CONASUPO's activities, local economic and political elites tended to concentrate their influence attempts not on the functionaries involved in policy formulation but at the more mundane level of policy implementation, as will be discussed in Chapters 5 and 6.

One CONASUPO program included in the scheme, however, did engender some opposition. This was the plan for the "People's Drug Stores," which were envisioned as means to dispense low cost medicines to disadvantaged sectors of the population, including those in rural areas. The program was specifically designed to minimize the opposition of the powerful pharmaceutical industry in Mexico, most of which is owned by transnational corporations. In spite of this precaution, however, the plan was rejected by the agency's Advisory Council. As a result of the political pressure on the President and a propaganda campaign which the industry mobilized, the plan for the drugstores was quietly and effectively shelved because "the time was not politically right for it," as one official reported. In contrast to the geographically dispersed commercial farmers, merchants, and intermediaries, the pharmaceutical industry maintained its national headquarters in Mexico City, kept abreast of rumors about what was being considered by the government, and used its impressive financial resources to manage an effective public relations campaign. This was the only part of the policy package which can be said to have been blocked at the formulation phase, but it was also the only part which met with significant resistance. When faced with potentially powerful opposition, the CONASUPO officials chose to abandon the program rather than fight for it and endanger the entire package.

In the absence of organized or vocal extragovernmental opposition, except that from the pharmaceutical industry, there was no imperative seen by CONASUPO officials to mobilize peasant support for the rural development policy. Significantly, few administrators in CONASUPO mentioned peasant demands for their services as an impetus to the generation of a reoriented policy. The lack of organized demands by low income groups for changes in the content of government policy conforms to a wider pattern of political paternalism in Mexico. Generally, government programs are designed by bureaucrats and then bestowed upon the lower classes in the absence of any sustained or organized demands for the services. Most demand making from this part of the population takes the form of individualized applications for resource allocation at the implementation phase. However, in the event that peasant support were required by CONASUPO, several company officials were influential within the peasant sector of the PRI and could be called upon to mobilize timely support if it became necessary.

Thus, in the formulation of the rural development scheme in CONA-SUPO, the planning process proceeded unnoticed and unheralded by the press, by public debate, or by official announcements. Neither the technical planning group in CONASUPO nor the agency's high level management was the focus of external demands for policy change.[18] Even the pharmaceutical industry preferred to pressure the President and his closest advisors rather than officials in the agency itself. The efforts to mobilize support for the policy were largely confined to attempts to influence the President and other organizations within the bureaucracy. Legislative representatives had no role whatever in the formulation of policy, and the tactics employed by the President and CONASUPO managers successfully prevented much opposition to the policy. Nor were functionaries of the PRI, even at high levels, consulted in the development of the scheme. Extragovernmental input into the policy was limited to the influence of a number of intellectuals who provided a theoretical foundation for examining rural underdevelopment and the opposition of the drug industry. Other than these, the process of planning, programming, and funding the rural development policy was an intrabureaucratic process. It involved, except for the middle level technical planning group in CONASUPO, only high level decision makers such as the President, various ministers of state, the agency director, and his immediate subordinates. The interplay of parties, groups, and interests, which have been noted in policy formulation processes in other Latin American countries, was not present in the creation of a new policy for agricultural development in Mexico.[19] Instead, the policy which emerged was the creation of a small number of individuals who worked quietly within the offices and corridors of the bureaucracy.

18. Similar findings are reported in Benveniste (1970: 12–13), and Purcell (1973).
19. More open policy formulation processes have been observed in Brazil (Daland, 1967), Chile (Kaufman, 1972), and Venezuela (Levy, 1973).

Policy Formulation and Interpersonal Exchange

How useful are exchange relationships in explaining the way the rural development policy was formulated and support for it mobilized? Clearly, they do not explain why an integrated rural development policy was considered to be vital if CONASUPO were to fulfill its legally defined role. However, both career-based alliances and calculations about resource allocations were significant factors in explaining the sensitivity of CONASUPO and other government agencies to presidential interests and concerns. Furthermore, bonds of mutual trust between individuals in CONASUPO were of fundamental importance in determining how the technical analysis of Mexico's developmental problems reached and influenced decision makers. More specifically, the recruitment of the technical planning department and the *confianza* between its manager and the general director were undoubtedly significant factors in the director's response to the plan.

More importantly, perhaps, it is clear that the acquisition of material resources affected the degree to which officials in CONASUPO became enthusiastic supporters of the policy of rural development. The response of various division and subsidiary managers to the policy was a reflection of their need to gain the resources they needed to accomplish job-related functions. The general director attempted to gain more thoroughgoing support for his policy by mobilizing career-based alliances where the bonds of resource dependence were not strong, as was seen in the case of DICONSA. Open opposition within the agency was discouraged because of the ultimate control the director had over the allocation of jobs.

Moreover, the use of interpersonal relationships was partly responsible for the ability of the general director to mobilize support for the policy within the government and to spearhead a drive for a coordinated agricultural policy. Ties to the Ministers of Finance and the Presidency, for example, were instrumental in influencing the President to support the agency both politically and financially. This allowed CONASUPO and its leadership to achieve more influence in the government. Finally, both career aspirations and resource allocation possibilities determined the degree to which the ministers and agencies responded to presidential initiatives and were willing to cooperate with other agencies in support of sectoral planning.

A number of conditions of the policy making environment in Mexico can be credited for the important role played by interpersonal relationships. As demonstrated in the example of CONASUPO, the demand making behavior of citizens and parties in support of policy alternatives plays a very insignificant part in the development or approval of government plans. Neither recipient groups, legislative bodies, nor the mass media are initiators of attempts to bring about changes in government services, although they may be appealed to after a presidential commitment to a particular policy is made in order to demonstrate widespread public support (see Purcell, 1975). Instead, efforts to influence policy are made in personal contacts with the President and those high level bureaucrats who are his confidants.

The secrecy surrounding the development of public policy in Mexico serves to strengthen the role of individual contacts and loyalty among government officials. In the absence of public debate, what is important is the quality of the personal relationships established with the President and his closest aids. Successful performance in high level bureaucratic roles is largely defined by the President and is measured both by political and financial support; he is in a position to make or break individual careers, and the aspirations which surround the *sexenio* change can be manipulated by him to achieve more cooperative and diligent performance than might otherwise be the case. The environment in which the policy is formulated, however, is a very different one from the environment in which the same policy is implemented. As will be demonstrated in Chapter 5, implementing a policy such as the rural development scheme of CONASUPO may be far more difficult than designing the policy in the first place.

5

Implementation I:
Responsiveness, Resources, and Careers

After months of laboring to design what they hoped would be an effective policy for rural development, many CONASUPO officials in Mexico City considered that the most important part of reordering the company's activities had been accomplished. After all, the scheme began with careful collection of data, analysis, and planning; a package of feasible programs had been formulated, and responsibility for tasks had been assigned; the general director of CONASUPO was firmly committed to the policy; all-important presidential support had been acquired and was reflected in a much expanded budget; and the first tentative steps toward sectoral planning had been taken by government agencies with responsibilities in rural areas. Therefore, many were willing to believe that the rural development policy was a reality. One planner dismissed all discussion of obstacles to plan implementation by declaring, "Jorge de la Vega, when he says something, he gets it done!" "Why is that?" he was asked. "Well, because he's the director!"

In spite of such admirable good faith, once a policy has been formulated, its consistent implementation is by no means automatic or assured. As discussed in Chapter 1, whether or not a policy becomes transformed into practice may depend upon the activities of administrators responsible for carrying out the programs. Even in the most regimented and routine of bureaucratic agencies, discretion in the making of decisions

cannot be eliminated; in a geographically dispersed organization characterized by imperfect channels of communication and authority,
whether or not the decisions of the individual bureaucrat are made in
pursuit of policy objectives can be a crucial determinant of overall
program results. In this sense, then, the responsiveness of bureaucratic
officials is one important factor which intervenes between policy formulated in central offices and the actual achievement of the ends specified
by the policy (see Kaufman, 1973; Van Meter and Van Horn, 1975).

Curiously enough, however, the role of bureaucrats as implementors
has received little attention from political scientists interested in public
policies in Latin America. In part, this may be due to the great centralization of the administrative apparatus in most Latin American countries.
Generally, all policy, even that which concerns the activities of local
governmental units, emanates from the national capital and from the
offices of federal bureaucratic agencies located there. Moreover, the
authority of the President is often perceived to be so extensive that his
political support may be considered all that is necessary to bring a policy
to life. At the same time, however, students of politics in developing
areas have long noted that a major difference between countries there
and in more developed regions is that in the former, attempts to influence
policy are typically made at the implementation or enforcement stage.[1]
This is in contrast to the United States and countries of Western Europe
where influence attempts tend to be focused on legislatures, bureaucratic
agencies, and political executives in order to shape the content of the
policy as it is being designed. This difference should be sufficient to
indicate the important role of policy implementors in countries such as
Mexico.

In the implementation of the rural development scheme of CONASUPO,
several variables affected the responsiveness of administrators to the
policy guidelines established by the central office. As might be predicted
from the data presented in previous chapters, both resource allocation
decisions and the alliances forged to achieve personal career goals
affected the degree to which administrators responded to the policy. The
implementation performance of these bureaucrats can be measured by
comparing the correspondence of their activities to central policy guidelines established to deliver an integrated package of services in rural
areas. Execution of the policy to transform subsistence agriculture would
occur if it could be established that, in their decision making, CONASUPO
officials were

1. Seeking to concentrate agency resources in rural areas;

2. Considering subsistence farmers as the primary recipients and
   beneficiaries of the agency's rural activities;

1. See Leff (1970), Riggs (1964), Scott (1969), and Weiner (1971: 163) for explanations
of demand making at the output stage of the policy process.

3. Seeking to achieve an integrated set of programs in any given community or region; and,

4. Evaluating local level rural needs in terms of economic exchange relationships.

A preliminary evaluation of bureaucratic responsiveness in terms of the first two measures—concentration of resources in rural areas and a focus on subsistence farmers as the target population—can be made with data on the two most important subsidiaries, BORUCONSA and DICONSA. As indicated in the previous chapter, they varied in the degree of open support they gave the policy. In practice, although both companies directed resources to rural areas, significant differences were also evident in their activities.

Policy Responsiveness in BORUCONSA and DICONSA

The policies of the parent company were communicated to the subsidiaries in a number of ways. The general director and his four division managers sat on the Advisory Council of each subsidiary and were officially kept informed of their activities. In addition, the offices of all subsidiaries except the regional DICONSA companies were located in Mexico City; CONASUPO management was normally in at least weekly contact with the heads of the companies on an informal basis. At times, telephone communication would occur daily. Moreover, subsidiary company managers were all appointed by De la Vega, often on the basis of prior acquaintance and personal loyalty. Finally, the parent company might have control over resources needed by the subsidiaries, and allocation might be perceived to be contingent upon responsiveness to central office policy. Given these instruments of influence, it is not surprising that data about both BORUCONSA and DICONSA indicate that they instituted a number of new programs in rural areas in response to the reoriented policy of the parent company. Decisions made in BORUCONSA, however, reflected a greater commitment to rural areas than in the other subsidiary.

BORUCONSA established the following set of policy guidelines in 1972 which mirrored the rural development policy of the parent company:

1. Organize, improve, and modernize our crop storage systems in order to become an effective instrument promoting marketing in rural areas;

2. Diversify our activities by making available various basic crop improvement inputs which *ejidatarios* are unable to obtain now because of market prices;

3. Extend the network of activities of BORUCONSA so that they become available to the communities and regions which do not now have

rural warehouses, in order to prevent these areas from becoming subject to the activities of intermediaries and hoarders at harvest time;

4. Provide the necessary aids for marketing crops to farmers so they
   can obtain a higher return for their harvests;

5. Pursue the better use of the subsidiary's installations;

6. Communicate with peasants in the most extensive form possible in
   order to ensure their solidarity, comprehension, and participation in
   the programs and activities developed by the subsidiary (CONASUPO,
   1973b).

Of course, BORUCONSA was established for the sole purpose of serving
rural low income communities with its warehouses, and it is to be
expected that this would be reflected in the company's statement of
principles. In addition, however, BORUCONSA's actual activities suggest
that it was committed to expanding its network and providing a
number of auxiliary services to low income rural inhabitants. Indicative
of this are figures which compare company activity in 1971, before the
rural development scheme was fully prepared, with its performance in
later years.

Table 19 provides data on the number of rural warehouses and the
extent of the services offered through BORUCONSA centers. Most significant, perhaps, are the figures indicating the growth in the amount of
total CONASUPO crop purchases made through the warehouse reception
centers—from 13 percent of the total amount in 1971 to 71 percent in
the 1973–1974 harvest cycle. The subsidiary expanded its rural outlets
by only 12.7 percent through 1974, but by the end of 1975, the subsidiary
reported that it was operating 2,434 centers. Investments in rural areas
rose from 5 million pesos in 1971 to 11.7 million in 1973. Over 200
defective warehouses were refurbished and enlarged, and the subsidiary
initiated a program to buy grain from the peasant in quantities as small
as one kilogram. This was specifically expected to benefit the subsistence
farmer as was a program established to lend peasants 25 percent of the
gunny sacks they needed for their crops and to enable them to rent or
buy the remainder.

In 1975, BORUCONSA took over operation of ANDSA warehouses with
the stated intent to "strengthen the meaning of ANDSA's original purpose
as a warehouse system established to provide services to the peasant
class" (Excelsior, June 14, 1975). Another important activity of the
subsidiary was its program to recruit and train reception center analysts,
those responsible for receiving, weighing, analyzing, and paying for the
grain delivered to the centers by local farmers. Prior to 1971, the
reception centers had been manned by CONASUPO or ANDSA officials who
had little interest in the local community and who very frequently
collaborated with intermediaries, local economic bosses, or truckers to

TABLE. 19.

Activities of boruconsa, 1971-1974

Services	1971	1972	1973	1974
Number of reception centers operating (1975 goal: 2,500)	1,109	1,119	1,131	1,250
Total purchase of CONASUPO through BORUCONSA centers	13%	42%	60%	71%
Number of reception centers offering				
Production inputs				
improved seeds	*	*	23	61
fertilizers	*	35	75	270
special credit program	*	*	*	135
Marketing aids				
interplot transportation	*	*	10	22
corn shellers	*	48	156	315
gunny sacks (no. sold in millions)	*	7.1	6.6	5.4
Other				
five basic products	*	*	*	1,142
medical centers	*	*	114	320
day care centers	*	*	4	19
Technical assistance brigades	*	*	7	N.A.**
Peasant communication				
Performances of peasant theater brigades	*	60	1,984	1,585
Copies of rural newspaper	*	91,000	156,000	N.A.
Radio programs	*	*	N.A.	300
Rural libraries	*	*	987	1,116

Source: CONASUPO "Informes de las filiales a la Gerencia General." Unpublished manuscript, 1973; *Gaceta,* No. 6 (August 15, 1974).

*Program not established.
**N.A. = Data not available.

defraud the peasants.[2] By 1974, BORUCONSA had trained 1,483 analysts who were members of the *ejido* communities where the reception centers were located. BORUCONSA reported making extensive efforts to promote the "social conscience" of the analysts to prevent a reoccurrence of corrupt practices.

2. This was frequently accomplished by refusing to buy small quantities of grain from an individual peasant. An intermediary might buy from the peasant at a lower price and

These figures do not reveal the extent to which allocation decisions were made in order to provide a package of services designed to break structural barriers to further development, but they do indicate the extent to which the company expanded its activities in rural areas and made available the services included in the policy. BORUCONSA administrators did attempt to concentrate resources in rural areas and to serve subsistence farmers in accordance with the policy guidelines of the parent company. But conforming to the rural development goals was easy for this subsidiary. Its main centers of activity were in these areas, as were its principal clientele and its primary function. And, as was seen in the last chapter, the need for increased resources made it highly rational for BORUCONSA to follow the new policy. A much more interesting case of policy responsiveness is that of DICONSA.

In 1972, DICONSA also proposed a set of principles for its activities:

1. Improve the living standards of sectors of the population which are economically weak, through the sale of food, shoes, clothing, and other articles of basic need at prices which are within their economic capacity;

2. Maintain the stability of prices of these articles in the consumer market by providing sufficient quantities to overcome supply deficiencies;

3. Improve the nutritional level of low income people through the sale of merchandise of certified quality and weight, whose variety and nutritional value encourages the development of balanced diets in terms of proteins, vitamins, and minerals.

These objectives do not single out rural inhabitants as special recipients of DICONSA's services. Rather, the target population specified by the subsidiary is the entire low income community in Mexico. As indicated in the last chapter, this had traditionally been defined by DICONSA administrators to consist primarily of low income urban dwellers. In 1970, of a total of almost 1,500 retail outlets, only 43 were in rural areas. To be responsive to the new rural development policy, DICONSA investment decisions would therefore have to undergo considerable change.

It had been DICONSA's experience that the operation of rural stores generally resulted in net losses for the company. Nevertheless, in 1972, DICONSA initiated a program for the development of a network of rural stores which was specifically designed to meet the needs of low income rural dwellers. Eighty-six percent of the company's total projected new stores were programmed for rural areas. Between 1970 and 1974, the company actually increased the number of rural stores to 25 percent

then resell it to CONASUPO for a higher price, frequently without physically moving the crop. Analysts also falsely analyzed the grain for impurities, paying the peasant for a more inferior delivery and pocketing the difference. At other times, they might weigh the grain incorrectly or demand a "tip" to fill out the proper form.

TABLE 20.

Growth of Urban and Rural DICONSA Outlets

Type of Store	1970	1971	1972	1973	1974	% Increase
Urban	1,424*	1,803*	1,875*	1,850	2,022	42.0
Rural	43	74	89	523	674	1,467.4
Total	1,467	1,877	1,964	2,373	2,696	83.8

Source: CONASUPO, "Informes de las filiales a la Gerencia General." Unpublished manuscript, 1973; DICONSA, "Curso de capacitación al Grupo Voluntario de visitas a tiendas." Unpublished manuscript, 1974.

*These figures exclude over 500 milk dispensaries which were transferred to another subsidiary in 1973.

of its total number of outlets. This contrasts with its record in 1970, when only 3 percent of its total network was in rural areas (see Table 20). Rural cooperative stores operated by organized groups of peasants contributed the greatest amount to the overall rural expansion. There were 418 of these stores operating throughout the country by October 1974. In view of these figures, then, it would seem that DICONSA's activities between 1971 and 1974 reflected a serious commitment to channel resources into rural areas. Given DICONSA's independent financial status, this response must be ascribed to the loyalty its high level administrators felt toward the managers of the parent company and the goals established by them.

The rural expansion of DICONSA, however, did not stop the growth of its urban network, as can be seen in Table 21. Although the rate of growth was much greater in rural areas than in urban ones, the rural expansion fell far behind what DICONSA officials had projected in early 1973. The major input into new rural outlets was to be in the form of 1,200 rural cooperative stores which were to be in operation by 1975. In October 1974, about 35 percent of the planned number had been opened (see Table 21). Of course, the inability of the company to reach the projected figures is easily attributed to overoptimistic calculations of the company's capability, to the difficulty of coordinating with other government agencies involved in rural cooperative efforts or to a policy of consolidation instituted in late 1973. However, during the same period, DICONSA managed to achieve 79 percent of its targeted growth in urban supermarkets, installations which required much more capital investment and organization than the small and simple rural stores. This variance would suggest that DICONSA continued to remain less committed to rural areas than to urban ones.

TABLE 21.

Goal Achievement in Opening Rural and Urban DICONSA Stores

Type of Stores	New Stores Programmed in Early 1973*	New Stores Established Early 1973– October 1974	% Programmed Growth Achieved
Rural cooperative stores	1,200	418	35
Urban supermarkets	142	112	79

Source: CONASUPO, "Informes de las filiales a la Gerencia General." Un-published manuscript, 1973; *Gaceta*, No. 10 (October 15, 1974).

*Total new stores of all categories programmed = 1,719; total new rural stores of all categories programmed = 1,472.

Additionally, the majority of the rural stores were set up with limited financial inputs from DICONSA. The cooperative stores, for example, were established with a working capital provided by the National Fund for *Ejido* Development, construction supervision from the National Institute of Community Development, materials and labor provided by the *ejidos,* and rural promotion from the Ministry of Agrarian Reform. DICONSA was assigned responsibility only for furniture and paint, training of community personnel, and routine distribution of merchandise. Most of the rest of the rural stores were largely financed by other government programs, such as those for indigenous groups in remote areas. In fact, over the five-year period, there was an absolute decline in the number of rural stores that DICONSA established and maintained by itself (see Table 22). Aid from other government agencies minimized the loss to DICONSA when the rural stores failed to show a profit. Thus, the urban areas continued to receive the great majority of DICONSA's investment capital. Nevertheless it is true that because of the absolute increase in its rural outlets, the subsidiary did make a substantial contribution to overall policy goal achievement.

At the national level, then, figures from both DICONSA and BORUCONSA indicate that the subsidiaries varied in the degree to which they were willing to concentrate their resources in rural areas and suggest that they differed in their commitment to the rural development policy. For BORUCONSA, pursuit of the policy directives of the parent company was the most rational course given the function of the agency and the fact that acquisition of resources was influenced by the active pursuit of policy goals. For DICONSA, on the other hand, extension to rural areas seems to have taken place without significantly altering the company's investment in urban areas. New resources became available to this

TABLE 22.

DICONSA Rural Growth
and Investment

Year	A Total Rural Stores	B Rural Stores Established Entirely by DICONSA	% B/A
1970	43	43	100
1971	74	48	65
1972	81	41	51
1973	523	36	7
1974	674	31	5

Source: CONASUPO, "Informes de las filiales a la Gerencia General." Unpublished manuscript, 1973; DICONSA, "Curso de capacitación al Grupo Voluntario de visitas a tiendas." Unpublished manuscript, 1974.

subsidiary through collaborative programs with other government agencies; it was not necessary to make a major shift in the allocation of its funds to implement the new policy.

If the study of policy implementation were to end here, it would be reasonable to conclude that CONASUPO's rural development policy was being executed as planned because the two subsidiaries most involved in the implementation process seemed to be more or less actively responding to central policy directives. Thus far, however, only the first two measures of policy implementation have been applied. That is, it has been considered whether officials at the national level sought to concentrate resources in rural areas and whether subsistence farmers were singled out as primary targets for company programs. But it has yet to be established that the infrastructure and activities of CONASUPO were reaching their intended beneficiaries. The relevant measures of policy implementation—delivery of an integrated set of programs and concern with viewing local level needs in terms of economic relationships—cannot be determined with data available at the national level. Information was collected on CONASUPO programs in a number of states, however, which is more suitable for evaluating these implementation activities of company officials. At this level, a number of factors other than policy directives from the central offices impinged upon resource allocation decisions.

Policy Implementation in the State Offices

> It is always, of course, more difficult to implement policy at the local
> level than to make decisions on a national level.

Prior to the initiation of the state offices in late 1973, the operations
of CONASUPO were complicated by the existence of multiple chains of
command extending from the national to the local level. In each state,
a representative of BORUCONSA and several zone chiefs supervised the
operations of the rural warehouses in accordance with BORUCONSA
directives; a state manager of DICONSA stores oversaw the activity of
these outlets as directed by DICONSA in Mexico City; a supervisor estimated crop production and reported directly to the Operations Division.
Agents representing Comisión Promotora and CECONCA carried out other
programs, each in response to directives emanating from his own
subsidiary. There was no state level coordination and frequently no
communication at all among these officials, in spite of the fact that all
were ostensibly working for the same federal agency. Even working
conditions, salaries, and time schedules varied considerably among
agents reporting to different subsidiaries. At times officials issued statements in which they purported to represent the views of CONASUPO but
which conflicted with those made by other representatives of the same
agency.

An attempt to remedy this confusion was made at the outset of the
Echeverría *sexenio*. At that time, a Coordination, Supervision, and
Special Projects Committee was established within the Operations
Division, and a representative of the committee was assigned to each
state. His tasks were to investigate abuses in the field operations of the
agency and to encourage greater coordination among the subsidiaries.
However, because the committee representative had no real authority
over those he was charged with supervising, the committee was unable
to bring about the desired changes; problems still had to be sent to
Mexico City for solution. The situation, as summarized by two state
representatives, was hardly conducive to the implementation of an
integrated rural development policy.

> Before the state representative program, . . . everyone was looking
> after his own garden.

> You know, before this office began, everyone here was a chief; no one
> paid any attention to what someone in another subsidiary was doing.

A second attempt to achieve greater coordination and responsiveness
was made in November 1973, when CONASUPO established offices in each
of 31 federal states in Mexico. In every state, a representative appointed
by the general director was empowered to coordinate all local activities

of the agency. He had the authority to correct abuses of official function locally, to hire staff, and to deal with state representatives of other federal government agencies. Most importantly, he was charged with the duty of establishing close working relationships with the state government and, specifically, of seeing that CONASUPO programs did not cause conflicts or political problems with the governor. It was also hoped that the personnel in the state offices, in touch with local conditions, would aid CONASUPO in selecting locations where effective programs could be implemented and in designing the most efficient mix of programs to meet community needs. The representative was expected to be able to identify problem spots early in order to correct them rapidly and avoid public disturbances. To provide coherence and respectability to the agency's image, CONASUPO's state representative was to be the only official source of public relations and news emanating from the agency at this level. Finally, in the event of natural disaster in the state, such as flooding, drought, or earthquake, the representative was to have extraordinary powers to coordinate CONASUPO's relief efforts.[3]

The new offices of CONASUPO consisted of a representative who considered himself a personal emissary of the general director in the state, a representative of BORUCONSA and one to eleven zone chiefs as his subordinates, a state manager of DICONSA and his staff of assistants, one or two community development workers of the Comisión Promotora, one to four supervisors reporting to the Operations Division, and whatever secretarial or administrative help was considered necessary and was authorized. In addition, several state offices included personnel of CECONCA, the subsidiary charged with providing training and extension programs for peasants. In three states there were local level representatives of MACONSA, the company in charge of stimulating the production of low cost construction materials. Some states also served as headquarters for regional offices of the DICONSA system, but these were not within the authority of the state representative to oversee. The ultimate organizational goal of the program, according to central office managers, was that "in each state they become a sort of mini CONASUPO with the same administrative organization that we have here in the center." The representative was to be the local level counterpart to the general director of CONASUPO.

Setting up the mini CONASUPOS, however, was to stop short of initiative in policy matters, according to the same officials in national headquarters. The state offices were established for the purpose of

3. Disaster relief has been a traditional function of CONASUPO. One of the subsidiaries, MACONSA, charged with regulating the construction materials market, was established in the wake of CONASUPO's efforts to aid victims of the severe earthquake of 1973 in the states of Puebla and Veracruz.

removing some of the burden of day to day problem solving from
Mexico City. "What this means now is that the solutions to local problems can be found locally, while still maintaining policy control from
the center." The representatives themselves were aware that their function was to be problem solving rather than policy making. One explained
the purpose of the program.

> The state offices were really set up as a tonic. . . . It was . . . an effort
> to decongest the problem solving system and see if some things couldn't
> be resolved right here in the state.

It was made clear to the representatives when they assumed their posts
that an important criterion by which they were to be evaluated was their
ability to find solutions to these problems. In regular reports to the
central offices, they were to keep Mexico City informed of the local
situation, but preferably *after* they had reached a satisfactory resolution
of the difficulty.

In 1974 and 1975, ten of the state offices set up by CONASUPO were
visited in order to interview the state representatives and agents of the
subsidiaries operating there. The offices were located in the state of
Aguascalientes, Guanajuato, Jalisco, México, Michoacán, Puebla,
Querétaro, San Luís Potosí, Veracruz, and Zacatecas. The offices were
chosen in consultation with CONASUPO personnel who were directly
responsible for overseeing the activities of the state headquarters. The
objective was to select and visit several state offices which functioned
adequately in terms of responsiveness to central policy directives as
perceived by national level administrators and others which were considered to be deficient in this respect. In addition, it was important that
the states all produce substantial amounts of staple products like corn
and beans and contain considerable populations of low income *ejidatarios* or small landowners. In the offices visited, it was apparent that
the requirement that the state representative be a local level problem
solver frequently made it difficult for him to be an effective policy
implementor at the same time.

Resource Exchange and Local Level Problem Solving

> We feel our principal goal in the State Offices Division is to make sure
> that the programs put in motion here in Mexico City actually reach
> the people they are designed to benefit.

> The more problems they send through to us, the worse we know their
> performance is. . . . The best state representatives solve problems at
> their own level.

The problem solving activities of the state representative occurred
on four different fronts where difficulties were likely to arise. The

organization itself, other federal agencies, the private sector, and the state government presented the representative with a myriad of decisional demands which required his attention daily. Theoretically, he could choose among a variety of methods to avoid or resolve a difficulty. He could, for example, use his authority to bring local CONASUPO officials to heel; he could communicate directly with the general director or with the governor to request that pressure be brought to bear on offending parties; he could deny valuable resources to those who opposed him and reward those who complied with his wishes; and he could refuse to cooperate with others unless reciprocal help were offered. In practice, the representatives in ten state offices evidenced a strong preference for a particular style of problem solving in which the formation of cordial and cooperative bonds of friendship and reciprocity were regarded as the most effective way to fulfill responsibilities and achieve a good record with their superiors.

This problem solving style was evident in their efforts to establish and maintain well-run local offices. Although the representatives had higher official status than any other local CONASUPO employees and although they had formal powers to direct these functionaries in overall policy, the CONASUPO agents were not direct subordinates of the representatives. Generally, they were appointed by home office officials and maintained direct reporting and supply relationships with their particular division or subsidiary. Consequently, their primary responsibility was to their own organizational hierarchy. Initially, the supervision of the state representatives was resisted and local agents often avoided reporting to them. Thus, one representative stated,

> When I began my job here, there were quite a few problems with the local functionaries thinking I was some kind of spy, or I was going to interfere in their work or their affairs. I had to work carefully and let them know I wasn't here to spy on them or impose orders on them or report them to Mexico.

The representatives were conscious of the problems of "human relations" at the state level, and the techniques for bringing about internal coordination were strikingly similar in the ten state offices. All representatives made statements which echoed the experience of one official,

> I have managed to achieve greater coordination at the state level through two strategies. One is respecting the hierarchies the agents have established within their own organization—that is, not intervening officiously—and the other is through dialogue with them.

The representatives reported that they attempted to demonstrate to the officials that mutual collaboration was useful to all parties involved.

For example, a representative would indicate that, supplied with relevant information, he could report favorably on the activities of the other local officials to Mexico City. He could also aid their projects by acquiring the help of the governor or federal officials, and he could defend them if they met with opposition in their work. In return, the state representative expected to have his suggestions accepted.

In the event that problems with local officials could not be solved through friendly relationships and mutual exchanges, the value of cordial relationships was perceived to be too great to jeopardize with open confrontations or exertions of official authority. Instead, problem solving tended to be pushed upward through the multiple hierarchies of the CONASUPO system, even though the representatives realized that this was a "bad" solution in terms of the criteria established by division management. One representative explained how the system worked.

> If I should have a problem with the state agent of BORUCONSA or DICONSA, for example—say opposing a "suggestion" I make—then I call my boss in Mexico and explain the problem to him, and then he gets in contact with the boss of the BORUCONSA or DICONSA man and presents the problem in the most subtle and friendly way possible. This fellow may then get in contact with the local agent of the subsidiary and again subtly try to resolve the problem.

In the one observed exception to this pattern of avoiding overt authority confrontations, a representative decided to exert direct pressure on unresponsive state level agents. Interestingly, however, it was not the authority of the representative which was brought to bear on the errant officials. Rather, the representative engineered a meeting in the state attended by the governor and national level officials in order to impress upon the agents that they should cooperate with him. Within CONASUPO itself, therefore, the preferred method to achieve effective working relations was to establish and maintain mutually beneficial informal exchanges of support and compliance.[4]

The representative was also responsible for coordinating activities with local level officials of other federal government agencies. CONASUPO might require the assistance of the state agent of the Commerce and Industry Ministry, for example, when merchants were found to be abusing retail price controls. Because payments for crop purchases were made through the official banks, the state representative was called upon to program payment schedules with them. The Agriculture Ministry, the Ministry of Agrarian Reform, the Water Resources Ministry, the

4. The ability to achieve intra-office cooperation, of course, frequently varied with the amount of informal authority the representative had. Some, for example, enjoyed strong support from either the central offices of the company or from the governor at the state level. This kind of backing enabled one representative to gain compliance from state agents through the transfer of all employees to other locations. Subsequently, newly appointed agents demonstrated a great desire to cooperate with the representative.

Social Security Agency, as well as numerous federally directed programs were also necessary to CONASUPO's activities. Among the representatives interviewed, collaboration between agencies was explicitly recognized to be based on exchanges of resources.

> Here at the state level, it's necessary for me to help out other government agencies; then they will help me out.

As with intra-agency coordination, however, interagency collaboration, when it occurred, was achieved through informal ties of friendship. One representative, for instance, reported no problems working with the local agent of the Ministry of Agriculture because of his close personal relationship with this official.

> I knew the state agent before I became a representative, and we get along well—we have very close ties, and I see him about once a week.

Initiatives at coordination which were not accomplished through *confianza* generally passed through the governor. He, in turn, acted as the intermediary to forge closer relationships among the agencies which were useful to him in accomplishing his own state level plans.

In addition to intrabureaucratic relationships, one of the most important duties assigned to the representative was to maintain non-hostile relationships with local level businessmen, generally through the Chambers of Commerce in the state. The task was a sensitive one because relationships with the private sector were strained under the Echeverría administration. Businessmen, identified with the political right in Mexico, had in the past waged vigorous propaganda campaigns against CONASUPO. The private sector in general tended to view CONASUPO's activities as an interference in the free market and as unfair competition because the agency's programs were not motivated by the need to show a profit. On a more specific level, installation of CONASUPO outlets and programs were perceived to be a real economic threat to merchants in the area serviced by the program. Attacks on the agency most commonly impugned the honesty and efficiency of the agency and its officials.

In the state offices, seeking an accommodation with local business was viewed as a means to improve CONASUPO's image. The goal of the state representatives was to keep the discontent or hostility of businessmen from escalating to a public level. The means by which they generally dealt with the problems presented by the local private sector was to use their influence over agency programs to benefit businessmen who were willing to take a sympathetic view of CONASUPO's activities. For example, one representative explained his strategy.

> I also try to improve relations with the Chamber of Commerce. I try to overcome the problem we have of lack of understanding. And I recently showed them a new contract we have in which CONASUPO

undertakes to sell them rice so they can sell it at reduced prices. I'm trying to help them get supplies of more CONASUPO products to distribute this way. When I first came here, they attacked us in the newspapers.

The reserves of foodstuffs maintained by CONASUPO could be assigned to friendly merchants and perhaps denied to hostile ones when they were distributed to private commercial establishments for retail sale at regulated prices. DICONSA had established the policy of purchasing merchandise, whenever feasible, through local and regional manufac-turers or processors, a practice which could be used as an inducement in return for cooperation from local industrial elites. In the event that a particular CONASUPO action, such as the installation of a DICONSA store, threatened influential private interests, the representatives could halt the project or relocate it to a less offensive site. In exchange for these accommodations, the state representative expected a more friendly acceptance of the agency's activities from the businessmen.

Perhaps most importantly, local problem solving for the state representative meant establishing and maintaining cordial relationships with the state government, particularly with the governor.[5] In Mexico, state governors can be selected to occupy their positions for a variety of reasons.[6] Some are important figures in national politics, members of what Brandenburg (1964) has dubbed the "Revolutionary Family." They are sent to the provinces by the President as his personal emissaries and can serve the useful purpose of bringing recalcitrant local groups within the purview of national politics. Other states are governed by *caciques* (or their henchmen) whose extensive political machines within the state have earned them impressive bargaining power when dealing with the President and national political leaders. The states of Chiapas, Puebla, and, until recently, Hidalgo are examples of leadership in this category. Still other states, such as Mexico and Veracruz have been governed by individuals typified by both national elite membership and strong local machines. Recent governors of the state of Mexico, for example, have generally alternated between national and state positions in their career trajectories. Finally, a few states are governed by those who have been "burned" at the national level and have been

5. As explained by one informant, the appointment of a state agent of a federal agency is a method commonly encountered in Mexico to foment good intergovernmental cooperation: "CONASUPO can really impose any program it wants to at the state level, even if the governor is against it. But what they try to do is 'coordinate' everything with the governor so conflicts don't arise. That's why the principal job of the state representative is to smooth relations with the local level *politicos*. Practically all government programs have such a person assigned to the state capital. They try to be great friends with the governor." Because of the political nature of such jobs, another respondent explained that "the position of the representative is one which requires a great deal of sensitivity."

6. Camp (1974) presents a useful discussion of the role of state governors in Mexican politics, the reasons they are selected, and their career ties to other political figures.

retired, at least for a *sexenio*, to the relative ignominy of a powerless governorship.

Whatever the reason behind their official appointment as PRI candidates and their subsequent election, governors are not often in a position to challenge presidential leadership openly. They may strike behind-the-scenes bargains with national leaders or attempt to isolate themselves from the influence of Mexico City, but failure to observe the rules of the political game can result in their precipitous removal, as governors of Guerrero and Hidalgo under Echeverría can attest. Moreover, most states, except for wealthier, more industrialized ones such as Mexico, Jalisco, and Nuevo León, control few financial resources and are greatly dependent on the federal government for money to carry out state level programs. Generally, relations between the federal and the state governments are characterized by mutual attempts at manipulation and accommodation. For example, state governors may attempt to acquire influence over federal programs in the state while federal officials may seek to gain the political support and aid of the governor but without unduly jeopardizing the objectives of their programs. Successful relationships therefore tend to be ones which emphasize the mutual benefit to be derived from cooperation. This was certainly true for CONASUPO at the state level.

The governors could be useful to CONASUPO when it attempted to carry out its activities at the state level. The governors, through their ties to the National Peasants Confederation (CNC), could mobilize peasants to cooperate with CONASUPO; they could make it convenient for other federal agencies to collaborate; they could use their legal powers to close state borders to shipments of grain and foodstuffs in order to prevent speculation and hoarding; and they could smooth relations with the private sector.[7] At the same time, the governors found CONASUPO to be a particularly useful agency. It had not escaped the attention of state governors, for example, that the opening of a CONASUPO store or rural warehouse might reflect on their administration and be valuable in solidifying support for the party. In other cases, it might be helpful for the governors to be able to halt the installation of a store or warehouse which threatened certain local interests, sometimes their own. In addition, disaster relief, emergency food programs, and pork-barrel

---

7. As explained to me by a number of officials, closing the borders of a state to commerce in particular items is considered necessary when a shortage of a given commodity occurs nationally. When there is a shortage, or even a rumor of one, speculators in Mexico City or other large cities buy up all stocks of the commodity they can for the purpose of profiting from skyrocketing prices. The governor, using the civil guard to enforce his ruling, can order the borders closed to the exit of whatever commodity is in short supply. Closing of state borders was particularly important to CONASUPO in 1973 and 1974 when extensive shortages in corn and beans occurred.

and patronage opportunities could all be made available through CONASUPO.

It is evident, then, that collaboration between CONASUPO and the governors could be mutually beneficial. The state representatives were very aware of their responsibilities to cooperate effectively with the state governor, and friendly relationships were considered necessary to gain access to him and his aid in solving local problems. The style of collaboration was vividly described by one representative.

> I have made it a point to become very good friends with the governor. I slap him on the back, shake hands with him, and go over often to talk with him. . . . I try to do what I can for him, to improve relations between the agency and him.

Another corroborated the need for friendly bonds and mutually beneficial exchanges.

> Relations with the governor couldn't be better. Actually, most of the communication we have with the governor is initiated by him—requests that we open a store here or look into such and such a problem. But then he reciprocates . . . it was the governor who gave the order to close the state border.

As with the other problem solving arenas, when dealing with the governors, close and personal relationships were considered to be the key to effective performance of official duties.

The goal of these problem solving activities, as defined by the state representatives interviewed, was the pursuit of CONASUPO operations without public conflict or scandal. Administrators at all levels were extremely concerned about the agency's public image; the hostility of the private sector and public distrust resulting from the past failures of agency programs and personnel were important stimulants for administrators to demonstrate that the company was currently operating properly and efficiently. Above all, avoiding scandal meant keeping unfavorable information about the agency from appearing in local newspapers. One representative, for example, explained that the press in his state, controlled by the private sector, "would seize upon the slightest statement or failure and make a big scandal of it." Moreover, the representatives interviewed all indicated awareness that their performance was being judged in Mexico City by their ability to solve problems without public discontent or attacks on the agency. They were also aware that some individuals at the state level might have influence in national politics and be in a position to complain of the performance of the agency or of the representative to public officials in Mexico City.

Given the strong emphasis on nondisruptive problem solving, the groups or individuals with the most power to create public disturbances or those with most national level connections were likely to be in a position to exert most influence on the state representatives. Thus, merchants in the private sector who were influential with the local press or chamber of commerce and who found themselves threatened by the installation of a DICONSA store would be in a good bargaining position to pressure for relocation of the outlet. Similarly, a governor with a strong local base of support would be able to "request" CONASUPO resources for his own political ends; the cost of noncompliance by CONASUPO might be a public attack or demand which would tarnish the agency's image or an unfavorable report about the representative.

Because of these pressures on the allocation of agency resources at the local level, the role of the state representative as a local level problem solver sometimes conflicted with his role as an implementor of central policy objectives. Thus, it was possible, for example, that CONASUPO installations might be located in areas selected by state political leaders for reasons other than meeting the needs of subsistence farmers; contracts might have to be signed with businesses whose operations were not always beneficial to the low income rural communities; or agency services might come under the control of the *caciques* or economic bosses who had traditionally exploited rural communities.

As indicated by the overview of the state representatives' problem solving mission, CONASUPO had an extensive variety of resources to distribute and the ways in which various groups might benefit from the acquisition of them was even more extensive. The position of the representative as the focus of a variety of demands is diagrammed in Figure 10. The circle represents his jurisdiction, the state. The most important local demands upon him come from the private sector, the governor, and other locally important political forces. In addition, he is the focus of performance demands from the central offices of CONASUPO. These demands are of two types: (1) to implement centrally determined policies, and (2) to solve local level problems without public scandal.

Significantly absent in this schema are demands made by peasants, except for those who are integrated and controlled through official organizations such as the CNC. As will be discussed in the next chapter, since the time of Lázaro Cárdenas in the 1930s, peasants in Mexico have not been in a position to make sustained independent demands on the political system for attention to their problems. At the state level in CONASUPO, the pressures for attending to the needs of the peasants tended to come not from the peasants themselves but from national level administrators of the agency. In Figure 10, these demands are represented by the arrow labeled "Implement Policies."

There were, of course, limits to the ability of the state representative to allocate the available resources as he wished. The hierarchies of the subsidiary companies in some cases determined how their own resources were to be allocated, and national level authorities in the agency itself might approve or reject the representatives' initiatives. In addition,

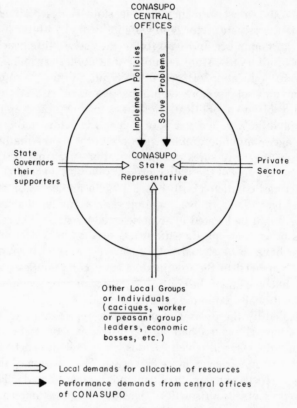

Figure 10. Demands on the State Representatives.

constraints imposed by bureaucratic routines and regulations limited the autonomy and power of the representative to make decisions.[8] Nevertheless, in most cases the representative had an important, if not decisive, voice in determining the use of agency resources; he had direct access both to the general director and to the governor, which provided him significant power; his decisions and support influenced when and

8. A good example of the regulations which imposed constraints on the decision making capacity of the representative is the process through which authorizations were made to transfer grain from one zone to another within the same state. A request for the transfer had to be made by the state chief of BORUCONSA to his own superiors in Mexico City. Then, BORUCONSA central offices relayed the request to the Operations Division of CONASUPO. If the transfer were justified, the authorization was relayed back to BORUCONSA central offices where it was then communicated back to the state chief of BORUCONSA. This process might take a month or more. While an interested state representative might be able to speed the routine through telephone calls to Mexico City, no action could be taken until the authorization was received.

where stores and warehouses were to be constructed, when training courses would be given, which merchants would receive regulatory supplies of important foods, which trucking companies would be hired to transport CONASUPO products, which communities would receive community development promoters, and how extensive the range of auxiliary CONASUPO services would be in the state. Depending upon circumstances in each state, these resources could be "spent" to achieve a variety of goals.

In the states visited, all representatives were under pressures similar to those illustrated in Figure 10. As discussed, it was part of their officially defined function to find nondisruptive solutions to local problems. In practice, therefore, it was virtually impossible for a state representative to make every decision on the basis of how best to implement the rural development policy. Political realities made such "perfect implementor" behavior unattainable. Nevertheless, it was observed that several state representatives generally attempted to be faithful policy implementors while others more frequently exerted their influence to serve state level interests which often conflicted with overall policy objectives. Differences in responsiveness were related to state level political conditions, the manner in which the representatives were selected, and their career aspirations.

Career Ties and Resource Allocation

> On the contrary, we're the ones who can help the governor by providing him the programs he needs here in the state.

Theoretically, of course, the requirements of federal policies, such as the ones established by CONASUPO, and those of state political actors are not necessarily in conflict. A state governor might be every bit as convinced as CONASUPO officials that rural development depends upon creating the conditions to liberate the subsistence farmer from his cycle of backwardness. In reality, however, governors find it necessary to make many compromises with competing interests in order to maintain their base of political support in the state. They are frequently dependent on the CNC, which in turn relies on local *caciques* to organize followings of peasants; CONASUPO policies which threatened the instruments of control used by the bosses were often subject to the attempts of the governor to modify them. This was explained by one official as a difficult problem for CONASUPO.

> Many governors, except in the most industrialized sates, have built their support on the CNC and are very hesitant to upset its state leaders. Thus, for example, we have this case in one state in which the community has gotten together to sack a dishonest analyst. But then the

general director gets a letter from the deputy of the area saying that the CNC does not want this fellow sacked. It obviously has the backing of the governor.

The attempts of the governors to modify CONASUPO programs were likely to be focused on its rural development efforts, and the influence they exerted tended to be directed at the CONASUPO agent closest at hand, the state representative.

In the spring of 1975, three state representatives of CONASUPO were relieved of their official responsibilities. The explanation for their removal which circulated within the agency was that each had been demonstrating "excessive enthusiasm for collaborating with the governor" in his activities. Evidently, the extent to which these administrators were enabling the governors to determine the distribution of CONASUPO resources had passed beyond the limits acceptable by central office management. In general, national level officials of CONASUPO were concerned about the problems which a governor could present for the agency. An administrator in the State Offices Division expressed doubts about overly close relations between the governors and the representatives.

> I'm very much against my representatives going out on political campaigns with the governors or the deputies or any other person running for office. If they must do it, I tell them very forcefully, "Look, don't offer *anything*—nothing at all—and don't promise anything either."

Regardless of such strict injunctions, data from five of the state offices demonstrate a significant difference between the responsiveness of administrators to state level political leaders and between the actual performance of the programs in those states.[9] In these five cases, the responsiveness of the representatives to state or national officials was closely related to the manner in which they were selected to fill the post.

It was unofficially acknowledged throughout CONASUPO that the entire category of state representatives had been chosen by the general director on the basis of "political" criteria. High level officials in the State Offices Division made little input into the selection of the representatives, even failing to influence the process in terms of minimal job requirements. Instead, reported one manager, "The general director made all the appointments to state representative positions. Using his own criteria—and I don't know what they were—he chose them all." In fact, due to the power of a number of governors and local political conditions, several representatives were actually chosen by the governors of

9. The five states were selected on the basis of the clarity of the career ties of the representative and the completeness of the data available. Their names are not revealed in order to protect the anonymity of the respondents.

the states where they were to be assigned. In private communication with the general director, these political leaders were able to indicate the person they wished appointed. A few representatives were chosen because of their relationship to other federal agencies. In a number of cases, the individuals chosen had ties to both national and state level influentials. And, finally, some of the representatives were chosen because of close personal relationships to high level officials in CONASUPO.

Table 23 presents data on socioeconomic characteristics of the five states to be compared and corresponding information on Mexico as a whole. The living conditions of the population, revealed by information on literacy, use of shoes, characteristics of homes, employment and language, have been used as general indicators of poverty and inequality in Mexico (see González Casanova, 1970; Wilkie, 1967). It can be seen that the states range from the relatively wealthy C and D, which have conditions generally better than the national average, to A, B, and E, which are poorer than the country as a whole on most indicators. Even for the most advanced states, however, the poverty of large segments of the population is impressive. It can be expected that these conditions of deprivation would be most acute in rural areas. At least one-third and in most cases half or more of the inhabitants live in rural areas, and significant proportions of the economically active are employed in agriculture. The five states, therefore, present differing environments for CONASUPO's activities, but all are suitable sites for the agency to implement its rural development programs. The states are all located in the central region of the country, and all are important corn production states.

Three of the states were served by representatives and a corps of other agents who were clearly linked to the national level leadership of CONASUPO; the other two were represented by officials who were selected for the post because of close ties to the state governor. When asked about how they came to occupy positions in CONASUPO, the statements made by the representatives clearly attest to differences in their recruitment. The first three clearly owe their jobs to the influence of administrators at the national level of CONASUPO.

A. I've worked in CONASUPO since the beginning of the *sexenio*. Before that, I worked in a number of government agencies but always in some connection with CONASUPO. I was part of the Coordination, Supervision, and Special Projects Commission, and then the director offered me this opportunity. We have a director who is first class. He's really on top of things.

B. I've known Jorge de la Vega since we were in school together. . . . We're from the same state. . . . He called me in January 1974 and asked me to take charge of this politically difficult state for him.

TABLE 23.

Socioeconomic Characteristics of Five States, 1970

Indicator	Mexico	State A	B	C	D	E
Total population (in thousands)	48,225	2,324	3,815	3,297	3,833	486
	(%)	(%)	(%)	(%)	(%)	(%)
pop. living in rural areas*	42.0	53.0	54.8	34.8	48.6	66.2
econ. active (12 years or older) in agriculture	39.4	59.0	53.1	34.1	30.3	48.1
pop. unable to read or write (10 years or older)	23.7	33.8	29.4	19.4	24.9	37.9
pop. speaking indigenous language	6.5	2.7	9.4	0.2	5.2	2.4
pop. not wearing shoes	21.5	23.0	25.5	22.5	11.2	28.1
homes with two rooms or less	69.1	77.2	75.1	60.8	68.4	74.7
homes without drainage	58.5	68.1	64.6	47.5	60.2	75.8

Source: Secretaría de Industria y Comercio, *Anuario estadístico, 1969; Noveno censo general de población, 1970.*

*1968.

C. "X" [a top level official in CONASUPO] suggested that I take charge of this for the company.

Two others, however, clearly had the governor to thank for their CONASUPO positions.

D. Before coming here, I had no connection at all with CONASUPO. There was another fellow who was going to be the state representative, but I beat him out. I know the governor well, and I have hundreds of friends in the state government, and what's more, I'm from here and I'm well known. . . . I had more friends than the other fellow. I'm here because of the governor, not because of anyone in CONASUPO.

E. The governor is a very good friend of mine. You see, I was his campaign manager and we've been friends for years.

There was a similar difference among the representatives in how they defined the objectives of CONASUPO in their state. The three representatives who were selected from the central office, for instance, made a point of explaining the relevance of CONASUPO programs to the subsistence agricultural sector.

A. The most important job CONASUPO has is the commercialization of agriculture for specific groups like *ejidatarios* and small farmers.

B. The two principal goals of CONASUPO . . . are to protect the income of the *campesino* by providing a guarantee price which really is delivered to him and to supply basic commodities to the population through its stores.

C. I consider the most important objective of CONASUPO to be the promotion of rural development. The second most important objective is to regulate the market in basic products. . . . CONASUPO is a very dynamic organization whose goal is to put an end to intermediaries and help the *ejidatario* of limited means.

The representatives selected by the governors, on the other hand, tended to define CONASUPO's objectives much more generally, avoiding specific mention of low income agriculturalists.

D. CONASUPO's purpose here is the commercialization of corn, buying and selling at guarantee prices.

E. The most important job of CONASUPO is to regulate the market.

In response to questions about problems at the state level and how CONASUPO should go about solving these problems, all of the representatives with national level ties indicated sensitivity to problems in the countryside and to the economic conditions which existed there.

A. It's very important for me to see all of the installations and communities and to know problems at the local level.

B. More attention should be given to the areas which are most inaccessible. In those areas the *cacique* really rules and has his *tienda de raya* [company store]. If CONASUPO could penetrate these areas it would really be fulfilling its social function.

C. It's necessary to do away with imposed programs—simply arriving in the countryside and putting in a well or electricity where people neither want it or need it. CONASUPO programs should not be subject to the *sexenio* in rural areas.

Similarly, one of the locally oriented representatives also explained problems and solutions in terms of the rural development goals of the central offices.

D. The problem with the idea of commercialization of corn is simply that the mechanisms don't work. . . . Until these problems of making the system more agile are solved, CONASUPO is going to go on having the same problems it has had for twenty-five or thirty years. The peasant is going to continue to fall into the hands of the hoarder. The mechanisms must be changed.

However, in an apparent contradiction of his expression of concern about the relationship between the peasant and the hoarder, this representative went on to explain, with evident approval, a program introduced by the governor which would actually fortify the position of the hoarder, usually the local boss or *cacique*.

D. The state government is going to act as endorser for any credit given to peasants to grow corn. This means that just about any peasant can qualify for credit and many problems I told you about will be solved because of the governor and the state government. Also this plan is designed to work through the hoarder, saying in effect, OK, go on giving credit to people in your community as you used to but do it with money of the government of the state. There's a saying in Mexico: If you can't beat 'em, join 'em, and that's what is being done.

The other representative suggested a problem and a solution which ignored the rural development policy.

E. CONASUPO must consolidate its present programs before expanding more. It is too heterogeneous right now.

Finally, the representatives indicated differences in the access they had to the governor and in their concern for coordinating CONASUPO programs with him.

Centrally Selected[10]

A. Yes, I'm also responsible for coordination with the state government. That's been something of a problem: trying to see the
governor. I've actually had to go to the Ministry of the Presidency
to get an appointment to see him. It's not he who's hard to see;
it's getting past the gorillas he keeps at the door who take your card
and there you sit for one or two hours until you give up.

B. I have no problems with the governor. We have very good working
relations and good personal relations although we are not close
friends. . . . I see him frequently at official meetings—once or
twice a month—but we only go to see him specially when there is
some new program started. Then I let him know about it. Generally, our functions go on pretty much without the need to consult
him, unless of course he hears of a problem and then he lets me
know of it. So much the better if the governor backs some program
of ours; that's just one more bit of support. But in any event, our
programs go on.

Locally Selected

D. Oh yes, we help the governor, too. For example, the President in
the past year made several trips to the state and the President very
much would like to see a DICONSA store in every town and village in
the country. So before he comes, the governor communicates with
us, and we have had a DICONSA store put in anywhere he was
programmed to go. . . . I speak at least once a week with the
governor either in person or on the telephone—sometimes twice a
week.

E. There is going to be a meeting to resolve the problem. . . . It's
going to be here in my office and the governor will be here because
he's my friend and he owes me this favor.

Taken together, these statements provide preliminary evidence that
a distinction between "center-oriented" and "local-oriented" state
representatives can be made. It seems reasonable to conclude, on the
basis of these statements, that the representatives who were chosen
because of links to national administrators were more likely to define
their responsibilities in terms of CONASUPO's objectives such as targeting
programs for subsistence farmers and providing the services which
would free the peasant from exploitive economic relationships. In the
states with locally tied personnel, on the other hand, the representatives
were more likely to focus their statements on the general objectives of
CONASUPO and to indicate the important role the governor has in
defining state level programs or solving problems. In terms of actual

10. The representative of state "C" did not respond to the question.

measures of performance, the offices with center-oriented representatives demonstrated a greater ability to deliver the rural development programs than did the other offices. Because of national decisions to concentrate resources in certain states, it is necessary to consider states with large programs separately from those with average size programs.[11] Within each category, however, center-directed states had better performance records in terms of the criteria established by central offices than local-directed ones.

Among the three with large programs, growth rates and service delivery figures are generally better among the two center-oriented offices than those of the local-oriented offices, as indicated by the figures in Table 24. Thus, for example, the percentage increase in the number of rural reception centers was 25 percent and 26.5 percent in the first category and less than 1 percent in the other. Similarly, the center-oriented offices tended to offer more auxiliary services than those of the local-oriented office. Programs for reaching and educating the peasant were given much greater impetus in the first two states than in the latter one. In terms of the distribution of rural and urban stores, states A and C were clearly more committed to the rural areas than state D.

Between the two average size programs, the differences are equally noticeable, especially as they concern the Five Basic Products project, an important emergency measure initiated by central offices in 1974 (see Table 25).[12] Because it was a program which directly threatened local merchants, especially in rural areas, it is not surprising to see that the center-oriented representative was more committed to extending this program to a large number of centers than the local-oriented official who had to be more sensitive to state level political forces. Once again, the commitments to establish rural stores and to extend the network of reception centers were evident in the center-oriented state as were its attempts to reach the peasant through literature, radio, and other special programs. This was less true in the state in which the representative was closely tied to the governor.

These data do provide some indication that performance levels may vary in relation to career dependency networks in Mexico. Because of the influence of the personnel change which occurs every *sexenio*, officials tend to be most responsive to the organization or individual which offers them the greatest chances for pursuing their own career aspirations. In

11. That is, in states where CONASUPO central headquarters have decided to concentrate resources, performance levels are likely to surpass those of average size program states, regardless of the career ties of the representative.

12. Under the Five Basic Products Program, corn, beans, rice, oil, and sugar were sold at cost, generally through the local warehouses but also through special dispensaries. This was done to help combat hoarding and speculation because of national shortages and inflation.

TABLE 24.

CONASUPO **Performance in Large Program States**

	Center-Oriented				Local-Oriented	
	A		C		D	
	No.	%	No.	%	No.	%
No. of rural reception centers						
1972	83		120		121	
1975	105		150		122	
% increase	26.5		25.0		0.8	
Centers with						
Library	72	80.9*	150	100.0	95	77.9
Clinic	0	0.0	28	18.6	6	4.9
Corn shellers	12	13.5	23	15.3	11	9.0
Inter-plot transport.	1	1.1	0	0.0	3	2.5
Five basic products, 1975	34	32.4	28	18.7	25	20.5
% of total national sale of						
Fertilizer	13.0		20.0		5.0	
Sacks	3		19		3	
Seeds	14		0		0	
No. radio stations carrying CONASUPO program	20		18		4	
Distribution per center						
Peasant mail (monthly)	16.1		20.0		15.1	
Flyers (monthly)	31.1		38.9		29.1	
Sports teams	1.0		0.74		0.64	
Training of analysts	1.0		1.1		0.61	
Stores						
Rural	42	38.0	30	21.9	7	9.5
Urban	69	62.0	107	78.1	67	90.5

*Percentages figured on the basis of number of centers existing in 1974. Unless otherwise indicated, all figures refer to 1974.

TABLE 25.

CONASUPO Performance in Average Program States

Services	Center-Oriented B		Local-Oriented E	
	No.	%	No.	%
No. of rural reception centers				
1972	39		27	
1975	48		30	
% increase	23.0		11.0	
Centers with				
Library	40	83.3*	15	50.0
Clinic	1	2.0	6	20.0
Corn shellers	3	6.3	0	0.0
Inter-plot transport.	0	0.0	0	0.0
Five basic products, 1975	69	143.0	6	20.0
% of total national sale of				
Fertilizer		1.0		0.4
Sacks		3.0		0.7
Seeds		1.7		0.0
No. radio stations carrying CONASUPO Program	34		3	
Distribution per center				
Peasant mail (monthly)		18.9		9.2
Flyers (monthly)		35.4		17.4
Sports teams		1.0		1.1
Training of analysts		0.8		0.8
Stores				
Rural	39	21.8	8	18.0
Urban	140	78.2	37	82.0

*Percentages figured on the basis of number of centers existing in 1974. Unless otherwise indicated, all figures refer to 1974.

Chapter 4, these tendencies were seen to have an effect on the formulation of the rural development policy. Now, in terms of the policy implementation functions of the state representatives of CONASUPO, this same
pattern of responsiveness has also been observed. That is, when the state
representative of CONASUPO was selected on the basis of the suggestion
of the state governor, it would be expected that the future career opportunities available to that individual would lie at the state level or be a
result of his willing cooperation with the state governor or the political
groups supporting him. The data suggest that representatives selected
in this fashion were less likely to be in the forefront of efforts to implement policy from central offices which threatened the economic or
political position of local power holders. On the other hand, an individual who thought his own employment in the future depended upon his
performance as defined by the national level administrators of the
agency tended to respond most faithfully to expectations emanating
from that level.[13]

Discovering explanations for the failure to implement public policies
is not difficult. One study even suggests that the successful initiation
of new projects is the exception rather than the norm. Given the extent
and variety of obstacles to program implementation, the authors state,
the most realistic expectation is that they will fail to become more than
words on paper (see Pressman and Wildavsky, 1973). Certainly in
CONASUPO, the performance of bureaucratic officials was problematic
for the implementation of the rural development policy of the agency.
Because of local circumstances, the representative heading the agency's
state office was called upon to be both an implementor of policy and
a local problem solver, roles which were frequently in conflict. Aware
of the dilemma in which the state representative was caught, a few
national level administrators of the agency attempted to establish other
mechanisms for achieving implementation at that level. One such
attempt was the Field Coordination Program which sought to involve
local level recipients in the planning and regulation of agency programs.
In Chapter 6, this program to achieve faithful execution of the rural
development policy is examined and the role of bureaucratic actors in the
resolution of grass-roots community problems is discussed.

___

13. As mentioned previously, all representatives had to respond to both local and
national level performance demands if they were to fulfill their duties adequately. Even
the most nationally responsive representative, for example, could not afford to offend
certain powerful local groups, and even the most locally responsive official was to some
extent controlled and directed in his decisions by the requirements of his official chiefs
in Mexico City. The difference between the two types of representatives was one of
general tendencies in responsiveness.

6

Implementation II:
Bureaucrats as Brokers

> The real problem is to get people standing up for their rights, working
> together to pressure governmental agencies into complying with their
> duties. If we can do this, we can achieve results which will last beyond
> the *sexenio*.

Official organizations and public functionaries in Mexico are frequently
in a position to ignore or exploit peasants, consumers, unskilled
workers, the unemployed, slum dwellers, and others, for these groups
have few effective means for making independent and forceful demands
on the government for the allocation of goods and services.[1] The lack
of autonomous demand making capacity among low status recipients
was one factor contributing to the failure of many CONASUPO officials
to perform their duties in accordance with the agency's rural development scheme.[2] Among those who could benefit from the use of agency
resources—merchants, middlemen, local political leaders, medium and
large landowners, truckers, *caciques*, and peasants—clearly the most
powerless were the peasants.

Since the Revolution of 1910, peasants have been gradually integrated into the political institutions of the Mexican regime. In the 1930s,
the support of President Cárdenas encouraged some independent peasant
political activity, but currently, the rural poor are organized and
represented by the most docile and least rewarded of the three sectors
of the official party.[3] Typically, local power wielders such as *caciques*
and *ejido* commissioners mobilize peasant followings through the use

1. The lack of political influence of low status groups in Mexico is discussed in
González Casanova (1970), Moreno Sánchez (1973), Reyna (1974), and Ronfeldt (1973).
2. Demand making, as it is used in Chapter 6, refers to "individual or collective
activities aimed at extracting certain types of benefits from the political system by
influencing the decisions of incumbent government officials. Demand making is thus
differentiated from political participation aimed at influencing government resource
allocation by replacing or retaining the incumbent authorities (i.e., electoral participation)
or by overthrowing or restructuring the political system itself (e.g., through revolutionary
violence)" (Cornelius, 1974: 1125).
3. See especially Adie (1970), Hansen (1971), Reyna (1974), Stavenhagen (1970),
Stavenhagen *et al.* (1968). An extensive historical analysis of peasant political activity
in one rural community is found in Ronfeldt (1973).

of economic rewards and sanctions and then deliver their support to municipal and state level officials of the National Peasants Confederation (CNC) which represents the sector in the PRI.[4] As a consequence, the votes of rural Mexico have long provided the regime with its most stable and reliable base of support (see Reyna, 1972). At the same time, government activity toward its agrarian population has generally been characterized by neglect and exploitation. Understandably, then, peasants have few political or organizational resources to use in pressing their claims upon government agencies like CONASUPO or upon their representatives.

Therefore, it is not surprising that CONASUPO's state offices were not always effective in ensuring that policies determined in Mexico City would actually be realized at the local level. While they were capable of achieving a degree of state level coordination and reducing some of the upward flow of decisions, the local offices were not able to guarantee that integrated packages of CONASUPO programs always reached their intended beneficiaries, the *ejidatarios* and peasant communities. Competing hierarchies within CONASUPO, the requirements of local problem solving, and the temptation to use agency resources for career advancement were factors which often prevented the faithful execution of the rural development scheme. As we have seen, the state representatives were subject to conflicting demands for services and performance. One official summed up the position of the chief local agent of the company,

> The state representative is often sandwiched between his responsibilities as a direct representative of CONASUPO or the general director in the state and the political pressures which are exerted upon him by the governor and local political forces. Many times he might be in a position of wishing to ignore of "not hear about" the malfunctioning or nonfunctioning of CONASUPO programs because of other pressures upon him.

It was much to expect that these individuals would become vocal and effective champions of subsistence farmers. Such activity on their part could easily result in public conflict and dissention, conditions which are anathema to Mexican officials and which can result in the loss of their jobs (see Fagen and Tuohy, 1972).

A small group of officials in CONASUPO, presented with the task of attempting to correct over thirty years of frequently misdirected efforts, decided that an experiment in program implementation should be undertaken. Execution of the rural development policy would be more effective, they suggested, if it depended on the participation and interest of community level recipients of CONASUPO's services rather than primarily on the motivations of the agency's state or national level officials.

---

4. The domination of peasant communities by local and state level bosses is analyzed in Instituto de Investigaciones Sociales (1975).

The delivery of a package of programs best suited to a specific community would most successfully occur if groups of *ejidatarios* and community members decided which services were most needed and then actively demanded satisfactory performance from agency personnel.

The idea to instrument grass-roots participation in the programs was not an obvious alternative for them to choose, however conventional such strategies have become in the United States. The Mexican political regime is preeminently paternalist and elitist in its activities and has, through various mechanisms, deliberately sought to limit the participation of the population in the policy process (see Reyna, 1974; Stevens, 1974). As will be remembered from Chapter 3, the PRI is not so much an aggregator of interests as it is an instrument to control the population through cooptation, political communication, and the individual allocation of rewards and sanctions. Within the bureaucracy, policies are generally designed with little input from the masses concerning their needs or interests (see Purcell, 1973, 1975). The rural development scheme itself was formulated in the absence of public demand for it, and peasant spokesmen were neither consulted nor kept informed about agency plans.

The Field Coordination Program, therefore, was a somewhat radical idea for a bureaucratic organization in Mexico, and one which could prove politically dangerous because it was predicated on the idea of mobilizing low status recipients of government services. It was approved and put into operation largely because of the high regard the general director had for his planning manager, whose enthusiastic promotion of the plan convinced him of its potential. Impressed with the capability and dedication of his chief planner, Jorge de la Vega promoted him to a specially created top level position where he was accorded strong support for most of his proposals.

The program was conceived as an attempt to achieve grass-roots control over state level agency personnel and organized community participation in both the design and delivery of an effective and appropriate package of services. It was also an experiment to ensure conscientious policy implementation and local level coordination. It was proposed that in selected experimental communities,

> groups of peasants will be organized to support directly CONASUPO's activities while at the same time they will serve as effective social linkages between the institution and the communities to promote new activities which will stimulate self-sustained development (CONASUPO, 1973a).

The overarching goal of the program was to enable the local community to establish and follow its own appropriate "development path." This was to be an alternative to the traditional method of imposing programs which conformed to idealized development models but which frequently had little relevance to local conditions. Additionally, it was expected that peasants could be taught, through utilization of the various programs of CONASUPO, to defend themselves vis-à-vis the government and to make effective demands upon it for increased attention and for the proper performance of its personnel and programs.

The manager of the program explained that there were two principal results to be achieved from this approach.

As you know, CONASUPO has a large and multifaceted program and the need has developed to coordinate it at the actual implementation phase. The second . . . is that it transfers many of CONASUPO's activities to the village level. There is simply no way to administer effectively a program such as CONASUPO. It is too large and has such a great variety of concession contracts and merchandizing systems that it is impossible to ensure honesty and effectiveness at the community level. If we were to have inspectors we would have to have inspectors for the inspectors and so on. So we decided to try this program of field coordination so that the peasants would become responsible for policing their own village CONASUPO activities.

The program was to be instrumented in a limited number of rural communities in several different states. In these communities, a development worker trained by CONASUPO was to stimulate the organization of development groups made up of village members. Once integrated, the groups would set out to identify the most immediate obstacles to local development and take appropriate action to resolve these problems. As each was attacked and vanquished, it was expected to bring to attention another structural barrier confronting the community. In its turn, the new obstacle would be dealt with. Ultimately, the community was to be able to achieve self-sustained development, first identifying and then acting to break economic constraints whose origin was external to the community.

As an example of this process, a development committee might begin its activities with the idea that a tractor was needed to help the community produce more. The group would subsequently lobby with various federal or state agencies until a tractor was made available on credit terms the community could meet. Hypothetically, in addition to teaching the community members to work together, cooperative use of the machine might highlight the fact that exorbitant prices were being paid to local merchants for fertilizers, seeds, insecticides, and other agricultural inputs and that the usurious credit charged for them was sapping the community of its economic surplus. The development committee would then approach CONASUPO and petition for the establishment of appropriate programs in its local warehouses so that the community could free itself from heavy economic obligations to the merchants. More adequate instruction at the local school, a community water supply, collective use of common lands, rural cooperative industries, and an effectively operating local health center responding to community needs were other solutions the groups were expected to be able to achieve.

Initial field experience in the communities, however, led program administrators to believe that structural change would not be easy if problems were attacked one by one. Instead, the committees and field agents were advised to meet together, carry out studies, and draw up a plan for the development of each community, centering on a package of essential programs. After the package had been designed, the community groups would be advised to concentrate first on acquiring those programs which CONASUPO could provide and then on those which could be obtained only through other government institutions. The development workers were to be available as resources, helping organize and suggesting channels for solving local problems. The end result, as explained by national program administrators, was "to have the government substitute for the local *caciques* who, through relationships of economic exchange, control the productivity and level of technology of local communities."

Regional coordinators of the program were assigned to aid the community workers and development groups. When possible, the coordinator was to assist the communities in dealing with the state office of CONASUPO; if state level personnel proved to be unresponsive, the coordinators could encourage the local group to present its problem directly to the program staff in Mexico City. These administrators in the capital had both formal authority and informal influence to seek solutions at executive levels. By mid-1974 there were eighty communities in which the Field Coordination Program was being tested. Visits to twelve communities and extended conversations with both the community development workers and the regional coordinators indicated that these bureaucrats frequently became intermediaries between the peasant committees and various agencies of the government, including CONASUPO.[5]

5. During the research, a series of visits to local installations of CONASUPO in rural areas was made. The visits to the field were made with four of the six regional coordinators active in the Field Coordination Program at the time. They provided extensive and intensive information on local level problems and the history of CONASUPO and Field Coordination operations in the area. They included me in their regular round of activities, such as attending conferences with community development workers and meeting with representatives of the rural communities. Field Coordination localities were observed in the states of Aguascalientes, Michoacán, Puebla, Querétaro, San Luís Potosí, and Zacatecas.

The use of the agents as brokers was often the most effective and rapid means to express community demands and achieve results. Where this was not possible because the officials lacked useful connections, the strategies which were suggested for local problem solving encouraged community groups to search out and mobilize other interpersonal networks. Thus, finding solutions to local problems often depended upon the timely activation of preexisting alliance networks which made it possible to by-pass bureaucratic bottlenecks and political resistance. The agency's grass-roots personnel also functioned as information brokers for the local communities, sharing with them privileged knowledge they acquired because of their access to the bureaucratic elite. The functioning of the Field Coordination Program can be described as an attempt to forge new alliances with the peasants which would redound to their benefit and replace the bonds which had been used to exploit them for centuries.

Until now, discussion has centered on intra-elite contracts which have a discernible effect on the policy process. The brokerage and advocacy role of CONASUPO agents introduces a different type of vertical alliance, one which is more commonly encountered in the literature on patron-client relationships. In CONASUPO, the pattern of mediation between low status actors and government officials was not oriented to the achievement of career mobility, as were the linkages among public officials already considered. Instead, a tacit bargain of collaboration with the field agents was exchanged for the delivery of material goods to the community.[6] Both elite-low status and intra-elite linkages were involved as bureaucrats formed alliances with local community groups and attempted to solve problems for them by mobilizing the ties they had to other officials.

Problem Solving Through Personal Mediators

> The most important thing is for us to penetrate the community. To do this we must go down to their level—work on their level, not as *patrones.* . . . Of course they are distrustful; they have reason to be. Government and party officials have come over and over again making promises which they never keep and at times deceiving and taking advantage of the people.

In the Field Coordination communities, peasants frequently perceived that problem solving would be facilitated if the CONASUPO community

6. Similar informal alliances have been reported by Schmidt (1974: 445). See also Heath (1972).

agent or regional coordinator could be mobilized on their behalf. As higher status actors, the bureaucrats would be able to communicate more easily with government officials. Those involved in the program reported some uneasiness about fulfilling the role of intermediary.

> That's something I've noticed about the way the peasants behave toward me. They try to use me because I'm a symbol of authority, even though I have no real connections and even though I'm living humbly in the community as they are.

Nevertheless, because of pressure upon these individuals to perform their assigned functions, the role was frequently accepted, albeit reluctantly.[7]

There were a number of reasons why the CONASUPO agents assumed the role of intermediaries or encouraged the mobilization of other alliances in the solution of local problems rather than merely stimulating the communities to work together to solve their own problems. First, the community development workers were under pressure to produce results as quickly as possible. They wanted to demonstrate their usefulness to the local communities and to gain the trust and confidence of their inhabitants. In addition, the existence of factions and widespread interpersonal distrust in the communities were cited as reasons for the need for rapid demonstrations of the efficacy of united action.[8] "They begin to understand," explained one development worker about the *ejido* committees, "when they begin to see results." Moreover, the only way the Field Coordination workers and administrators thought they could avoid problems of political resistance from local powers was to work quickly to undercut the economic base of the *caciques* or economic bosses. Thus, commented an experienced member of the team,

> We are becoming more and more aware . . . that change in relationships of exchange cannot occur over extended periods of time. It must be done rapidly to break the chain of extraction and exploitation.

In addition, the effective and efficient resolution of problems was considered the key to overcoming apathy and dependence in the peasant community when dealing with the government. The paternalistic attitude of the government toward the low income population was frequently cited by Field Coordination agents as an obstacle to the development of self-help efforts in the local communities. In many villages, these individuals reported, the dominant attitude among peasants was that the government was responsible for providing all

---

7. In Colombia also, bureaucrats were observed to acccept brokerage roles when dealing with local communities, even though they were often uncomfortable with the "traditional" relationships (see Schmidt, 1974: 437–441, 445).

8. On the existence of factionalism in *ejido* communities, see Carlos (1974: Chaps. 5 and 6).

goods and services and that to acquire them, one could only ask and wait. In one Field Coordination region, for example, an agent described this relationship of paternalism and dependence.

> The habit of paternalism is very strong here. The people, who are very poor, are in the habit of looking to the government for everything and not doing anything on their own to help themselves. The government has created this feeling in them because it's the poorest region in the country and officials have come with the attitude of "Oh, the poor peasants here. Let's give them some help."

This attitude among politicians and bureaucrats had encouraged the proliferation of specialized federal agencies whose officials were accomplished at making promises to alleviate a host of problems in every community they visited. "Unfortunately," explained a beleaguered development worker, "our government has the habit of going around making promises left and right which it has no intention of fulfilling." The lack of performance by the government inevitably affects the attitudes of the population. An *ejido* leader was heard to reply bitterly to a question about the delivery of a tractor to the community, "With all the tractors which have been *promised* us, we have more than enough! I don't care how little you help us, but please let it be *real*, not just more promises." Because of such attitudes, the community workers of CONASUPO thought that a firm and speedy demonstration of good faith was required if the local groups were to develop the unity and enthusiasm necessary to continue functioning actively.

Another reason the community development agents found themselves assuming a brokerage role was simply that this kind of approach to problem solving is highly institutionalized in the Mexican political system. Demands made on the government very frequently take the form of personal applications for the allocation of public goods and services.[9] So great is the perception that problems are solved only through personal channels that one observer has referred to the "myth of the right connection" in Mexican society (Stevens, 1974: 94). Particularly where powerless groups such as peasants are concerned, it is not surprising that the approach to those holding answers to local problems would be made first through the more traditional forms of petition and personal intervention (see González Casanova, 1970). Nor is such a strategy ill-conceived or unfruitful. Mexican peasants have learned, through generations of practice, that the use of personal networks is perhaps the most effective means to acquire what they need from the government.

As a consequence of these circumstances, the acceptance of a mediatory role by the community workers and coordinators was perhaps to

9. Cornelius (1975: Chap. 7) and Scott (1974) discuss this phenomenon in Mexico.

be expected once they identified themselves with local problems and attempted to find solutions to them. This pattern of problem solving was repeated in cases recounted by CONASUPO's field agents. In some of the situations described by these individuals, it was apparent that the agent-as-broker formed part of an extended chain of alliances which would be activated to solve any given problem. These chains began with alliances between the low status village committees and the community agent and continued to those among higher level officials of the government. This was, for instance, how the community of San Marcos sought to find a solution to its drainage problem.[10]

Case I: Drainage for San Marcos

The *ejido* of San Marcos had no system of drainage. During rainy periods, the local roads and fields became almost impassable and the huge puddles of water which collected were viewed by residents as a hazard to health and safety. A number of times since the formation of the *ejido* in 1934, groups had been organized to petition government agencies for help in solving the drainage problem. In turn, the groups went to the Water Resources Ministry and the Ministry of Agrarian Reform with their request and waited, after each visit, for a study to be carried out to determine a feasible solution. Always they were met with the promise that the problem would be studied, analyzed, and attacked. No action was ever taken, however. At one point, the community had even collected a sizable amount of money from individual residents to help pay for the needed improvement, but still no official cooperation was forthcoming.

When the community worker arrived in the area in February of 1974, a development committee was activated around the drainage issue, as this was the problem community members wanted most to resolve. The committee went to the state level agents of the Water Resources Ministry and once again presented a petition. Once again, a study of the problem and action to resolve it were dutifully promised, and once again, no action was forthcoming. At this time, however, the community developer felt under some pressure to prove his usefulness to the community and to demonstrate that the development group could be efficacious in the resolution of local problems. This was the first project attempted under his tutelage, and he admitted wanting to produce results quickly. Moreover, the community was factionalized politically and economically, and he thought that one way to unite it would be to show that group action could result in benefits for the entire community.

10. The names of the communities, municipalities, and states are fictitious although the events described actually occurred, according to reports of the community development workers.

Therefore, he sought out a means to make a more effective request of the Water Resources Ministry. He communicated his problem to the regional coordinator; this individual in turn communicated the local need to the Field Coordination headquarters in Mexico City. A high level official from the central office soon paid a visit to the community and listened to the development group discuss its problems and frustrations. He then proceeded to the state capital where he visited the Water Resources offices to contact a friend of his, the state agent of the ministry, to present the problem of San Marcos to him. Very soon after that, the Water Resources study team arrived in San Marcos to begin the necessary studies.

In this example, the community acting alone was not able to make an effective demand, but the use of higher status actors as advocates for the local level group achieved a rapid response from the official agency in question. Such brokerage and advocacy roles were not only useful to the communities in dealing with other government agencies; they also helped solve intra-CONASUPO bottlenecks. This was the case in the state of Oriente, where the community agents adopted the role of intermediary and mobilized a chain of interpersonal alliances in order to facilitate the establishment of DICONSA stores in rural areas.

Case 2: DICONSA Stores for Oriente

One of the problems frequently noted by community development workers was that they were always identified as agents of CONASUPO. Therefore, the issues around which the development committee co-alesced tended to be a reflection of what the peasants thought the worker could get for them rather than what were, in fact, the most important community needs. This characteristic situation was sum-marized by one of the Field Coordination agents, who explained,

> The peasants know what their real needs are—they know them very well. But they also know what you have to offer. So often they ask for the things you have to offer even though this has nothing to do with their real needs.

"The peasants recognize that I am CONASUPO," complained another development agent, "and all of a sudden they want stores." Because of such perceptions, many development groups decided that their major problem was that they did not have a CONASUPO store in their commun-ity. Privately, the community workers and field coordinators often thought that opening a store would not be a developmentally useful service provided by the government. At the same time, however, they were committed to encouraging self-generated proposals for projects. Additionally, they felt under the same pressure to produce quick results as the worker in San Marcos.

Therefore, in the state of Oriente, a number of community groups were not discouraged from contacting the state agent of DICONSA and the representative of CONASUPO to petition for stores. After presenting their requests to these officials, all groups were informed that DICONSA had established a temporary policy of opening up no new stores until it could resolve some of its supply and control problems. The various development committee members returned to their communities with nothing to show for their efforts. Faced with the inability to achieve positive results at the state level offices, the field workers contacted the regional coordinator who was responsible for all program communities in the state. He met with several of the development committees to hear of their petitions and experiences. He then made a special trip on their behalf to Mexico City, where he spoke with Field Coordination administrators. These higher level officials then contacted friends among national level officials of DICONSA to discuss the establishment of stores in Oriente. Shortly after this, the coordinator returned to his region to report, "They are going to let us continue with plans and proposals for rural stores just in this zone."

In the *ejido* of San Marcos and the state of Oriente, the local communities, represented by their development committees and tutored by the community workers, sought solutions to their problems through the mobilization of intermediaries and advocates. The peasant communities, as relatively powerless units in the political system, found it unrewarding to present their problems directly to the federal and state administrative authorities who controlled the resources they sought. Instead, the means to achieve results was perceived to be through the use of a bureaucratic broker. In the two examples cited, the CONASUPO workers had access to individuals who in turn had access to the resources needed by the communities. The problem solving system, diagrammed in Figure 11, makes use of both vertical and horizontal channels of influence. The strategic value of employing higher status intermediaries is made clear in the case of community development efforts in the municipality of Zapata where no brokers were utilized and, perhaps consequently, the communities were unable to achieve a rapid solution to their petitions.[11]

Case 3: The Municipality of Zapata and
the Five Basic Products

A community worker was assigned to organize development committees in three communities in the municipality of Zapata. When he

11. A municipality, or *municipio*, is a political division of territory which corresponds most closely to a county in the United States. Within each *municipio* are a number of communities, *ejidos*, and villages.

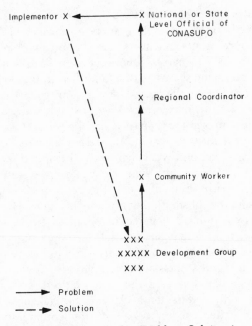

Figure 11. Channels for Problem Solving in
the Field Coordination Program.

arrived there in March 1974, he noticed immediately that the population
was being exploited by local merchants who were charging exorbitant
prices for the staple goods which were the basis of the traditional diet in
the area. Beans were sold at prices more than double the official rate,
for example, and cooking oil was 45 percent more expensive in the area
than elsewhere. Therefore, as soon as the communities were organized
the agent informed them of the Five Basic Products Program which was
being publicized and implemented at that time by BORUCONSA. Widespread shortages of a number of staple goods in Mexico in 1974 had
resulted in equally widespread hoarding and price scalping. As an
emergency measure, CONASUPO had organized the Five Basic Products
Program which was to operate from BORUCONSA warehouses, or where
these did not exist, from small community distribution centers. In each
dispensary, corn, beans, rice, sugar, and oil were to be sold at official
prices in order to ensure that communities had access to the products
they needed at prices they could afford. In order to have the maximum
impact on local price structures, the program was designed for easy
and rapid implementation, necessitating only the delivery of the products
to a preexisting outlet and the commissioning of a community member,
usually the warehouse analyst, to sell them. The communities of Zapata
were told that they, too, could qualify for this program.

The three development committees drew up a single petition requesting that the Five Basic Products Program be established in their communities. A group of committee members agreed upon a mutually convenient
day to travel to the state capital where they would present the petition,
first to CONASUPO's state representative and then to the official in charge
of BORUCONSA activities in the state. The community worker accompanied
the group in order to provide moral support but refused to speak for
the group. Before presenting themselves at the office, they met in a café
and discussed how they were going to present their request, what their
arguments were to be, and what their overall demand making strategy
would be. Later, after waiting some time to see the state officials, the
group was received by both of them; the petition was duly presented
and accepted and the substantiating arguments given. After this, neither
official took any action on their request. A number of months later, in
spite of several follow-up visits by the development committees, the
petition had still not been acted upon. The community worker summed
up the reception found at the state offices bitterly, "I was always treated
by the state representative as a third-class citizen, and he treated the
campesinos as if they were tenth class." The lack of a higher status
intermediary to intervene on behalf of the communities of Zapata
undoubtedly contributed to their failure to obtain results.

On some occasions, the CONASUPO agents were not able to act as
brokers for the local community because they, too, lacked the personal
connection needed for solution of specific problems. Recognizing the
value of the higher status intermediary, the agents might, therefore,
encourage the peasant groups to seek out other brokers who could help
them. Such was the situation in the ejido of El Maguey where the community group attempted to mobilize traditional political patrons on its
behalf.

Case 4: El Maguey and Its Padrinos Políticos

The development worker found the ejido of El Maguey seriously
divided into two competing factions. One faction was led by the ejido
commissioner while the other was identified with the three-man vigi-
lance committee, which is responsible under the Mexican agrarian code
for making sure that the commissioner performs his duties correctly and
fairly. The leadership of both factions had used the official positions to
acquire economic and political rewards for their followers. Each group
supported a different extracommunity political faction at the municipal
and state levels of the PRI. The politicians who relied on their support
served as padrinos políticos (political godfathers) to the respective ejido
factions, and each local clique had established the practice of approaching them when it wished to receive governmental aid or special consideration for its members. In return, the peasants provided whatever political
support the patrons requested.

The community worker made some attempt to organize a group which included representatives of both factions, but the development committee which emerged after community elections was entirely formed by members of the stronger faction. The formation of the development group itself seemed to stymie any effort to have the community work together for a common purpose. Presented with this situation, the community worker decided that the best strategy would be to encourage the development committee to work on projects which would of necessity benefit the entire community and whose use could not be restricted to members of one faction only. "The only way to begin to break down these divisions is to produce results," he concluded. Producing results in El Maguey meant that the development committee would begin its demand making efforts by approaching the appropriate *padrinos políticos*. These politicians, motivated by the desire to strengthen the dependence and loyalty of the faction, would be willing to act as intermediaries for the development committee in presenting its demands to bureaucratic agencies.

On other occasions, too, CONASUPO agents were not able to act as brokers for the communities because special personal ties did not exist, and the communities themselves were unable to provide the right connection. This situation sometimes occurred when the assistance of other government agencies was needed. The regional coordinators and community workers affirmed that any impersonal activity on their part to approach a government agency would only result in harming the chances of the community to achieve what it wanted. Thus, for example, the preferred strategy was that of a silent partner in development efforts.

> When dealing with the other agencies, presenting petitions and such, it's best to stay in the background, to be completely invisible as an agent of CONASUPO. This is in order to prevent jealousies and reactions and competition from other agencies. It's necessary to work sort of behind the scenes to get things from other agencies.

In situations such as these, in which neither the CONASUPO agents nor the community had any preexisting alliances which would be useful for problem solving, the function of the CONASUPO field workers was most commonly that of an information broker. In this role, they used the access they had as educated and urban bureaucratic actors to gather information which they could share with the development committees. Subsequently, they attempted to advise the groups on the most promising strategies to follow in their demand making.

Information Brokerage

> What's got to happen in this country is that people have got to organize and *force* the government to function properly. . . . I've been telling

lots of groups of peasants to do what Don José [an *ejido* commissioner]
and his group did: when the BORUSCONSA agent just couldn't be located
to attend to them, they simply said, "OK, he'll surely be here in the
morning. We'll just sleep here and wait for him." Believe me, the agent
showed up like magic then!

One of the objectives of their efforts often described by the community
workers and regional coordinators was to "leave the peasants with a
sense of how to do things on their own." Aware that their own tenure
and perhaps their own programs would expire in 1976 with the end of
the Echeverría administration, they thought the value of their work
depended on building a community structure which would transcend
the *sexenio* because it had resulted in grass-roots learning of how to
solve problems. It was important to the community level bureaucrats
to spread the idea that many community problems were capable of
solution through self-help measures which required only minimal
material inputs from the government agencies. For instance, a CONASUPO
Field Coordination agent explained,

> In the work of our program we try as little as possible to rely on other
> government agencies, or even on CONASUPO. We think that the peasant,
> through organization and becoming aware of his basic needs, can do
> a lot for himself. He doesn't need always to be running to the govern-
> ment or waiting for new things to fall out of the sky.

In fact, however, most self-help efforts did require some input from
government agencies. Most commonly, rural communities were simply
too poor to acquire the resources they needed without official support
for credit and special authorizations or to handle the opposition of those
who would be harmed by any local change. In the Field Coordination
communities, when it was necessary to deal with government agencies,
the CONASUPO agents attempted to school the peasant groups in the most
effective way to make their demands felt.

In Mexico, a myriad of special government programs, agencies,
ministries, and development funds are often charged with similar and
overlapping functions. At other times, the division of function among
them is strict, arbitrary, and jealously guarded. Knowledge of this
complex bureaucratic maze of responsibilities and constraints is not
easy to acquire, especially by rural community members who have
limited experience in dealing in such matters.[12] Advice about which
agency to approach as well as the most effective strategy for demand

12. Friedrich (1969) describes the case of a rural *cacique* in Mexico whose base of
power in the community derived in part from his ability to read and interpret the complex
and extensive agrarian code for community residents. In Mexico City, urban *caciques*
perform similar functions in low income communities (Cornelius, 1975: Chap. 6). Stevens
(1974) uses the term "information broker" to denote an "inside dopester" in Mexico. On
rural *caciques* in general, see Ugalde (1973).

making was provided by CONASUPO agents in meetings with the development committees. Additionally, an important aspect of this information provision role was indicating to the committees which of the officially made promises could be believed. The Field Coordination agents were sensitive to the problems created by making promises which could not be fulfilled. Part of their function, as they defined it, was to "Let the peasants know which of their requests have no chance of getting results and which do. . . . We should never promise anything we aren't going to do, aren't certain that can be done."

A number of development committee meetings in several different rural communities were attended, and the role of the community development workers was observed. The pattern of interaction they established with the peasant groups demonstrates clearly their function as information brokers. In meetings in a number of different locations, members of the groups generally initiated discussion by presenting what they considered to be their problems and needs—the malfunctioning of a BORUCONSA warehouse, the construction of a local rural industry, or the purchase of a tractor, for example. The Field Coordination personnel at the meetings then encouraged the peasants to think of different strategies for reaching a solution. When these were forthcoming, the CONASUPO agents evaluated the suggestions and indicated which ones seemed the most likely to lead to success.

The agents stressed that there existed a number of channels through which the committee could try to resolve community problems. The most effective strategy, they recommended, was to try the most promising one and, if the attempt proved unsuccessful, to try another one. The regional coordinator, if he were present at the meeting, might share his knowledge of which officials in the state capital were or were not worth talking to and who among agents of the bureaucracy seemed ready to fulfill his function and who was not at all interested in helping the rural communities. Peasants were warned of unresponsive or ineffective subsidiaries within CONASUPO and advised that it was best to work through other parts of the agency if possible.

In the meetings, the field agents suggested that a useful strategy for the group was to press particular officials to state a firm date before which action on a petition would be taken. On that date, the group was told to present itself before the official to inquire about the petition. If no action had been taken, the group should press for a firm date once again. If still no action resulted, other means to bring pressure to bear should then be attempted. For example, in one meeting a group indicated its concern that a state level functionary was not carrying out his duties. The regional coordinator shared with them the story of a development group in a neighboring community which had resolved a similar problem by writing a letter to the official's superiors in Mexico City to complain of his behavior. "Now," the group was told in an attempt to stimulate action, "that same official falls all over himself trying to help the *ejido* he used to ignore."

The relative usefulness of various institutions and individuals for problem solving meant that the Field Coordination agents did not usually encourage the community groups to work through the PRI. In fact, the party was considered by the field officials to be part of the reason the community was not developing. Therefore, concluded one worker, "It's best for CONASUPO to stay clear of dealings with the party, controlled by the same group which is exploiting the community." "However," confessed another, "if they can be of some help to us, we don't hesitate to accept it from them." This was, in fact, the opinion behind encouraging the community of El Maguey to work through its political patrons. On another occasion, a regional coordinator suggested that the development committee contact the federal deputy from the area to present a complaint. In most cases, however, the use of the party was not thought to be an effective way to achieve results.

> We don't generally go to political figures to solve local problems. We go to the agencies concerned. Now, for example, if the peasants should suggest taking their petition to the governor, we of course don't discourage them. There's nothing to be lost by trying. But the best results come from dealing directly with the agencies involved. . . . And it's much better for CONASUPO to appear apolitical.

In addition to providing information for the purpose of initiating activity, the CONASUPO Field Coordination officials also functioned as intermediaries to keep the development committees informed about what had become of their requests. As a result of their trips to the state capitals and frequent telephone contacts with Mexico City, they were able to report on the status of particular petitions at official levels. Particularly when a problem required action to be taken in the national capital, the regional coordinators, as elite actors working on behalf of rural communities, kept tabs on its progress through bureaucratic channels. The privileged information was then passed on to the peasant groups, and they were advised about when and where to take more action. This information brokerage and the advocacy role of the field workers were considered necessary to help the peasant communities escape from the exploitive relationships which characterized their powerless condition.

New Alliances for Old

> We have the idea of planting new things in our program, but we have realized that it's necessary to make the old things function first before starting new things.

> If we run into local opposition, we report it to our superiors all the
> way up to the President if need be.

The description of how the Field Coordination Program functioned
makes it clear that although the objectives of the program might be
considered radical within the context of the Mexican political system,
the strategies employed or encouraged by local level change agents
were far from revolutionary. Violence or organized public demand
making or demonstrations of dissatisfaction were never suggested by
the community workers as useful methods to present their grievances.
Instead, reliance on the tried and proved effectiveness of personal
contacts to achieve solutions to community problems was the most
common means employed by the development workers and committees.[13] Of course, the role of CONASUPO agents as advocates and brokers
to assist local development efforts was not explicitly foreseen in the
original proposal and plan for the program. However, the structure
and characteristics of the Mexican political system tended to encourage
the development of this role. Community groups acting on their own
were often unable to achieve response from government officials who
were not in the habit of responding to those with low status or with
little power. In addition, the imperative to find rapid solutions to
community problems encouraged reliance on personal networks.

A number of problems confronted the Field Coordination Program
as it attempted to foment new alliances between the rural areas and
responsive government agencies. For instance, at times even the most
effectively staged demand making attempts failed because no agencies
had enough resources to allocate to the problem. Venality of public
officials sometimes went uncorrected even when exposed because the
individuals in question had powerful political backing, as indicated by
the statement of a CONASUPO official on pages 131–132. Or the problems
of a local community might be physically impossible to solve, such
as when poor soil or lack of water meant that agriculture in an area
might never develop. In some communities, the apathy of the peasants,
caused by decades if not centuries of experientially based cynicism,
made failures of all attempts at community organization. And the
Field Coordination Program was able to affect only a small number
of localities.

In addition, from the outset of the program, personnel problems
absorbed a considerable amount of the time and energy of national
level administrators and seriously affected the ability of community

---

13. Similar nonviolent strategies are preferred by urban migrants in Mexico City (see
Cornelius, 1975: Chap. 9). For the problems inherent in protest activities of low status
actors in the United States, see Lipsky (1968).

agents to provide long term assistance to the local areas. Most of these problems were directly related to the manner in which the community development workers were recruited. In Chapter 3, the recruitment of the *equipo* of regional coordinators was described, and it was shown that strong ties of *confianza* existed between individual coordinators and national program directors. As a result, these officials remained in the program and continued to perform their functions with dedication and zeal even when their zones were changed and their responsibilities redefined. The development workers, however, were recruited without the aid of personal introductions or the assurances of *confianza*. Instead, because the salaries offered were low, the field conditions difficult, and the program rapidly put into operation, the development workers were recruited through public notices to rural teachers and students of the social sciences at UNAM. One hundred and six trainees began their service in November 1973. Eighteen months later, only sixteen development workers remained in the program. The relationships they had with their superiors, the national administrators of the program, were not strong enough for them to operate effectively under difficult conditions. Gradually, the community workers became disillusioned or discouraged and left the program until only a few remained.

The most pervasive problems of the program, however, were related to the role of CONASUPO officials as change agents in situations in which their activities threatened traditional economic and political relationships. Based as it was on the idea of fomenting community level participation in demand and decision making, the Field Coordination Program was likely to encounter challenges from the local *caciques*, notables, and bosses who controlled economic and political activity in the communities. CONASUPO officials were well aware of the potential problems which could result from attempting to circumvent and ultimately destroy local power holders.

> CONASUPO wants to break the power of the *cacique* or the sons and grandsons of *caciques* who are often allied with the PRI and the CNC. There is some danger in this—pistols are still worn in many rural areas to deal with this kind of threat.

Another community worker reported, "Going out and meeting with peasants can be a dangerous business in Mexico. It threatens a lot of people." In some remote areas, the *caciques* were considered to be an unassailable force, even by the party. In one state, the reaction of such local influentials had caused the governor to request that CONASUPO completely remove the Field Coordination Program from his state.

In addition, the hold of the traditional alliances on the peasants could be resilient. The local *caciques* and bosses, frequently integrated as members of the community, generally had strong personal ties with local inhabitants and were people to whom others would go in time of need. Although the "aid" provided by these individuals might be detrimental to the long term interests of those "aided," the services they provided were numerous, the terms of repayment flexible, and the help immediate (see Bartra, 1975). One of the goals cited by many CONASUPO officials was to "make the agency as agile as the *cacique* and the *coyote*." To the extent that it did not fulfill this objective, local communities might find it convenient or necessary to continue dealing through the traditional relationships.

Politically, the control exercised by the party and local *caciques* in rural areas was firm and based on years of experience. As explained by one Field Coordination administrator,

> You must realize that government here, especially in rural areas and especially where the state government is concerned is made up of a number of leaders, each tied to the next leader higher up. Thus, at the local community level, there will be one man with his group which will effectively control the whole community. This leader will be tied to a leader in a larger area and thus it goes growing in pyramidal form. Thus, it is often possible, with 10 percent of the agrarian structure, to control the rest very effectively.[14]

Moreover, while some CONASUPO agents might be eager to organize peasant groups to participate actively in the achievement of their self-defined goals, not many of the workers thought that active local demand making was an idea which conformed to the objectives of the regime as a whole.

> A peasant leader said to me the other day, "I know you have come here to organize us," and I immediately replied to him, "No, we've come to help you resolve your problems." We don't want to talk anything about "organization." That's what this government will not allow—organization. You can say what you wish and write what you wish and criticize as much as you like now and get away with it. But the moment you try to organize, they'll be right on top of you. This government will stand anything except organization.

At both the local and national levels, then, there were limits on the extent to which members of the bureaucracy or their low income clients could challenge politically important interests in their efforts to "replace the *cacique* with the government." These constraints help explain a number of strategic changes which occurred in the program between 1973 and 1975. In the lapse of one year's time during which the activities

14. For a general discussion, see Flynn (1974). Analysis of time series voting data in Mexico has demonstrated that rural regions tend to support the PRI more faithfully than do urban areas (see Reyna, 1972). Arterton (1974: Chap. 7) presents data on the type and frequency of political participation in four rural villages in central Mexico.

of the Field Coordination Program were observed and its officials interviewed and reinterviewed in an attempt to evaluate program results,
the initial objectives of the program were modified. Most importantly,
perhaps, new and self-generated proposals for community development
were subordinated to attempts to make the programs already in operation function more effectively. Thus, greater attention was directed
toward pressing demands for proper conduct on the state level functionaries of CONASUPO itself.

It became evident that the local CONASUPO warehouse could not serve
as a locus for the services needed by the community until the representative, the BORUCONSA agent, and the analyst were willing to respond to
community pressure. It was more fully realized, then, that effective
community participation depended not only on the attitudes and activities of local recipients but also on the performance of the public institutions themselves. As a reflection of this changed perception of how
bureaucratic responsiveness is achieved, the regional coordinators
assumed the advocacy-brokerage role more explicitly. They were
assigned to specific state offices to function as facilitators and promoters
of CONASUPO activities in the state. They made their own field visits to
the communities and reported on the implementation problems they
encountered. Consequently, the seventy-five development committees
which remained functioning gradually assumed the role of passive
informants about local problems.

The peasants, precisely because they were low status actors, were
often unable to achieve response to their petitions. As was seen in
Chapter 5, the system of accommodation which functioned at the state
level tended to benefit those with most political and economic resources.
On a number of occasions, Field Coordination Program officials
attempted to circumvent local resistance by appealing for support to
national level administrators such as the program manager and the
agency director. As the presidential selection process neared in 1975,
however, these officials tended to become more cautious and wary of
provoking disturbances at the local level. Instead, it became part of the
strategy of the program to involve state, municipal, and *ejido* authorities
in the initiation and delivery of the programs. The politicians could
assume, therefore, their traditional roles as political patrons and have
a voice in the distribution of CONASUPO resources.

To some degree, then, the attempt to stimulate grass-roots participation was abandoned, and the operation of the program became
oriented toward "stimulating effective operation from the top down
rather than from the bottom up," as one official reported. That the
program itself ultimately proved less effective than hoped is mute
witness to the strength and durability of traditional patron-client
alliances and the constraints these place on the ability of bureaucrats

to act as effective change agents. More positively, however, the program also suggests the possibility that highly motivated and sensitive officials can become advocates for local communities. In spite of failures and the limitations on fulfilling the brokerage role, the Field Coordination project at times resulted in greater responsiveness within CONASUPO itself and was instrumental in bringing about the solution to a number of specific community problems.

The setbacks and reorganizations experienced by this experiment in policy implementation seem to have resulted more from the difficulty of bringing about rapid social change which makes demands on the interests and loyalties of politically significant individuals than from defects in the experiment itself. Change in bureaucratic performance, as the Field Coordination personnel came to realize, depends not only on the mobilization of recipient groups but also on the motivations and responsiveness of the officials of the government who make implementation decisions.[15] Finally, this program, as well as the entire CONASUPO organization, was affected by the rhythm of the *sexenio*, which places major limitations on the policy process in Mexico and upon the capacity of the regime to foment and direct social and economic change.

15. For an interesting study of this proposition in India, see Eldersveld, Jagannadham, and Barnabas (1968).

7

Public Policy and Political Change in Mexico

> Change is an opportunity for me to do something more, to begin a new program or to build something. During a *sexenio* in the first year practically nothing gets done—we are planning and evaluating. In the next three years we implement and organize all sorts of new programs, and in the last two years we consolidate the programs we have begun.

> The presidential succession is so close now that the officials are afraid to make any decisions or begin any programs because they might fail, and then these people would be out of a job in the next *sexenio*. So we call them and are told to call back tomorrow or the *licenciado* is out or in a meeting or something. They just put us off and put us off.

During the Echeverría administration, the activities of CONASUPO and the behavior of its officials were clearly influenced by the tempo of national political life and responsive to the course of the *sexenio*. At the outset of the administration, a new director was chosen by the President, and by early 1971 he had recruited his top level staff; these new managers selected their subordinates in the following months. By August 1971, the management was ready to point out the past failures of the company and to announce the need for sweeping changes in its operations, the most significant of which were related to a rethinking of agricultural problems in Mexico. A policy for rural development was formulated in the technical planning department, and the remainder of the second year of the *sexenio* was devoted to refining the plan, mobilizing political and financial support for it, and making sure that internal procedures were developed to facilitate it. As a result of these activities, 1973 was critical for the implementation of the rural development policy. Both the state offices and the Field Coordination Program were initiated, and significant advances were made in the institution of new programs and the delivery of services. Although the hours were long and the tasks demanding, spirits were high among the agency's management personnel throughout 1973 and 1974.

By the spring of 1975, however, a subtle change had occurred within the organization. Because of the approach of the presidential selection process, agency personnel became more discrete in their activities and less innovative in their work. It was reported that high level meetings were held with subsidiary company managers to sensitize them to the political objectives of the agency. Increased emphasis was placed on instrumenting the Five Basic Products Program widely and respondents alluded to its relationship to the impending presidential campaign. In addition, the state representatives were in more frequent contact with Mexico City offices for advice and consultation about decisions they had to make at the state level. The hours were still long, but more and more administrators reported spending them engaged in public relations and image-building activities.

The influence of the *sexenio* on CONASUPO was clear, and the patterns of behavior it encouraged are repeated in hundreds of other public agencies in Mexico with predictable regularity. At the beginning of each presidential term, bureaucratic agencies are assigned leaders who must then set about learning the intricacies of their new responsibilities. Soon, they begin to replace the middle and top level officials who have remained, uncertain and virtually inactive, from the previous administration. At the same time, the new managers evaluate the organizations they have acquired and attempt to introduce revised policies and new programs. This process takes time. A year or more might go by before a satisfactory team has been recruited; another six or twelve months might be devoted to study, reorganization, and policy development. During this period, the regular functions of the organizations are reduced to a minimal level as "old" administrators equivocate and "new" ones acquire experience.

Administrative routines are firmly established by the third year of the *sexenio*, and new programs and policies are given further impetus. During this and the succeeding year, officials in the agencies and ministries are generally optimistic about the success of the changes instituted under their direction. Public announcements are frequently made that definitive solutions to agency-relevant problems are being applied and that the future of the country will be determined by the new programs. For these two years, national level administrators are absorbed in the tasks of delivering the services and programs which have been promised and conscientious attempts are made to streamline administrative procedures and resolve bureaucratic bottlenecks. The accent is on reform, implementation, and even innovation.

By the fifth year of the *sexenio*, however, the shadow of the impending presidential selection begins to be felt. Administrators become increasingly concerned with institutionalizing and routinizing the programs under their direction. There is a push to expand the activities and impact of the organizations, and attempts to evaluate program performance are abandoned under the pressure to increase public awareness of the agencies. At the same time, middle and high level administrators themselves become more cautious, less concerned with reform and innovation, and more sensitive to problems which might bring unfavorable publicity. Organizational leadership is watched carefully by subordinate management personnel for cues about making decisions which will enhance the career opportunities of those at the top of the hierarchies. Gradually but inexorably, policies are abandoned or modified to accommodate conflicting interests and the ambitions of those who are politically significant both within the organizations and outside them.

The last year of the *sexenio* is characterized by intense but behind-the-scenes politicking and by equally intense inattention to official duties. At the national level, decisions are delayed and avoided; secretaries increasingly report that their bosses are "in conference" and cannot be disturbed; all become less inclined to discuss problems or programs openly; discretion is the rule of the day. Before allocation decisions are made, extensive consultations with central offices occur. In addition, local political figures are increasingly courted and efforts to deliver services to low status clienteles may be greatly expanded, curtailed, or abandoned, depending upon their impact on local political chieftains. As one observer of this process has commented, politics in the last part of the *sexenio* means "reviving old friendships and acquaintances, as well as making new ones . . . the normal functioning of the organization suffers from general inattention and decisions are not made so that 'the new administration will not be compromised'" (Saldaña Harlow, 1974: 13). This is also the time for selling influence and for granting concessions in return for political support. The last year is, therefore, characterized by intense activity on the part of groups and individuals who deal with the bureaucracy. With the inauguration of a new President and the selection of his top level subordinates, the cycle is completed, and the new administrators once again tackle the appointment of staffs and the formulation of policies.

Public Policy and the *Sexenio*

It is to be expected that as a predictable characteristic of political life in Mexico, the *sexenio* would also have definite consequences for the policy process. One effect is that it introduces constraints on the ability of bureaucratic agencies to plan and implement policies. Valuable time and experience are lost every six years because bureaucrats must "re-tool" for their new positions and cannot be certain that the policies they champion will endure beyond their own short tenure. Moreover, personal and regime priorities effectively eliminate most allocation planning from policy formulation processes. In spite of these negative effects, the *sexenio* also enables the bureaucratic apparatus to respond to changing conditions and to presidential leadership in the definition of national problems. The *sexenio*, then, sets limits on the capacity of bureaucratic officials to accomplish major tasks of policy change and implementation, but it also encourages the development of an administrative system which is both flexible and responsive to the national political elite.

Memory and Time

As decision making elites in Mexico set about engineering solutions to national problems, they are constrained by their own limited "memory" of the programs and policies of the agencies they head. Although this is not a characteristic unique to Mexican policy makers, having been singled out by Hirschman (1965: 243–244) in Brazil, the regularity with which previous "definitive solutions" are abandoned without serious evaluation and the limited familiarity with alternatives and antecedents are clearly the results of the personnel change which accompanies the beginning of a *sexenio*. Each new administration is concerned with making its own impression on public programs quickly, and newly recruited officials take over their duties with little commitment to preexisting plans. As a result, old policies which have failed are reintroduced in the guise of new solutions; old mistakes are repeated by the inexperienced cadres; and many programs which prove to be promising in one administration are shelved by the next. The experience which is accumulated by individual administrators as they move from agency to agency during their careers is the subtle capacity to persist through the management of human relations and politics; it generally has little relevance to the more specific tasks of designing and implementing policy.

In CONASUPO, few officials had much knowledge of the agency prior to 1970 or 1971, and the initial planning of new efforts consumed considerable time and energy because basic data relevant to rural development and past agency programs had to be gathered and carefully analyzed. How much time is expended in research and data collection each *sexenio* cannot be calculated, but the example of CONASUPO is suggestive of the problems caused by the limited historical memory and practical experience of bureaucratic personnel. Limited memory also made it difficult for CONASUPO to evaluate the causes and consequences of past agency programs. As a case in point, the unsuccessful *Graneros del Pueblo* Program was not systematically evaluated for its relevance to new policies. Of course, officials at both national and state levels admitted that the program had been a political boondoggle; many considered that corruption and the failure of the program to deliver what it promised had left the peasants distrustful and hostile toward CONASUPO. Yet these same administrators tended to assume that peasant distrust and corrupt officials had disappeared with the initiation of the new administration because a different and dedicated group was managing the agency with good intentions and high ideals.[1] That previous *equipos* might have shared their concerns and motivations and still have failed to achieve positive results was not seriously considered. It was evident that there was a reluctance among CONASUPO officials to think beyond the confines of the Echeverría administration or to inquire deeply into organizational or systemic problems of the agency. The memory of the peasants, however, extended far beyond these limits and affected their willingness to accept and cooperate with the agency.

Additionally, in Mexico there are time limits which are strictly observed in the formulation of new plans. Because it is unknown who will head any agency or who will man its responsible positions and because the temperament, commitments, and ideals of the next President are a mystery to policy makers, there is little incentive or rationale for making long term plans. From one *sexenio* to the next, a public agency might skyrocket from insignificance into the President's inner circle of favorites and acquire control of great amounts of money and influence. It can just as rapidly sink to ignominy in the succeeding *sexenio*.[2] In CONASUPO, the possible lack of continuity of the agency's position was admitted even in 1974.

> CONASUPO could go up or down depending on the person who is put in as chief. No one knows what will happen. . . . And already you can notice people beginning to look around and say, "Oh, this person or that person," and figuring out who's going to come out ahead.

So inexorable is the *sexenio* change of personnel that few attempts are made to plan beyond the next election in terms of policy, and public officials such as those in CONASUPO generally limit themselves to attempts to routinize programs and procedures. In the event they fail, it is unlikely they will be around to deal with the consequences.

1. Agents in the field, however, were generally very much aware of the distrust and hostility of the peasants. "Many peasants have a phobia about CONASUPO," a local level administrator reported in accounting for problems he found in his work. He went on to recount numerous methods used by CONASUPO agents to deceive and take advantage of the peasants. For a specific example, see Arterton (1974: 160–161). For general orientations toward government officials, see Almond and Verba (1963), Coleman (1972), Cornelius (1975: Chaps. 3 and 8), Fagen and Tuohy (1972: Chap. 5), Kahl (1968: 116).

2. One informant expanded on this theme, using the example of the National Institute for the Protection of Children (INPI), a government organization "adopted" by Echeverría's wife. "Yes, the *sexenio* is a tragedy for many programs. They change in importance and function completely from one *sexenio* to another. Take INPI, for example. That was started by López Mateos and was well financed and organized. In rural areas particularly it carried out a number of highly useful activities with children and mothers. Then came Díaz Ordaz, and the program practically disappeared. When I asked people about it in rural areas, they were disillusioned about it: 'Oh, that disappeared,' or 'Oh, that doesn't do anything anymore,' they'd say. Now under the wife of the President the program has again become very important; we'll see what happens."

The same time limits affect the implementation process. What is not accomplished in the first four or five years of a *sexenio* has little chance of being done at all. During the final year of an administration, officials may reflect on the difficulties they have encountered in putting their grand plans into operation, but they have little opportunity to correct their errors. In terms of the expectations of the planners and managers who designed the rural development strategy, for example, the implementation of CONASUPO's new policy for transforming subsistence agriculture probably had not been as effective as they planned by 1975. After almost three years of effort, the network of reception centers and stores in rural areas had been significantly fortified, but the spread of auxiliary services offered through them was still thin. Unfortunately, the opportunity to reinforce their efforts was almost over.

As the end of the *sexenio* neared, relations with other government agencies became especially difficult. Each agency, with its own programs and political priorities, was competing to expand its influence and to gain the recognition of the President and was less inclined to give attention to cooperative efforts. Significantly, those rural services whose delivery depended entirely on CONASUPO—peasant orientation and training, communications, the Five Basic Products—were the ones most likely to be offered in the reception centers. When other agencies were involved—in the clinics, the provision of improved seeds, fertilizers, and credit—the delivery levels were lowest. Typical of the implementation problems faced by CONASUPO was the failure to provide production or consumer credit to more rural areas. By late 1974, only two states had programs for rural production credit, and only twelve *ejidos* in the entire country had CONASUPO stores offering consumer credit. The failure of these particular programs to grow was the result of reluctance on the part of the agricultural banks to commit themselves to any large scale program in 1974 and 1975 when the *sexenio* was almost over. In short, the very clear time limits of the *sexenio* tend to establish equally clear constraints on the policy process.

Resource Allocation and Planning

The *sexenio* also has considerable impact on public investment decisions. As has been amply demonstrated, all high and middle level positions in the bureaucracy have both explicit and implicit functions. The explicit function, of course, is to get the job done: regulate the market; make sure grain is stored correctly; train analysts to weigh products accurately; distribute merchandise, etc. Implicit in all activities, however, is the need to promote one's own career or that of one's superior. Thus, for example, one administrator in CONASUPO admitted,

> In Mexico, much activity is directed toward maintaining an image. It might be the image of the President or of the director or of the manager.

> It's obvious why: we have a single six-year term with no reelection
> and a single party and therefore much is done not because it's the best
> way to do a thing but according to the need to maintain a personal
> image.

Because of the certainty and regularity of personnel change, programs
are often established with a view to their consequences for the future
of individuals involved rather than to the needs of the society or even
of the organization.

In addition to the use of government programs to establish and
extend personal careers, public organizations themselves have explicit
and implicit functions. The maintenance of stability, the fortification
of the populist myths of the Revolution, and the enhancing of regime
support are the most important of the implicit goals of bureaucratic
agencies in Mexico. Certainly many of CONASUPO's activities were
directed toward these ends. In the Díaz Ordaz administration, the
Graneros del Pueblo Program was inspired partly by the desire to
demonstrate the government's presence in rural areas. Under Echeverría,
the Five Basic Products, the expansion of the urban supermarket chain,
and newly constructed state office buildings seem to be the contribution
of the agency to strengthening its own image and that of the regime.
The entire 250 million dollar retail chain operated by DICONSA was
considered by many CONASUPO officials to constitute the agency's
principal "political" input while the important work of the company
was carried out in its price support and crop purchasing programs.
All of these programs can of course be justified on other grounds; but
most administrators were candid in admitting their more subtle objectives also.

This need to establish and maintain an image encourages what two
observers have dubbed "plazismo," or the propensity to invest in highly
visible but developmentally questionable projects such as remodeling
public parks and thoroughfares.[3] In addition, the fragility of their careers
and the implicit functions of their organizations mean that bureaucratic
decision makers may lack the capacity to resist political pressures in the
allocation of public resources. They must protect themselves by entering
into the kinds of alliances which have been the theme of much of this
study and by offering public resources in return for political quiescence
and support. In CONASUPO, it was demonstrated that the allocation of key

3. See Fagen and Tuohy (1972: 28–29). These authors go on to state, "The attractions
of such projects to cautious office holders are legion: They are physically and politically
visible; they can be completed in a relatively short time and thus accrue wholly to the
reputational capital of the incumbent; they are for all the people and thus require no hard
choices as to what sector or project should receive scarce resources; they are uncontro-
versial in the tradition of 'good works'; they can often be partially funded through the
donations of others eager to have their names associated with civic improvements"
(Fagen and Tuohy, 1972: 29).

positions was often made not on the basis of policy or management-relevant criteria but because of the need to establish career alliances or mobilize a political following. As a consequence, there may be a considerable gap between the formulation of public policies and their effective implementation because of the need to compromise, reward, accommodate, or avoid confrontations with those who have the ability to affect one's career or the reputation of the agency one represents.

We have seen, then, that a multitude of factors impinge on decisions to provide resources to individuals, groups, or institutions in Mexico. Some scholars have noted that there seem to be no effective guidelines for determining the distribution of public investments and no basis for establishing priorities among development needs (see Fagen and Tuohy, 1972: 28–29). There is, moreover, little reason to expect that the decision of one bureaucrat, agency, or *sexenio* administration will be honored or implemented by the next. These characteristics, however, do not seem to be a result of administrative carelessness or of a failure to emphasize planning or rationality in the making of public policy. Rather, they are a result of a planning process from which serious efforts to establish and maintain specific allocation criteria have been deliberately *excluded*, as the case of CONASUPO has indicated.

The agency, of course, did operate on the basis of a general statement of priorities: Programs were directed at low income consumers who earned less than 2,000 pesos a month and producers who earned less than 12,000 pesos a year. However, these two categories include 90 percent of the economically active consumers and 94 percent of all farmers in the country, and these general guidelines are hardly a sufficient basis for making hard decisions about who should benefit, why, and how from agency activities. Nor was the budgetary planning instrumented by the new administration a suitable guide for making these kinds of decisions. How were specific choices of this nature made, then?

In interviews, many agency officials were asked how they determined where new CONASUPO installations would be located. Their answers indicate the difficulty policy makers would encounter should they attempt to establish and enforce allocation criteria based on economic, social, and other policy relevant information:

> The primary criteria for locating installations are political. Once a place has been suggested by the governor or someone, then a study is done.
>
> I chose the sites mostly on the criteria of knowing the people involved.
>
> We of course carry out socioeconomic studies to set up the stores—to select the most adequate places—but really, the selection of sites is mostly a political question. A municipal president or even the governor or the representative will determine when a store is to be opened.

We get probably five or six applications for stores a day. Some arrive even from the President of the Republic, some from the general director, some from the governor. . . . My criterion is whether I can supply a store.

Naturally, we get a lot of political pressure for carrying out programs. That's one reason why often our plans fail to match up to what actually happens. The director may tell us to carry out a certain project, or it may come from the manager or from the governor of the state, a municipal president or even from the presidency. When we get this kind of pressure, there's nothing really we can do about it. We just change our plans in accordance with it. Take our sewing centers, for example. We had originally programmed ten for three states; now we have twelve in about seven states.

There is *lots* of political pressure in this job, above all for large contracts. Nearly every day I hear from somebody's friend, from some big-shot or from someone who has a recommendation. I tell them it doesn't make any difference. Except, of course, when the recommendation comes from the director. You see, he often has information or is responding to pressures we don't know about.

One store we are working on now is a case resulting from the presidential campaign. When Echeverría came to this particular place during the presidential campaign, he promised the people a CONASUPO store. Later the director came and confirmed this.

Two programs . . . are a direct result of political pressures. One . . . was pushed through by "X" who had friendships and a great interest in the program . . . a few telephone calls were made and promises of help made so the program was set up. The other . . . was similarly set up through someone in a high position . . . who had interests there.

It is apparent that political influence and information were recognized by public officials to present the only truly operative priorities for resource distribution. And, in fact, in CONASUPO, little serious attention was given to analyzing need for installations or programs during the planning stage. Indeed, this was generally not considered to be a task relevant to planning at all. Undoubtedly, excluding allocation guidelines from planning might easily lead to repetitions of the *Graneros* experience or DICONSA's pre-1970 financial and control problems, but in the case of CONASUPO, both career advancement and an emphasis on the need to avoid political disturbances meant that allocation was largely determined on the basis of specific local political conditions. There were, then, widely recognized criteria for making allocation decisions, but they tended to be so specific to time and place that they were impossible to codify or rationalize during the planning process.

Power and the Bureaucracy

In spite of characteristics of the political system which inhibit the capacity for effective policy making, there is also considerable opportunity in Mexico for fomenting change in public policies should the

President and his lieutenants in the bureaucracy choose to champion reform or innovation. A good example of the capacity of the system to respond to change is the difference between the Díaz Ordaz administration (1964–1970) and that of Luís Echeverría (1970–1976). The former was typified by conservative, pro-business policies and repressive—even paranoid—responses to attempts to expand political participation. Under Echeverría, however, redistributive policies were stressed to some extent, rural areas received greater attention, and a rapprochement with liberal intellectuals and students was engineered through greater freedom of expression and a more open presidential style. To a considerable degree, bureaucratic agencies adopted the policies of the Echeverría administration as their own. Changes such as these are made possible by characteristics of the regime which have been explored in this study.

First, as we have seen, the politico-administrative career system means that top level bureaucratic personnel are extremely sensitive to presidential initiatives. In CONASUPO, for example, the President's evident interest in rural areas was viewed as a golden opportunity to enhance both the individual positions of management personnel and the importance of the agency. Thus, the career alliances which pervade the public administration and the party are potentially available for manipulation by the President to achieve his overall goals. There are, of course, limits to his ability to marshall response—competing factions and *camarillas* and the very size and unwieldiness of the apparatus—but nevertheless, he has considerable power to ensure that bureaucratic leaders respond more to him than to the internal pressures of the individual agencies or their clienteles. At the level of the individual agency in Mexico, the top leadership mirrors the President's influence. For example, we have seen that the director of CONASUPO was able to manipulate career alliances to acquire support for his policy preferences. And the case of the state representatives indicates that where personal linkages are strong between bureaucratic officials, more effective performance in terms of policy implementation can be expected. Career ties, therefore, can be a powerful lever for leaders who wish to establish change-oriented policies for social or economic development.

Second, opposition to policy changes can be managed through the calculated distribution of public resources. The fact that demands are focused on the allocation process tends to discourage widespread public debate, the coalescence of hostile organizations and publics, or proposals of alternative solutions while policy is being formulated. As we have seen, particularistic arrangements with the private sector, *caciques*, and other political figures were frequently resorted to in CONASUPO in order to ameliorate opposition to the agency and its policies. Ultimately, of course, this kind of problem solving through resource distribution threatens the successful implementation of policy, as happened in several of the state offices; nevertheless, it remains an instrument whose judicious use can be instrumental in bringing about policy change with a minimum of public opposition.

Related to both the foregoing factors is the contribution of extended personal alliances to maintaining the regime, even when policy change is introduced. This study has provided considerable evidence that the patron-client linkage is pervasive in Mexico and is instrumental in integrating the society. Present in the interaction of local *cacique* and peasant, of national politicians and their *camarillas*, of the economic elite and the bureaucratic leadership, of union bosses and their syndicalized followers, it is a mechanism which permits the accommodation of diverse and often conflicting interests within the political arena. In perhaps the most corporately organized political system in Latin America, these bonds between individuals tie Mexican society together and enable the governmental regime to survive and to regulate the flow of demands made upon it.[4] Pyramided into extensive and complex networks linking members of various social classes, economic interests, and political persuasions, the personal relationships explain much about the persistence and the flexibility of the political regime itself.

The networks and linkages examined in the Mexican case are pre-eminently pragmatic alliances and are entered into when they are deemed useful for the achievement of individual goals. For the elite they are established when and where the exigencies of career mobility dictate; for peasants they are a means of responding to an insecure environment (see Scott, 1975). Because they are pragmatic accommodations to the system, based on personal advantage and loyalty rather than on ideology, class, or program, they can be manipulated by the President and bureaucratic leaders should they seek to instrument policy changes. They provide the regime with a capacity for flexible response to changing political, economic, and social conditions.

These conditions of presidential power and personally oriented political alliances increase the role of the public administration in the formulation of policy and the distribution of resources in Mexico. As we have seen, few interests or groups actively initiate demands, advise, consult, or directly influence the bureaucrats as they formulate plans for the development of the country.[5] In most countries, of course, the

4. The corporatist ideal of society, found widely throughout Latin America, is rooted in a heirarchical, personalistic, and authoritarian perception of man in an organic social and political family (see Chalmers, 1972; Cotler, 1972; Hanson, 1974; Newton, 1970; Pike and Stritch, 1974; Schmitter, 1971: 108–133; Wiarda, 1974b). In Mexico, the maintenance of the corporate political system in which functional groupings are tied directly to the government and party and directly dependent upon it, depends upon the integrative and cooptive mechanisms provided by the clientele bond.

5. Organized business and industrial groups are recognized by students of Mexican politics to have considerable influence on public policy. The designing and implementation of the rural development policy in CONASUPO, however, provided little opportunity to

role of the public administration in policy development has increased significantly in the twentieth century. But in Mexico there is little of the multiparticipant bargaining, negotiation, public debate, and scrutiny which typify countries in which legislatures, interest groups, public opinion, and judicial bodies each intervene in and influence the policy making process. The bureaucracy, then, is an important locus for the study of political change in Mexico.

Bureaucracy and Political Development

One definition of political development is that the national state has the capacity to regulate the behavior of its citizens in certain areas of activity, to formulate and implement programs it deems in the public interest, and to call upon the population for material and moral support for its activities.[6] The bureaucracy is deeply implicated in all three of these aspects of governmental capability, and its efficient performance is, therefore, vital to the level of political development of the country as a whole. It is often expected that as modernization proceeds, the public administration will take on more and more characteristics of the ideal type bureaucracy described by Weber. Riggs' (1964) model of bureaucratic change is also closely related to expectations about development. He has posited that as a society emerges from the transitional stage of political development, the public administration will gradually lose the particularism, formalism, elitism, obstructionism, and corruption which characterize the stage itself.

The foregoing study of a bureaucratic agency in Mexico, however, calls into question both these formulations. The public administration in Mexico is capable of using modern, rational, and technical methods to gather, analyze, and employ information relevant to policy making. The case of CONASUPO has demonstrated the bureaucracy's ability to design comprehensive plans for social and economic development. To some extent, the public administration also has the capacity to escape the stalemates of conflicting clientele demands and of executive disinterest in change-oriented programs. Moreover, it has a limited but real ability to implement the policies it has designed, perhaps the most difficult task in the policy process. And it accomplishes this within the confines of a highly politicized, particularistic, and ascription-oriented administrative apparatus which has more in common with the Mexican

---

study this assertion. As with relations with political influentials, however, much of the accommodation with business interests takes place at the implementation phase. As one informant stated, "The private sector gets along by coming to private and individual terms with the government." For a general view, see Purcell (1975) and Shafer (1973).

6. On political development as governmental capability, see Almond and Powell (1966), Huntington (1968), Pye (1966).

political system itself than with the public administrations of the United States, Great Britain, Germany, or France. Using the models of either Weber or Riggs, its capacity to function relatively effectively is not one which would be predicted.

What is evident from the study of CONASUPO is that the requirements of a modern society for thoughtful, innovative, and development-oriented public policy need not be in conflict with characteristics of a social or political order long considered traditional or transitional. In fact, what is remarkable in the Mexican case is the extent to which "nonmodern" relationships and attitudes are used and manipulated to achieve the development policy goals espoused by the politico-adminis-trative leadership. Rather than hindering the performance of the bureau-cracy, such characteristics can even be instrumental in the pursuit of public objectives. The officials in CONASUPO who sought to formulate and operationalize the rural development policy freely embraced such mechanisms as kinship relationships, political influence, personal loyalty, and career dependence to achieve their goals. In the Mexican system, these instruments are recognized as highly efficacious and legiti-mate means to obtain program and policy results, as was evident in a statement made by one respondent.

> It has been a great help in our program that the Chief is the brother of the wife of the President. It has opened many doors for us. He worked for many years in the CNC and he was a deputy and so he has great knowledge of the countryside and its organizations. I find that in many cases, just mentioning his name has been a boon to a program. It gets results!

If characteristics such as personalism and particularism are instru-mental to the achievement of policy goals, there is little reason to expect that they will be abandoned simply because the public administration becomes more technically skilled, more development-oriented, or more highly rationalized. Certainly in CONASUPO, an agency staffed by young, educated, and innovative administrators, the incidence and utility of face-to-face exchange relationships was pervasive and has shown no tendency to diminish over time. In spite of this, the operation and efficiency of market regulation in Mexico has changed considerably during four decades and CONASUPO has adapted and responded to newer, more demanding circumstances. Moreover, the mechanisms useful for achieving policy objectives designed to encourage economic and social development are the same instruments relied upon by the regime to maintain itself. Therefore, it cannot easily be argued that pressures from the political system will bring about a diminution of the "nonmodern" characteristics in the administrative apparatus and the emergence of a Weberian-like bureaucracy.

Nor can it be maintained that the personalism, politicization, and particularism which characterize the public administration in Mexico are simply variants of the spoils system which typified the bureaucracy in the United States in the nineteenth century. The patronage system in Mexico does not operate within the context of a two-party system nor within an environment in which there is a large, organized, and committed movement for reform of its operations. There is no conflict over appointments between the legislative and the executive branches as there was in the United States. Nor are there significant alternative means for providing or acquiring resources such as developed in the United States and contributed to the decline of institutions like the urban machine.[7] Instead, the public bureaucracy in Mexico shares and reiterates characteristics and values found widely in Mexican society and politics (see Wasserspring, 1974).

In the study of the rural development policy as it emerged in CONA-SUPO, the extent to which bureaucratic organizations in Mexico are shaped by the political system has become evident. Because of the methods by which bureaucratic leadership and middle level management are selected and because of the intertwining of administrative and political functions and personnel, the dominant influence on the political system—the *sexenio*—is also the most important determinant of bureaucratic performance and behavior. The public administration in Mexico functions in close collaboration with the political elite, and its style is congruent with that of the regime itself. The view of the Mexican political system that has emerged in this case study is that of a corporate and authoritarian regime, dominated by a party-bureaucratic apparatus and pervaded by extensive clientelist relationships among the population and the political elite.[8] It is, nevertheless, a flexible system with considerable capacity for self-perpetuation and adaptation. The government's control over economic and political resources is decisive, and there are few societal norms which constrain the governing elite from using these resources as it deems necessary. It is a political structure which has endured for several decades despite changes in economic development, industrial capacity, and technical knowledge. Considering the cohesive and durable structure of political relationships in Mexico, can it be expected that the authoritarian system will give way to a more open, equitable political society?

7. On the spoils system in the United States, see Hoogenboom (1961, 1970), Mosher (1968). On the urban machine, see Banfield and Wilson (1963: Part 3), Gosnell (1937).

8. For descriptions of authoritarian regimes, see Anderson (1970), Linz (1970), Malloy (1974, 1975), Newton (1970), O'Donnell (1973), Purcell (1975), Skidmore (1973), Stevens (1975), Wiarda (1974b).

Sources of Political Change in Mexico

> There are, if you will, changes which are made in order not to change.

> I think the reason this administration decided to channel more resources to the rural areas was because it saw that in order to maintain the current political structure—and the economic and social structure also—it would have to make some accommodations.

Thus far, political development has been discussed in terms of the capacity to govern, and it has been concluded that under this definition the Mexican regime is considerably advanced. Another dimension of political development may be the ability of a citizen population to participate in the decision making process of the government (see Weiner, 1971: 161–165). By this definition, political development can be judged by the ability of citizens to express political opinions, to demand equitable treatment from the judicial and administrative systems, to vote in elections in which viable alternatives are offered, and to defend or promote individual or group interests within the rules of the political community. Using these criteria, as we have seen, Mexico cannot be considered highly advanced. Moreover, prospects for the emergence of a more open political system are not encouraging.

Given the focus of this study, an obvious place to begin searching for sources of changing political relationships in Mexico is with the bureaucratic elite. Its influence in public life cannot be doubted; middle and upper level bureaucrats are melded to the political elite, are linked to the economically powerful in the private sector, and are tied to leaders of the urban and rural working classes through networks of personal ties. Together with the rest of the political class in Mexico, the bureaucratic elite has developed vertical power relationships throughout the society and has derived from these individual and particularistic linkages power to pursue policies and programs which it defines to be in the public interest.

As indicated, its position of dominance in the policy process provides the bureaucratic leadership with the potential to introduce change-oriented policies. Especially in the initial years of a *sexenio*, there are considerable opportunities for public officials to influence the President in the definition of national goals. However, it is important to note that the policy direction of the bureaucrats occurs within limits acceptable to the President and the party leadership and conforms to the established rules of the game. That the young, dynamic, and development-oriented CONASUPO administrators adapted to the hierarchical and secretive policy making style of the regime and acquiesced to given resource allocation patterns is reason for doubting the capacity of the rest of the bureaucracy to foment a significant change in political relationships in the society.[9]

As we have seen, many CONASUPO administrators were intensely interested in redistributive policies and were dedicated advocates of solutions to social and economic problems suffered by the poor. They developed a policy which they hoped would alleviate these problems and then worked actively on its implementation. But the changes they sought did not include a radical redistribution of political power. Even the most daring attempt to work for a change in the distribution of economic rewards, the Field Coordination Program, relied on socially legitimate and time-honored political mechanisms to aid the peasant communities. Indeed, most of the programs espoused by the bureaucratic leadership in CONASUPO and elsewhere generally result in strengthening the governing apparatus and in increasing popular dependence on the regime. If the example of bureaucratic leadership in CONASUPO can be generalized, it would seem that high and middle level personnel are well integrated into the system and are benefiting from the present distribution of political power. As a consequence, bureaucrats in Mexico, whatever their ideals or self-perceptions, are likely to continue to work within the structure of the political system rather than to promote more open political participation.

Still less leadership can be expected from the dominant party. As has been discussed, the PRI is based upon a multitude of leader-follower relationships which depend for their persistence on personal loyalty and opportunity. The resources of the regime are distributed through hierarchical levels of party chieftains and are instrumental in maintaining the PRI's control of political participation. Moreover, the leaders of the party do not occupy their positions because they represent the views of their members but because they have reflected the wishes of the President and his advisors in each *sexenio* and have responded first to their leadership. At the local level, as the example of CONASUPO's state representatives indicates, governors, deputies, senators, municipal presidents, and village leaders serve the party by mobilizing and delivering the support of their followers and are rewarded for their efforts with a variety of government controlled goods and services, which are frequently channeled through the bureaucracy.

In the resultant system of accommodation and payoff, the governors, the *caciques*, and other political actors have far more to gain from the present system than they would if they championed the political rights of their followers. In the absence of deep convictions about popular

9. Similarly, in Central America, Wynia (1972: 83) considers the role of technical advisors to have "adjusted to traditional policy making conditions and patterns rather than vice versa."

participation, the opportunities for personal advancement are too great within the system to encourage many party leaders to step outside the fold. One serious attempt to democratize local level political participation, the effort spearheaded by party head Carlos Madrazo in the mid-1960s, was abruptly squelched by the President and party influentials.[10] Moreover, losers in factional struggles are regularly reintegrated into the system, thus diminishing the potential for political opposition. In fact, the party may even oppose efforts to redistribute social and economic resources. It has been demonstrated that CONASUPO's strategy for rural development was often met at the local level by the resistance of state or local party chiefs whose personal interests would be harmed if the peasants were encouraged to escape from the bonds of dependency and exploitation.

What, then, about the President? Certainly he has a great capacity to lead; the system of personal loyalties and the structure of career advancement concentrate both formal and informal influence in his hands. The politico-administrative elite is sensitive to his concerns and responds to his initiatives. In some respects, his ability to direct the bureaucracy may be increasing, in spite of the size and lack of organization of the apparatus. As the Ministries of the Presidency and Finance increase their technical capacity for oversight and their legal or customary influence over the approval of projects and the disbursement of funds, this will enable the President to extend his power and ability to elicit compliance from the administration if he should decide to introduce reform or innovation.

But the President of Mexico is also a creature of the system; he has emerged from the ranks of the PRI and has learned to be skilled in the arts of accommodation and reward which bind the system together; he depends upon these mechanisms to maintain the regime. Under Echeverría, the rechanneling of resources to the rural zones was in part an attempt to ensure stability and conformity in the countryside, especially at a time when urban labor and business interests were less easily satisfied. As long as social peace remains a paramount value and objective of the Mexican elite, it is unlikely that the President will move to abolish the authoritarian structure which has ensured it for more than thirty years. Even his potential for charismatic leadership is limited; the undisputed aura of authority he enjoys as President deserts him at the end of the fifth year of the *sexenio* to reappear in the person of the presidential candidate. Charisma, therefore, inheres in the institution,

10. At the outset of the Díaz Ordaz administration, party chief Madrazo encouraged the participation of local communities in the voicing of opinions and planning of proposals for government activities. He also championed more democratic local elections for party positions and official candidates. As a result, internal conflict in the party became a serious problem, and Madrazo was ousted from his position in 1965.

not in the man. Through the selection of Finance Minister José López Portillo as the official candidate for President, Echeverría made an attempt to maintain his influence after his *sexenio* is over, but there is no doubt that López Portillo will be the boss, the *jefe máximo*. While López Portillo is widely acknowledged to be a *técnico* rather than a *político*, it is nevertheless true that only by observing the rules of the game could he have reached such political heights. Thus, the President of Mexico would seem to have a great capacity to lead and to influence the definition of public goals, but his power stops far short of being able to restructure the political regime more equitably.

What about the capacity of the mass of the Mexican population to demand political change? The study of CONASUPO makes it possible to comment on only one sector of this mass, the peasants who constitute close to 40 percent of the population. It was demonstrated how the peasantry has been the most docile of "revolutionaries" in the past three decades, regularly offering its firm support to the regime. This sector has traditionally been the one most tied to exploitive power relationships and the least able to defend itself against rapacious political and economic bosses. Moreover, the means by which the peasants approach the political system and make requests for government goods and services militate against their capacity to make independent and forceful demands for changes in political relationships, and the particularistic mobilization of patron-client networks tends to hinder attempts to achieve broader participation.

On some occasions, however, peasants have used land invasions, marches to the state or national capitals, and demonstrations to reach the attention of "public opinion" which, in Mexico, is most importantly defined by the political elite. In some cases, their grievances have been listened to and attended, given the sensitivity of the regime to those who threaten public disturbances. Potentially, protests and demonstrations are instruments which might be exploited more fully by peasant groups to achieve response to their demands. Nevertheless, the power of the regime to squelch unwanted or embarrassing opposition remains overwhelming (see Ronfeldt, 1973). From the buying off of dissident leaders to the use of physical force, the instruments of the regime to maintain itself are legion. Ultimately, then, peasants, who generally lack trustworthy leaders and effective organizations to represent them, are not easily in a position to demand significant changes in the regime.

There are other groups in Mexican society which may or may not have the potential to demand or foment political change—urban and rural guerrillas, university students, urban labor, or conservative business interests, for example. Specific predictions about their capacity to cause a reordering of political relationships cannot be made on the basis of material presented in the study of CONASUPO. However, the same characteristics which constrain the political role of the bureaucracy, the party, the President, and the peasants are likely to affect them also. The monopoly of resources enjoyed by the regime as well as the personal opportunity structure and the lack of organizations for policy-oriented demand making are probably a hindrance to their ability to spearhead change. Once again, it is likely that the regime itself can outmaneuver their demands and persist.

Some have suggested that political systems such as the Mexican one are becoming more subject to change as they are forced to listen and attend to the accumulation of demands of various social groupings and publics, demands which are frequently conflicting.[11] Others have considered that the fundamental character of the Mexican regime is altering because of a loss of legitimacy resulting from increased use of repression.[12] However, it has been stressed here that the strength of the authoritarian system in Mexico is precisely its capacity to meet a large number and variety of unaggregated demands in individual and particularistic fashion and to avoid widespread public dissent. In the cases in which opposition has become public, as in the student strikes of 1968 and 1971, the school text book and fiscal reform issues of 1974, and agrarian unrest in the northwest in 1975, the regime has still monopolized enough resources to meet the crises and come through with its underlying structure unscathed. More and more demands on the system may be made, but there appears no reason to expect that these will result in a breakdown of the political structure itself; they may continue to be channeled through and resolved in the same elite-dominated apparatus.

The possibilities for a more equitable distribution of power in Mexico are stark. There is within the current authoritarian structure sufficient flexibility to redistribute economic resources marginally and to allow widespread individual social mobility without endangering the mechanisms of control dominated by the government. The Mexican regime has proved itself remarkably astute in ameliorating the tensions and opposition which have developed from time to time. Echeverría's attention to rural areas and his attempts to bring young university graduates into the fold have demonstrated the ability of the regime to make the necessary adaptations to deal with potential threats to stability. And, indeed, this is a perspective shared by many Mexicans. One informant, for example, summarized this view of a system whose fundamental structure remained unchanged under Echeverría.

> I think this administration has attempted to reformulate the myths of
> the government and is attempting to strike a new pose of populism

---

11. This is an interpretation presented in Anderson (1967), Needler (1971), Ronfeldt (1975: 27–29), Scott (1974), Tuohy and Ronfeldt (1969).

12. See especially Cockroft (1972).

in order to maintain its control. In order to deal with the demands that are being made on the system, it is fomenting this populist propaganda. In reality nothing has changed. This is an authoritarian regime and is not becoming "democratized" as some think.

The prognostication for the future of the Mexican political system is that it will prove a durable regime.[13] It is firmly institutionalized throughout the society and definitively in control of crucial social, economic, and political resources. Within the government apparatus itself, policy making, decision making, and implementation styles are all congruent with the present distribution of power. That it is an authoritarian and ultimately exploitive system does not seem to make it incompatible with the requirements of economic development, industrialization, or modern mass society. Perhaps the most that can be hoped is that pressures from within the regime will continue to encourage greater economic and social equity, if not increased political equality.

13. Similar conclusions are reached in a number of recent studies. See Hansen (1971: Chap. 8), Purcell (1975: Chap. 6), Ronfeldt (1973: Chap. 8).

Appendix A

The Methodology and Conduct of the Study

The field research for this study of the policy process in Mexico was initiated in March 1974 and completed in May 1975. The primary tool for the research was the open-ended interview, a format particularly appropriate for the kind of data sought in the study (see Dexter, 1970; Gorden, 1969; Richardson *et al.*, 1965; Schatzman and Strauss, 1973). The research included seventy-eight interviews of CONASUPO administrators at high and middle levels and nineteen interviews with members of the Mexican academic community and administrators in other government agencies who had frequent contact with CONASUPO. The interviews lasted an average of two hours each; a number lasted six to twelve hours and extended over the course of several days. All interviews were conducted in Spanish.

Included in each interview were a number of questions to obtain information on the following topics:

1. Individual job responsibilities as formally defined and as personally perceived.

2. Administrative responsibilities and operating procedures of the unit under the respondent's direction; budgetary allocations; programs in operation and those planned for the future.

3. Perception of problems in the unit when the respondent took command; measures taken to solve the problems.

4. Specific and important problems perceived in carrying out assigned responsibilities; activities or perceptions of means to

solve these problems; perceptions of why organizational and program problems exist (i.e., vested interests, personalities, administrative organization, ideology, base motives of others, etc.).

5. Strategies pursued for control and coordination of personnel and programs; tactics used and lines of authority followed in the solution of specific problems.

6. Perception of important changes affecting both the agency and unit the respondent is responsible for; perception of future development and activities of the agency.

7. Personal definition of agency goals and objectives; awareness of overall policy thrust of the central organization of CONASUPO.

8. Process of policy formulation as individual was involved, especially as this touched upon rural operations; steps, influences, and procedures involved in initiation and approval of policy changes.

9. Specific activities and directives within the unit directly affecting its pursuit of rural development and agricultural projects; principal agency of government or units of CONASUPO with which it deals; problems encountered.

10. Personal data on education, geographical origins, previous employment; involvement in professional and other organizations; other sources of income; CONASUPO employment; party involvement; future career aspirations; etc.

A second type of data collected in the research was from documentary materials. Four general sources for CONASUPO-related information were tapped. First, officials in CONASUPO were generous in providing extensive internal reports, newsletters, analyses, lectures, and brochures which specified agency activities, described specific projects, reported financial data, and commented on important agency problems. The organization and procedure manuals of the agency were also thoroughly reviewed. A second source of written information on CONASUPO came from newspaper archives. Although sketchy in coverage, these sometimes provided the only information available on the past history of the agency and its predecessors. A third, but much less important source because of its scarcity, was a limited number of books and articles which analyze or describe CONASUPO activities. The fourth source was Mexican government publications such as census reports and financial and agricultural statistics which were useful for acquiring information on Mexican social and economic conditions.

Aspects of the research topic and methodologies selected for studying it are significant for the limitations they impose on the research. Perhaps most important is the problem inherent in a case study, the problem of inference (see Riley, 1963: 68–75). Selecting any given agency as the site for a case study involves variables of subjective evaluation and ease of access. During the investigation, however, attempts were made to ascertain the wider existence of the patterns observed through informant perspectives and by consulting previous scholarly research. In addition, by including linkages between CONASUPO administrators and outside actors in the policy making process, it can be reasonably proposed that exchange relationships are more widely found within the Mexican political system. Moreover, as most actors were involved in career alliances before coming to CONASUPO, it is reasonable to expect that the research findings can be generalized to a broader environment.

The second problem of inference in the research is that interviews were conducted with a nonrandom sample of public administrators within CONASUPO. Two methods of compensating for sample bias were followed in the research and analysis. During the interview series, an attempt was made within several departments to interview virtually all top and middle level officials in the unit (see Coleman, 1970: 119). This was true of programs at the national level and the objective of all visits to state headquarters. Second, in the analysis of data and writing of the study, a conscious attempt was made to avoid presenting quantitative information on respondents which might lead to misinterpretation of the data. Thus, for example, wherever possible, diagrams and charts were employed to describe significant patterns rather than the use of absolute numbers or percentages. It was hoped that in this way systematic and nondistorted use of the information obtained through interviews could be achieved.

Finally, while a more rigorous testing of principal research hypotheses might have resulted from the use of quantitative budget and allocation data, much of this information was not available, either because it did not exist in CONASUPO archives or because it was considered of too sensitive a nature to provide to an outside observer. In many cases, the figures which appear in the analysis have been culled from a variety of sources. Every attempt was made to assure the reasonable accuracy of the figures, but in many cases it was thought most wise to omit the use of contradictory or unclear figures.

Appendix B

The Size, Growth, and Distribution of the Public Bureaucracy in Mexico

TABLE B-1.

Absolute Growth of the Public Administration, 1900–1969

Year	No. of Persons	Year	No. of Persons
1900	25,188	1940	191,588
1910	22,415	1950*	263,261
1921	63,074	1960*	334,934
1930	147,301	1969**	406,607

Source: Ministerio de Fomento, *Resúmen general del censo de la Republica Mexicana*, 1900; Secretaría de Agricultura y Fomento, *Tercer censo de población*, 1910; Secretaría de la Economía Nacional, *Anuario Estadístico, 1938; Sexto censo de población, 1943; Séptimo censo general de población*, 1950; Secretaría de Industria y Comercio, *Octavo censo general de población*, 1960; *Noveno censo general de población*, 1970.

* Estimated.
** See note 8, Chap. 3.

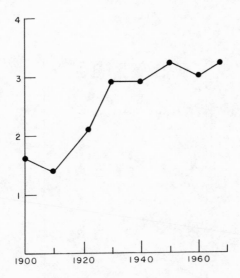

Figure B-1. The Growth of the Public Administration as a Percentage of the Economically Active Population. Note: Percentage for 1921 is estimated.

TABLE B-2

Distribution of Employees of the Public Administration in Mexico, 1969

Level of Government Employment	No.	%
Federal	305,281	75.0
State	50,640	12.5
Municipal (county)	41,649	10.3
Unspecified	9,037	2.2
Totals	406,607	100.0

Source: Secretaría de Industria y Comercio, *Noveno censo general de población,* 1970.

TABLE B-3.

Public Sector Organizations in Mexico, 1972

Type of Organization	Agriculture and Forestry	Social Welfare	Finance	Interior	Industry, Commerce, Fishing	Communications and Public Works	Foreign Relations	Services	Total
Ministries and Department of State	3	3	1	7	1	2	1	0	18
Decentralized agencies	9	43	3	46	14	6	1	1	123
State participation industries	23	0	40	0	186	20	0	23	292
Committees, commissions, and councils	68	25	2	38	17	22	14	1	187
Trusts	36	39	2	5	50	23	1	4	160
Totals	139	110	48	96	268	73	17	29	780

Source: Secretaría de la Presidencia, *Bases para el programa de reforma administrativa del poder ejecutivo, 1971–1976.*

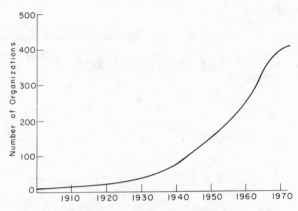

Figure B-2. Growth of Decentralized Agencies and State Industries. Source: Secretaría de la Presidencia, *Bases para el programa de reforma administrativa del poder ejecutivo federal, 1971–1976.*

TABLE B-4.

Distribution of Public Investment Expenditures in Mexico, 1966

Level of Government	%
Central government	34.0
States and municipal governments	10.8
Autonomous agencies and public enterprises	55.2

Source: United Nations, *Estudio económico*, p. 113.

Appendix C

Recent Data on Agriculture in Mexico

TABLE C-1.

Use of Agricultural Lands in Mexico, 1960–1970

	1960	*1970*
Total hectares	169,084,208	144,637,051
	(%)	*(%)*
Cultivated area	14.1	19.0
Natural pastures	46.8	48.2
Forest	25.8	12.8
Productive uncultivated area	6.6	5.8
Other (desert, unimproved, rocky, constructions, roads)	6.7	14.2
Totals	100.0	100.0

Source: Secretaría de Industria y Comercio, *Quarto censo agrícola-ganadero ejidal*, 1960; *Quinto censo agrícola-ganadero ejidal*, 1970.

TABLE C-2.

Gross Internal Agricultural Product at 1960 Prices

Year	Millions of Pesos	% Change
1965	19,921	
1966	20,214	1.5
1967	20,165	-0.2
1968	20,489	1.6
1969	20,145	-1.7
1970	21,140	4.9
1971	21,517	1.8
1972	20,955	-2.6
1973	20,829	-0.6
1974	21,287	2.2

Source: Banco Nacional de Comercio Exterior, *Comercio exterior de México,* 1975.

TABLE C-3.

Private Farms and *Ejidos,* 1960–1970

	No. of Holdings	% of Total	Hectares	% of Total	Average Holding Size (Ha.)
Private farms					
1960	1,337,232	47.3	102,831,770	69.4	76.9
1970	993,888	35.1	75,221,983	52.0	75.7
Ejidos* and agrarian communities					
1960	1,491,455	52.7	45,370,624	30.6	30.4
1970	1,834,422	64.9	69,415,068	48.0	37.7
Totals					
1960	2,828,687	100.0	148,202,394	100.0	52.4
1970	2,828,310	100.0	144,637,051	100.0	51.1

Source: Secretaría de Industria y Comercio, *Quarto censo agrícola-ganadero ejidal,* 1960; *Quinto censo agrícola-ganadero ejidal,* 1970.

*Figures are based on the number of communities, not number of individuals.

TABLE C-4.

Farm Size and Agricultural Production, 1950–1960

Farm Size (in annual production)	% of All Holdings		% of Total Value of Production	
	1950	1960	1950	1960
Below subsistence $0–80	54	50	7	4
Subsistence $80–400	32	33	21	17
Family $400–2,000	12	13	32	25
Multifamily $2,000–8,000	1	3	15	22
Large Multifamily $8,000 +	0.3	0.5	25	32

Source: Centro de Investigaciones Agrarias, *Estructura agraria y desarrollo agrícola en México*. Mexico: Fondo de Cultura Económica, 1974, p. 200.

TABLE C-5.

Federal Public Investment in Agricultural Development, 1959–1970

Year	Total (millions of pesos)	Irrigation (% of total)	Other Investments (% of total)
1959	1060.1	76.9	23.1
1960	817.8	75.5	24.5
1961	1141.4	83.3	16.7
1962	1134.6	75.9	24.1
1963	1958.3	76.8	23.2
1964	2254.8	79.3	20.7
1965	1524.5	71.7	28.3
1966	1177.5	82.3	17.7
1967	2405.0	84.2	15.8
1968	2940.0	81.6	18.4
1969	3631.6	67.7	33.3
1970	3921.4	68.6	31.3

Source: 1959–1968, Centro de Investigaciones Agrarias, *Estructura agraria y desarrollo agrícola en México*. Mesico: Fondo de Cultura Económica, 1974, p. 135; 1969–1970, Secretaría de Industria y Comercio, *Anuario estadístico*, 1970–1971.

Bibliography

Adams, J. S.
 1965 "Inequity in Social Exchange," in Leonard Berkowitz (ed.), *Advances in Experimental Social Psychology*, Vol. 2. New York: Academic Press.

Adie, Robert F.
 1970 "Cooperation, Cooptation, and Conflict in Mexican Peasant Organization," *Inter-American Economic Affairs*, Vol. 24, No. 3 (Winter).

Aguilar Monteverde, Alonso, and Fernando Carmona
 1967 *México: riqueza y miseria, dos ensayos*. Mexico: Nuestro Tiempo.

Alisky, Marvin
 1974 "CONASUPO: A Mexican Agency Which Makes Low Income Workers Feel Their Government Cares," *Inter-American Economic Affairs*, Vol. 27, No. 3 (Winter).

Almond, Gabriel, and G. Bingham Powell, Jr.
 1966 *Comparative Politics: A Developmental Approach*. Boston: Little, Brown.

Almond, Gabriel, and Sidney Verba
 1963 *The Civic Culture*. Boston: Little, Brown.

Ames, Barry
 1970 "Bases of Support for Mexico's Dominant Party," *American Political Science Review*, Vol. 64, No. 1 (March).
 1973a "From Response to Behavior: The Need for Contextual Anchoring in the Study of Latin American Bureaucrats." Paper prepared for 1973 meeting of the Comparative Administration Group of the American Society for Public Administration, April 1–5.

Anderson, Bo, and James Cockroft
 1966 "Control and Cooptation in Mexican Politics," *International Journal of Comparative Sociology*, Vol. 7, No. 1 (March).

Anderson, Charles
 1967 *Politics and Economic Change in Latin America*. Princeton, N.J.: Van Nostrand.
 1970 *The Political Economy of Modern Spain: Policy Making in an Authoritarian System*. Madison: University of Wisconsin.

Anderson, Eugene, and Pauline Anderson
  1970 "Bureaucratic Institutionalization in Nineteenth Century Europe," in
       Arnold J. Heidenheimer (ed.), *Political Corruption.* New York: Holt,
       Rinehart & Winston.
Argaez, Ignacio, *et al.*
  n.d. "Las condiciones del desarrollo de la agricultura de subsistencia de la
       península de Yucután." Unpublished manuscript.
Arterton, Christopher F.
  1974 *Political Participation as Attempted Interpersonal Influence: Test of
       a Theoretical Model Using Data from Rural Mexican Villages.* Un-
       published doctoral dissertation, MIT.
Baer, Werner
  1974 "The Role of Government Enterprises in Latin America's Industrializa-
       tion," in David J. Geithman (ed.), *Fiscal Policy for Industrialization
       and Development in Latin America.* Gainesville: University of Florida.
Bailey, F. G.
  1963 *Politics and Social Change: Orissa in 1959.* Berkeley: University of
       California.
Bailey, John J.
  1975 "Policy Making in Colombian Decentralized Agencies: Presidential
       Control Versus Agency Autonomy." Paper prepared for delivery at
       the annual meeting of the American Political Science Association,
       San Francisco, September 2–5.
Banco de México
       Indicadores económicos.
  1971 *La distribución del ingreso en México: Encuesta sobre los ingresos y
       gastos de la familia, 1968.* Mexico: Fondo de Cultura Económica.
Banco Nacional de Comercio Exterior
       Anuario estadístico.
  1970 "Aspectos económicos del discurso de toma de posesión del Presidente
       de México," *Comercio exterior,* Vol. 20, No. 12 (December).
  1971 *La política económica del nuevo gobierno.* Mexico.
  1975 "Reflections on Agricultural Development Policy," *Comercio exterior
       de México,* Vol. 21, No. 3 (March).
Banco Nacional de México
       Review of the Economic Situation of Mexico.
Banfield, Edward C., and James Q. Wilson
  1963 *City Politics.* New York: Vintage Books.
Barkin, David
  1970 "Agricultural Development in Mexico: A Case Study of Income Con-
       centration," *Social Research,* Vol. 37, No. 2 (Summer).
  1975 "Regional Development and Interregional Equity: A Mexican Case
       Study," in Wayne A. Cornelius and Felicity M. Trueblood (eds.)
       Latin American Urban Research, Vol. 5. Beverly Hills, Calif.: Sage
       Publications.
Barnard, Chester
  1938 *The Functions of the Executive.* Cambridge, Mass.: Harvard University.

Barraclough, Solon, and Juan Carlos Collarte
   1973 *Agrarian Structure in Latin America.* Lexington, Mass.: Heath
      Lexington.

Bartra, Roger
   1974 *Estructura agraria y clases sociales en México.* Mexico: Ediciones Era.
   1975 "Campesinado y poder político en México," in Instituto de Investi-
      gaciones Sociales, *Caciquismo y poder político en el México rural.*
      Mexico: Siglo XXI.

Beltrán, Luís, S.
   1971 "La 'Revolución Verde' y el desarrollo rural latino-americano," *Desa-
      rrollo rural en las américas,* Vol. 3, No. 1.

Bennett, Peter D.
   1968 *Government's Role in Retail Marketing of Food Products in Chile.*
      Austin: University of Texas, Bureau of Business Research.

Bensman, J., and A. Vidich
   1962 "Power Cliques in Bureaucratic Society," *Social Research,* Vol. 29,
      No. 4.

Benveniste, Guy
   1970 *Bureaucracy and National Planning: A Sociological Case Study in
      Mexico.* New York: Praeger.

Berger, Morroe
   1957 *Bureaucracy and Society in Modern Egypt: A Study of the Higher
      Civil Service.* Princeton, N.J.: Princeton University.

Betley, Brian J.
   1971 "Otomí Juez: An Analysis of a Political Middleman," *Human Organi-
      zation,* Vol. 30, No. 1.

Blank, David E.
   1973 *Politics in Venezuela.* Boston: Little, Brown.

Blau, Peter
   1955 *The Dynamics of Bureaucracy.* Chicago: University of Chicago.
   1957 "Formal Organization: Dimensions of Analysis," *American Journal of
      Sociology,* Vol. 63.
   1964 *Exchange and Power in Social Life.* New York: Wiley.

Blau, Peter, and Richard W. Scott
   1962 *Formal Organizations.* San Francisco: Chandler.

Boissevain, Jeremy
   1965 *Saints and Fireworks: Religion and Politics in Rural Malta.* New York:
      Humanities Press.
   1966 "Patronage in Sicily," *Man,* New Series 1, No. 1 (March).
   1974 *Friends of Friends: Networks, Manipulators, and Coalitions.* New
      York: St. Martin's.

Brandenburg, Frank
   1964 *The Making of Modern Mexico.* Englewood Cliffs, N.J.: Prentice Hall.

Camp, Roderick Ai
   1974 "Mexican Governors Since Cárdenas: Education and Career Contacts,"
      Journal of Inter-American Studies and World Affairs, Vol. 16, No. 4
      (November).

1975   "The National School of Economics and Public Life in Mexico," *Latin American Research Review*, Vol. 10, No. 3 (Fall).

Campbell, J. K.

1964   *Honor, Family, and Patronage*. Oxford: Clarendon.

Carlos, Manuel L.

1974   *Politics and Development in Rural Mexico: A Study of Socioeconomic Modernization*. New York: Praeger.

Carlos, Manuel L., and David Brokensha

1972   "Agencies, Clients, and Goals: A Cross-Cultural Analysis," *Studies in Comparative International Development*, Vol. 7, No. 2 (Summer).

Carrillo Castro, Alejandro

1973   "Capacidad política y administrative del estado mexicano," in *Política y administración pública*. Mexico: Universidad Nacional Autónoma de México, Facultad de Ciencias Políticas y Sociales, Serie Estudios 30.

Castellanos, Rosario, David Alfaro Siquieros, Renate Leduc, Enrique Ortega A., Arturo Warman, Jorge Carrión, and Guillermo Montaño

1969   *La corrupción*. Mexico: Nuestro Tiempo.

Centro de Investigaciones Agrarias

1974   *Estructura agraria y desarrollo agrícola en México*. Mexico: Fondo de Cultura Económica.

Chalmers, Douglas A.

1972   "Parties and Society in Latin America," *Studies in Comparative International Development*, Vol. 7, No. 2 (Summer).

Chapman, Brian

1959   *The Profession of Government*. London: Unwin.

Chevalier, François

1967   "The *Ejido* and Political Stability in Mexico," in Claudio Veliz (ed.), *The Politics of Conformity in Latin America*. London: Oxford University.

Clark, Peter, and James Q. Wilson

1961   "Incentive Systems: A Theory of Organization," *Administrative Science Quarterly*, Vol. 6 (June).

Cleaves, Peter S.

1974   *Bureaucratic Politics and Administration in Chile*. Berkeley: University of California.

Cochrane, James D.

1967   "Mexico's New *Científicos*: The Díaz Ordaz Cabinet," *Inter-American Economic Affairs*, Vol. 21, No. 1 (Summer).

Cockroft, James D.

1972   "Coercion and Ideology in Mexican Politics," in James D. Cockcroft, Andre Gunder Frank, and Dale L. Johnson, *Dependence and Underdevelopment: Latin America's Political Economy*. New York: Anchor.

cocosa (Comité Coordinador del Sector Agropecuario)

1973   "Lineamientos de política agropecuaria." Unpublished manuscript.

Coleman, James S.

1970   "Relational Analysis: The Study of Social Organizations with Survey Methods," in Norman K. Denzin (ed.), *Sociological Methods*. Chicago: Aldine.

Coleman, Kenneth M.
1972 *Public Opinion in Mexico City About the Electoral System.* Chapel
     Hill: University of North Carolina, The James Sprunt Studies in
     History and Political Science, No. 53.
CONASUPO
     Gaceta
1971a *Informe Especial al Consejo de Administración.*
1971b "Diagnóstico de treinta años de acción reguladora de CONASUPO."
      Unpublished manuscript.
1972a "Análisis programático de la operación global." Unpublished man-
      uscript.
1972b "Programa Maíz: Bases para un plan de acción." Unpublished
      manuscript.
1972c "Esquema general para la transformación de la agricultura de sub-
      sistencia." Unpublished manuscript.
1972d "Programa de acción para la agricultura de subsistencia." Unpublished
      manuscript.
1973a "Programas de CONASUPO." Unpublished manuscript.
1973b "Informes de las filiales a la Gerencia General." Unpublished manu-
      script.
1974 "El presupuesto por funciones en CONASUPO." Unpublished manuscript.
Conklin, John G.
1973 "Elite Studies: The Case of the Mexican Presidency," *Journal of Latin
     American Studies,* Vol. 5, No. 2 (November).
Cornelius, Wayne A.
1973 "The Impact of Governmental Performance on Political Attitudes and
     Behavior: The Case of the Urban Poor in Mexico City," in Francine F.
     Rabinovitz and Felicity M. Trueblood (eds.), *Latin American Urban
     Research,* Vol. 3. Beverly Hills, Calif.: Sage Publications.
1974 "Urbanization and Political Demand Making: Political Participation
     Among the Migrant Poor in Latin American Cities," *American Polit-
     ical Science Review,* Vol. 68, No. 3 (September).
1975 *Politics and the Migrant Poor in Mexico City.* Stanford, Calif.: Stan-
     ford University.
Cotler, Julio
1970 "Traditional Haciendas and Communities in a Context of Political
     Mobilization in Peru," in Rodolfo Stavenhagen (ed.), *Agrarian Prob-
     lems and Peasant Movements in Latin America.* New York: Doubleday.
1972 "Bases del corporativismo en el Perú," *Sociedad y Política,* Vol. 1
     (October).
Crozier, Michel
1964 *The Bureaucratic Phenomenon.* Chicago: University of Chicago.
Daland, Robert T.
1967 *Brazilian Planning: Development Politics and Administration.* Chapel
     Hill: University of North Carolina.
1972 "Attitudes Toward Change Among Brazilian Bureaucrats," *Journal of
     Comparative Administration,* Vol. 4, No. 2.

Dalton, M.
 1959 *Men Who Manage.* New York: Wiley.
Davis, Charles L., and Kenneth M. Coleman
 1974 "The Regime Legitimizing Function of External Political Efficacy in an
       Authoritarian Regime: The Case of Mexico." Paper presented at the
       annual meeting of the American Political Science Association, Chicago,
       Ill., August 29–September 2.
Davis, Stanley M.
 1968 "Managerial Resource Development in Mexico," in Robert R. Rehder
       (ed.), *Latin American Management: Development and Performance.*
       Reading, Mass.: Addison-Wesley.
Denton, Charles F.
 1969 "Bureaucracy in an Immobilist Society: The Case of Costa Rica,"
       Administrative Science Quarterly, Vol. 14, No. 3 (September).
Dexter, Lewis A.
 1970 *Elite and Specialized Interviewing.* Evanston, Ill.: Northwestern Uni-
       versity.
DICONSA
 1974 "Curso de capacitación al Grupo Voluntario de visitas a tiendas."
       Unpublished manuscript.
Dogan, Mattei, and Richard Rose
 1971 *European Politics.* Boston: Little, Brown.
Durán, Marco Antonio
 1967 *El agrarismo mexicano.* Mexico: Siglo XXI.
Eckstein, Salomón
 1966 *El ejido colectivo en México.* Mexico: Fondo de Cultura Económica.
 1968 *El marco macroeconómico del problema agrario mexicano.* Mexico:
       Centro de Investigaciones Agrarias.
Economist Intelligence Unit
       Mexico, Annual Supplement.
Eldersveld, S. J., V. Jagannadham, and A. P. Barnabas
 1968 *The Citizen and the Administrator in a Developing Democracy.* Glen-
       view, Ill.: Scott, Foresman.
Erasmus, Charles J.
 1968 "Community Development and the *Encogido* Syndrome," *Human
       Organization,* Vol. 27, No. 1 (Spring).
Esman, Milton J.
 1972 *Administration and Development in Malaysia.* Ithaca, N.Y.: Cornell
       University.
Fagen, Richard R., and William S. Tuohy
 1972 *Politics and Privilege in a Mexican City.* Stanford, Calif.: Stanford
       University.
Feder, Ernest
 1971 *The Rape of the Peasantry.* New York: Anchor.
Felix, David
 1968 "The Dilemma of Import Substitution—Argentina," in Gustav Papanek
       (ed.), *Development Policy: Theory and Practice.* Cambridge, Mass.:
       Harvard University.

Fernández y Fernández, Ramon, and Ricardo Acosta
  1961 *Política agrícola*. Mexico: Fondo de Cultura Económica.
Flores, Edmundo
  1961 *Tratado de economía agrícola*. Mexico: Fondo de Cultura Económica.
Flynn, Peter
  1974 "Class, Clientelism, and Coercion," *Journal of Commonwealth and Comparative Politics*, Vol. 12 (July).
Foster, George
  1967a *Tzintzuntzan: Mexican Peasants in a Changing World*. Boston: Little, Brown.
  1967b "Peasant Society and the Image of the Limited Good," in Jack Potter, May Diaz, and George Foster (eds.), *Peasant Society: A Reader*. Boston: Little, Brown.
  1967c "The Dyadic Contract: A Model for the Social Structure of a Mexican Peasant Village," in Jack Potter, May Diaz, and George Foster (eds.), *Peasant Society: A Reader*. Boston: Little, Brown.
Friedrich, Paul
  1969 "The Legitimacy of a *Cacique*," in Marc Swartz (ed.), *Local Level Politics*. Chicago: Aldine.
Geertz, Clifford
  1960 "The Changing Role of Cultural Brokers: The Javanese Kijaji," *Comparative Studies in Society and History*, Vol. 2.
Glade, William P., and Charles Anderson
  1963 *The Political Economy of Mexico*. Madison: University of Wisconsin.
Gomez, Rudolph
  1969 *The Peruvian Administrative System*. Boulder: University of Colorado, Bureau of Governmental Research and Service.
González Casanova, Pablo
  1970 *Democracy in Mexico*. London: Oxford University.
Gorden, Raymond L.
  1969 *Interviewing: Strategy, Techniques, and Tactics*. Homewood, Ill.: The Dorsey Press.
Gosnell, Harold F.
  1937 *Machine Politics: Chicago Model*. Chicago: University of Chicago.
Graham, Lawrence
  1968 *Civil Service Reform in Brazil*. Austin: University of Texas.
Graziano, Luigi
  1973 "Patron-Client Relationships in Southern Italy," *European Journal of Political Research*, Vol. 1.
Greenberg, Martin
  1970 *Bureaucracy and Development: A Mexican Case Study*. Lexington, Mass.: Heath Lexington.
Greenfield, Sidney M.
  1972 "Charwomen, Cesspools, and Road Building: An Examination of Patronage, Clientage, and Political Power in Southeastern Minas Gerais," in Arnold Strickon and Sidney Greenfield (eds.), *Structure and Process in Latin America: Patronage, Clientage, and Power Systems*. Albuquerque: University of New Mexico.

Gruber, Wilfried
  1971 "Career Patterns of Mexico's Political Elite," *Western Political Quarterly*, Vol. 24, No. 3 (September).
Hansen, Roger D.
  1971 *The Politics of Mexican Development*. Baltimore: Johns Hopkins.
Hanson, Mark
  1974 "Organizational Bureaucracy in Latin America and the Legacy of Spanish Colonialism," *Journal of Inter-American Studies and World Affairs*, Vol. 16, No. 2 (May).
Heady, Ferrel and Sybil L. Stokes (eds.)
  1962 *Papers in Comparative Public Administration*. Ann Arbor: Institute of Public Administration, University of Michigan.
Heath, Anthony
  1971 "Review Article: Exchange Theory," *British Journal of Political Science*, Vol. 1.
Heath, Dwight B.
  1972 "New Patrons for Old: Changing Patron-Client Relationships in the Bolivian Yungas," in Arnold Strickon and Sidney Greenfield (eds.), *Structure and Process in Latin America: Patronage, Clientage, and Power Systems*. Albuquerque: University of New Mexico.
Heeger, Gerald A.
  1973 "Bureaucracy, Political Parties and Political Development," *World Politics*, Vol. 25, No. 4 (July).
Henry, Laurin L.
  1958 "Public Administration and Civil Service," in Harold E. Davis (ed.), *Government and Politics in Latin America*. New York: Ronald Press.
Hicks, F.
  1971 "Interpersonal Relations and *Caudillismo* in Paraguay," *Journal of Inter-American Studies and World Affairs*, Vol. 13, No. 1 (January).
Hinojosa, Juan José
  1974 "El Estado: Empresario por distracción," *Excelsior* (Mexico City), December 4, 1974: 6.
Hirschman, Albert O.
  1965 *Journeys Toward Progress*. Garden City, N.Y.: Anchor.
Hollnsteiner, M. R.
  1967 "Social Structure and Power in a Philippine Municipality," in Jack Potter, May Diaz, and George Foster (eds.), *Peasant Society: A Reader*. Boston: Little, Brown.
Homans, George C.
  1958 "Social Behavior as Exchange," *American Journal of Sociology*, Vol. 63, No. 6 (May).
  1961 *Social Behavior: Its Elementary Forms*. London: Routledge & Kegan Paul.
Honey, John C.
  1968 *Toward Strategies for Public Administration Development in Latin America*. Syracuse, N.Y.: Syracuse University.
Hoogenboom, Ari
  1961 *Outlawing the Spoils*. Urbana: University of Illinois.

1970 "Spoilsmen and Reformers: Civil Service Reform and Public Moral-ity," in Arnold J. Heidenheimer (ed.), *Political Corruption*. New York: Holt, Rinehart & Winston.

Hopkins, Jack W.
1967 *The Government Executive of Modern Peru*. Gainesville: University of Florida.

Huntington, Samuel P.
1968 *Political Order in Changing Societies*. New Haven: Yale University.

Ike, Nobutaka
1972 *Japanese Politics: Patron-Client Democracy*. New York: Knopf.

Ilchman, Warren F.
1965 "Rising Expectations and the Revolution in Development Administra-tion," *Public Administration Review*, Vol. 25, No. 4.

Ilchman, Warren F., and Norman Uphoff
1969 *The Political Economy of Change*. Berkeley: University of California.

Instituto de Investigaciones Sociales
1975 *Caciquismo y poder político en el México rural*. Mexico: Siglo XXI.

Jaguaribe, Helio
1968 *Economic and Political Development: A Theoretical Approach and a Brazilian Case Study*. Cambridge, Mass.: Harvard University.

Jaquette, Jane S.
1972 "Revolution by Fiat: The Context of Policy Making in Peru," *Western Political Quarterly*, Vol. 25, No. 4 (December 1972).

Johnson, Kenneth
1971 *Mexican Democracy: A Critical View*. Boston: Allyn and Bacon.

Jones, William O.
1972 *Marketing Staple Food Crops in Tropical Africa*. Ithaca, N.Y.: Cornell University.

Kahl, Joseph A.
1968 *The Measurement of Modernism*. Austin: University of Texas.

Kaplan, Marcos
1969 "El estado empresarial en la Argentina," *El Trimestre Económico*, Vol. 36 (January March).

Kaufman, Herbert
1973 *Administrative Feedback: Monitoring Subordinates Behavior*. Wash-ington, D.C.: Brookings.

Kaufman, Robert R.
1972 *The Politics of Land Reform in Chile, 1950–1970*. Cambridge, Mass.: Harvard University.
1974 "The Patron-Client Concept and Macro-Politics: Prospects and Prob-lems," *Comparative Studies in Society and History*, Vol. 16, No. 3 (June).

Kenny, M.
1961 *A Spanish Tapestry: Town and Country in Castile*. Bloomington: Indiana University.

Kriesberg, Martin
1965 *Public Administration in Developing Countries*. Washington, D.C.: Brookings.

Landé, Carl
  1973 "Networks and Groups in Southeast Asia: Some Observations on the
        Group Theory of Politics," *American Political Science Review*, Vol.
        67, No. 1 (March).
La Palombara, Joseph
  1964 *Interest Groups in Italian Politics*. Princeton, N.J.: Princeton Uni-
        versity.
Leeds, Anthony
  1965 "Brazilian Careers and Social Structure: A Case History and Model,"
        in Dwight B. Heath and Richard N. Adams (eds.), *Contemporary
        Cultures and Societies of Latin America*. New York: Random House.
Leff, Nathaniel H.
  1968 *Economic Policy Making and Development in Brazil, 1947–1964*. New
        York: Wiley.
  1970 "Economic Development Through Bureaucratic Corruption," in
        Arnold J. Heidenheimer (ed.), *Political Corruption*. New York: Holt,
        Rinehart & Winston.
Lemarchand, René, and Keith Legg
  1972 "Political Clientelism and Development," *Comparative Politics*, Vol.
        4 (January).
Levy, Jr., Fred D.
  1973 "Economic Planning in Venezuela," in Clarence E. Thurber and
        Lawrence S. Graham (eds.), *Development Administration in Latin
        America*. Durham, N.C.: Duke University.
Linz, Juan
  1970 "An Authoritarian Regime: Spain," in Erik Allardt and Stein Rokkan
        (eds.), *Mass Politics*. New York: Free Press.
Lipsky, Michael
  1968 "Protest as a Political Resource," *American Political Science Review*,
        Vol. 62, No. 4 (December).
Lomnitz, Larissa
  1974 "The Social and Economic Organization of a Mexican Shantytown,"
        in Wayne A. Cornelius and Felicity M. Trueblood (eds.), *Latin
        American Urban Research*, Vol. 4. Beverly Hills, Calif.: Sage
        Publications.
Lowi, Theodore J.
  1967 "Machine Politics—Old and New," *Public Interest* (Fall).
Malloy, James M.
  1974 "Authoritarianism, Corporatism and Mobilization in Peru," in F. B.
        Pike and T. Stritch (eds.), *The New Corporatism: Socio-Political
        Structures in the Iberian World*. Notre Dame, Ind.: University of
        Notre Dame.
  1975 (ed.), *Authoritarianism and Corporatism in Latin America*. Pittsburgh,
        Penn.: University of Pittsburgh.
Martínez Ríos, Jorge
  1972 "Los campesinos mexicanos: Perspectivas en el proceso de marginali-
        zación," *El perfil de México en 1980*, Vol. 3. Mexico: Siglo XXI.

Mayntz, Renate, and Fritz W. Scharpf
  1975 *Policy Making in the German Federal Bureaucracy.* New York: Elsevier.
Ministerio de Fomento (Mexico)
  1900 *Resúmen general del censo de la República Mexicana.*
Mintz, Sidney W., and Eric R. Wolf
  1950 "An Analysis of Ritual Co-Parenthood (*Compadrazgo*)" *Southwestern Journal of Anthropology,* Vol. VI (Winter).
Montgomery, John D. and William Siffin (eds.)
  1966 *Approaches to Development: Politics, Administration, and Change.* New York: McGraw Hill.
Moreno Sánchez, Manuel
  1973 *Mexico: 1968-1972: Crisis y perspectiva.* Austin: Institute of Latin American Studies, University of Texas.
Mosher, Frederic C.
  1968 *Democracy and the Public Service.* New York: Oxford University.
Mouzelis, Nicos P.
  1967 *Organization and Bureaucracy: An Analysis of Modern Theories.* Chicago: Aldine.
Musalem López, Omar
  1974 "La renta de la tierra, el desarrollo agrícola y la migración rural." Paper presented to the XLI Congreso Internacional de Americanistas, Mexico, D.F., September 2-7.
Nathan, Andrew J.
  1973 "A Facionalism Model for CCP Politics," *The China Quarterly* (January-March).
Navarrete, Ifigenia M. de
  1970 "La distribución del ingreso en México," en *El perfil de México en 1980.* Mexico: Siglo XXI.
Needleman, Carolyn, and Martin Needleman
  1969 "Who Rules Mexico? A Critique of Some Current Views on the Mexican Political Process," *Journal of Politics,* Vol. 31, No. 4 (November).
Needler, Martin
  1971 *Politics and Society in Mexico.* Albuquerque: University of New Mexico.
Newton, Roland N.
  1970 "On 'Functional Groups,' 'Fragmentation,' and 'Pluralism' in Spanish American Political Society," *Hispanic American Historical Review.* Vol. 50 (February).
O'Donnell, Guillermo A.
  1973 *Modernization and Bureaucratic-Authoritarianism: Studies in South American Politics.* Berkeley, Calif.: Institute of International Studies, University of California (Politics of Modernization Series, No. 9).
Padgett, L. V.
  1966 *The Mexican Political System.* Boston: Houghton Mifflin.
Palerm, Angel
  1968 *Observaciones sobre la planificación regional.* Washington, D.C.: Union Panamericana.

1972 *Agricultura y sociedad en mesoamerica.* Mexico: Secretaría de Educa-
      ción Pública.
Pan American Union
1965 *Public Administration in Latin America.* Washington, D.C.
Parrish, Charles J.
1973 "Bureaucracy, Democracy, and Development: Some Considerations
      Based on the Chilean Case," in Clarence E. Thurber and Lawrence S.
      Graham (eds.), *Development Administration in Latin America.* Dur-
      ham, N.C.: Duke University.
Pellicer de Brody, Olga
1974 "Mexico in the 1970s and Its Relations with the United States," in
      Julio Cotler and Richard Fagen (eds.), *Latin America and the United
      States: The Changing Political Realities.* Stanford, Calif.: Stanford
      University.
Petras, James
1969 *Politics and Social Forces in Chilean Development.* Berkeley: Univer-
      sity of California.
PIDER (Programa de Inversiones para el Desarrollo Rural)
1973 "¿Qué es el PIDER?" Unpublished manuscript.
Pike, Frederick B., and Thomas Stritch (eds.)
1974 *The New Corporatism: Socio-Political Structures in the Iberian World.*
      Notre Dame, Ind.: University of Notre Dame.
Pinto, Rogerio Feital
1969 "Political Functionality and Administrative Effectiveness: Three Models
      of Latin American Public Administration," *International Review of
      Administrative Sciences,* Vol. 35.
Pitts-Rivers, Julian
1954 *People of the Sierra.* New York: Criterion.
Poitras, Guy E.
1973 "Welfare Bureaucracy and Clientele Politics in Mexico," *Administrative
      Science Quarterly,* Vol. 18, No. 1 (March).
Poitras, Guy E., and Charles F. Denton
1971 "Bureaucratic Performance: Case Studies from Mexico and Costa
      Rica," *Journal of Comparative Administration,* Vol. 3, No. 2 (August).
Pollock, John C.
1974 "The Political Attitudes and Social Backgrounds of Colombia's Urban
      Housing Bureaucrats," in Francine F. Rabinovitz and Felicity M.
      Trueblood (eds.), *Latin American Urban Research,* Vol. 3. Beverly
      Hills, Calif.: Sage Publications.
Powell, John Duncan
1970 "Peasant Society and Clientelist Politics," *American Political Science
      Review,* Vol. 64, No. 2 (June).
1971 *The Mobilization of the Venezuelan Peasant.* Cambridge, Mass.:
      Harvard University.
Pressman, Jeffrey L., and Aaron Wildavsky
1973 *Implementation.* Berkeley: University of California.
Prieto Vazques
1969 "La distribución del ingreso en México," *Comercio exterior,* Vol. 19,
      No. 9.

Purcell, Susan
    1973 "Decision Making in an Authoritarian Regime: Theoretical Impli-
         cations from a Mexican Case Study," *World Politics*, Vol. 25, No. 3
         (April).
    1975 *The Mexican Profit-Sharing Decision: Politics in an Authoritarian
         Regime*. Berkeley: University of California.
Purcell, John F. H., and Susan Kaufman Purcell
    1976 "Mexican Business and Public Policy," in James Malloy (ed.),
         Authoritarianism and Corporatism in Latin America. Pittsburgh,
         Penna.: University of Pittsburgh.
Pye, Lucian W.
    1962 *Politics, Personality and Nation Building*. New Haven: Yale University.
    1966 *Aspects of Political Development*. Boston: Little, Brown.
Quinn, Michael Alan
    1972 *Technicians Versus Politicians, Administrative Reform of Local Gov-
         ernment in a Developing Country: A Case Study of Pôrto Alegre,
         Brazil*. Unpublished doctoral dissertation, University of Illinois.
Ray, Talton
    1969 *The Politics of the Barrios of Venezuela*. Berkeley: University of
         California.
Reyes Osorio, Sergio, and Salomón Eckstein
    1971 "El desarrollo polarizado de la agricultura mexicana," in Miguel
         Wionczek *et al. ¿Crecimiento o desarrollo económico?* Mexico:
         SepSetentas.
Reyna, José Luís
    1972 *An Empirical Analysis of Political Mobilization: The Case of Mexico*.
         Ithaca, N.Y.: Cornell University Dissertation Series, No., 26.
    1974 *Control político, estabilidad y desarrollo en México*. Mexico: El
         Colegio de México, Cuadernos del Centro de Estudios Sociológicos,
         No. 3.
Reynolds, Clark W.
    1970 *The Mexican Economy: Twentieth Century Structure and Growth*.
         New Haven: Yale University.
Richardson, Stephen A., Barbara S. Dorhenwent, and David Klein
    1965 *Interviewing: Its Forms and Functions*. New York: Basic Books.
Riggs, Fred
    1964 *Administration in Developing Countries: The Theory of Prismatic
         Society*. Boston: Houghton Mifflin.
Riley, Matilda W. (ed.)
    1963 *Sociological Research*. New York: Harcourt, Brace and World.
Roett, Riordan
    1972 *Brazil: Politics in a Patrimonialist Society*. Boston: Allyn and Bacon.
Ronfeldt, David
    1973 *Atencingo: The Politics of Agrarian Struggle in a Mexican Ejido*.
         Stanford, Calif.: Stanford University.
Rourke, Francis E.
    1969 *Bureaucracy, Politics, and Public Policy*. Boston: Little, Brown.
Rudolph, Susanne H., and Lloyd I. Rudolph
    1974 "Service Families in Princely India: The Patrimonial Politics of

Authoritarian Regimes." Paper prepared for the annual meeting of the American Political Science Association, Chicago, Ill., August 29–September 2.

Saldaña Harlow, Adalberto
1974 *Observaciones sobre prácticas administrativas en México.* Toluca, Mexico: Instituto de Administración Pública del Estado de México.

Sandbrook, Richard
1972 "Patrons, Clients, and Factions: New Dimensions of Conflict Analysis in Africa," *Canadian Journal of Political Science,* Vol. 5, No. 2 (March).

Sarfatti, Magali
1966 *Spanish Bureaucratic-Patrimonialism in America.* Berkeley: Institute of International Studies, University of California.

Schatzman, Leonard, and Anselm L. Strauss
1973 *Field Research: Strategies for a Natural Sociology.* Englewood Cliffs, N.J.: Prentice Hall.

Schmidt, Steffen W., James C. Scott, Laura Gausti, and Carl Landé
1976 *Friends, Followers, and Factions.* Berkeley: University of California.

Schmidt, Steffen W.
1974 "Bureaucrats as Modernizing Brokers? Clientelism in Colombia," *Comparative Politics,* Vol. 6, No. 3 (April).

Schmitter, Philippe
1971 *Interest Conflict and Political Change in Brazil.* Stanford, Calif.: Stanford University.

Schuh, G. Edward
1970 *The Agricultural Development of Brazil.* New York: Praeger.

Scott, James C.
1969 "Corruption, Machine Politics, and Political Change," *American Political Science Review,* Vol. 63, No. 4 (December).
1972 "Patron-Client Politics and Political Change in Southeast Asia," *American Political Science Review,* Vol. 66, No. 1 (March).
1975 "Exploitation in Rural Class Relations: A Victim's Perspective," *Comparative Politics,* Vol. 7, No. 4 (July).

Scott, Robert E.
1964 *Mexican Government in Transition.* Urbana: University of Illinois.
1966 "The Government Bureaucrats and Political Change in Latin America," *Journal of International Affairs,* Vol. 20, No. 2.
1974 "Politics in Mexico," in Gabriel Almond (ed.), *Comparative Politics Today: A World View.* Boston: Little, Brown.

Secretaría de Agricultura y Fomento
1910 *Tercer censo de población.*

Secretaría de Industria y Comercio (Mexico)
Anuario estadístico.
1960a *Octavo censo general de población.*
1960b *Quarto censo agrícola-ganadero ejidal.*
1970a *Noveno censo general de población.*
1970b *Quinto censo agrícola-ganadero y ejidal.*

Secretaría de la Economía Nacional (Mexico)
1938 *Anuario estadístico.*

1943 *Sexto censo de población.*
1950 *Septimo censo general de población.*
Secretaría de la Presidencia (Mexico)
  *Bases para el programa de reforma administrativa del Poder Ejecutivo,
  1971–1976.*
Seidman, Harold
  1970 *Politics, Position, and Power: The Dynamics of Federal Organization.*
  New York: Oxford.
Shafer, Robert J.
  1966 *Mexico: Mutual Adjustment Planning.* Syracuse, N.Y.: Syracuse
  University.
  1973 *Mexican Business Organizations: History and Analysis.* Syracuse,
  N.Y.: Syracuse University.
Sherwood, Frank P.
  1970 "The Problem of the Public Enterprise," in Fred W. Riggs (ed.),
  Frontiers of Development Administration. Durham, N.C.: Duke
  University.
Silva Michelena, José A.
  1967 "The Venezuelan Bureaucrat," in Frank Bonilla and José A. Silva
  Michelena (eds.), *A Strategy for Research on Social Policy.* Cam-
  bridge, Mass.: MIT.
Silverman, Sydel F.
  1967 "The Community Nation Mediator in Traditional Central Italy,"
  in Jack Potter, May Diaz, and George Foster (eds.), *Peasant Society.*
  Boston: Little, Brown.
Simon, H. A.
  1957 *Administrative Behavior.* New York: Free Press.
Singelmann, Peter
  1974 "Campesino Movements and Class Conflict in Latin America: The
  Functions of Exchange and Power," *Journal of Inter-American Studies
  and World Affairs,* Vol. 16, No. 1 (February).
Skidmore, Thomas E.
  1973 "Politics and Economic Policy Making in Authoritarian Brazil, 1937–
  1971," in Alfred Stepan (ed.), *Authoritarian Brazil: Origins, Policies,
  and Future.* New Haven: Yale University.
Smith, John (pseud.)
  1969 "The Campesino's Perspectives in Latin America," *Inter-American
  Economic Affairs,* Vol. 23, No. 1 (Summer).
Smith, Peter H.
  1974 "Making It in Mexico: Aspects of Political Mobility Since 1946." Paper
  presented at the annual meeting of the American Political Science
  Association, Chicago, Ill., August 29–September 2.
Solís, Leopoldo
  1971 *La realidad económica mexicana: Retrovisión y perspectivas.* Mexico:
  Siglo XXI.
Stavenhagen, Rodolfo
  n.d. *Aspectos sociales de la estructura agraria en México.* Centro Latino-
  Americano de Investigaciones en Ciencias Sociales.

1970 "Social Aspects of Agrarian Structure in Mexico," in Rodolfo Staven-
      hagen (ed.), *Agrarian Problems and Peasant Movements in Latin
      America.* New York: Doubleday.
Stavenhagen, Rodolfo, Fernando Paz Sánchez, Cuauhtemoc Cárdenas, and
Arturo Bonilla
  1968 *Neolatifundismo y explotación: De Emiliano Zapata a Anderson
         Clayton & Co.* Mexico: Nuestro Tiempo.
Stevens, Evelyn P.
  1974 *Protest and Response in Mexico.* Cambridge, Mass.: MIT.
  1975 "Protest Movements in an Authoritarian Regime: The Mexican Case,"
         Comparative Politics, Vol. 7, No. 3 (April).
Stinchcombe, Arthur L.
  1974 *Creating Efficient Industrial Administrations.* New York: Academic
         Press.
Strickon, Arnold, and Sidney Greenfield (eds.)
  1972 *Structure and Process in Latin America: Patronage, Clientage, and
         Power Systems.* Albuquerque: University of New Mexico.
Stuart, W. T.
  1972 "The Explanation of Patron-Client Systems: Some Structural and
         Ecological Perspectives," in Arnold Strickon and Sidney Greenfield
         (eds.), *Structure and Process in Latin America: Patronage, Clientage,
         and Power Systems.* Albuquerque: University of New Mexico.
Suleiman, Ezra N.
  1974 *Politics, Power, and Bureaucracy in France: The Administrative Elite.*
         Princeton, N.J.: Princeton University.
Tarrow, Sidney
  1967 *Peasant Communism in Southern Italy.* New Haven: Yale University.
Tello, Carlos
  1971a "Un intento de análisis de la distribución personal del ingreso," in
         Miguel S. Wionczek (ed.), *Disyuntivas sociales.* Mexico: SepSetentas.
  1971b "Notas para el análisis de la distribución del ingreso en México," *El
         Trimestre Económico* (Mexico), Vol. 150 (April).
Thibaut, J. W., and H. H. Kelley
  1959 *The Social Psychology of Groups.* New York: Wiley.
Thirsk, Wayne R.
  1973 "Income Distribution Consequences of Agricultural Price Supports in
         Columbia," Rice University, Program of Development Studies, Paper
         No. 43.
Thurber, Clarence E., and Lawrence S. Graham (eds.)
  1973 *Development Administration in Latin America.* Durham, N.C.: Duke
         University.
Tuohy, William S.
  1973 "Centralism and Political Elite Behavior in Mexico," in Clarence E.
         Thurber and Lawrence S. Graham (eds.), *Development Administration
         in Latin America.* Durham, N.C.: Duke University.
Tuohy, William, and D. Ronfeldt
  1969 "Political Control and the Recruitment of Middle Level Elites in

Mexico: An example from Agrarian Politics," *Western Political Quarterly*, Vol. 22, No. 2 (June).

Turner, Frederick C.
1973 "Mexican Politics: The Direction of Development," in William P. Glade and S. R. Ross (eds.), *Críticas constructivas del sistema político mexicano: Critiques of the Mexican Political System*. Austin: University of Texas.

Ugalde, Antonio
1970 *Power and Conflict in a Mexican Community*. Albuquerque: University of New Mexico.
1973 "Contemporary Mexico: From Hacienda to PRI, Political Leadership in a Zapotec Village," in R. Kern (ed.), *The Caciques: Oligarchical Politics and the System of Caciquismo in the Luso-Hispanic World*. Albuquerque: University of New Mexico.

United Nations
1972 *Statistical Yearbook*.

Van Meter, Donald S., and Carl E. Van Horn
1975 "The Policy Implementation Process: A Conceptual Framework," *Administration and Society*, Vol. 6, No. 4 (February).

Vernon, Raymond
1963 *The Dilemma of Mexico's Development*. Cambridge, Mass.: Harvard University.

Waldman, Sidney R.
1972 *Foundations of Political Action: An Exchange Theory of Politics*. Boston: Little, Brown.

Waldo, Dwight
1970 *Temporal Dimensions in Development Administration*. Durham, N.C.: Duke University.

Wasserspring, Lois
1974 *Politics and Authority in Corporatist Society: A Study of Mexico*. Unpublished doctoral dissertation, Princeton University.

Weiner, Myron
1971 "Political Participation: Crisis of the Political Process," in Leonard Binder *et al.*, *Crises and Sequences in Political Development*. Princeton, N.J.: Princeton University.

Wennergren, Boyd E., and Morris D. Whitaker
1975 *The Status of Bolivian Agriculture*. New York: Praeger.

Wharton, Jr., C. R. (ed.)
1969 *Subsistence Agriculture and Economic Development*. Chicago: Aldine.

Whyte, William F.
1969 *Organizational Behavior: Theory and Application*. Homewood, Ill.: Irwin and Dorsey.

Wiarda, Howard J. (ed.)
1974a *Politics and Social Change in Latin America: The Distinct Tradition*. Amherst: University of Massachusetts.
1974b "Corporatism and Development in the Iberic-Latin World: Persistent Strains and New Variations," in Frederick B. Pike and Thomas Stritch

(eds.), *The New Corporatism: Socio-Political Structures in the Iberian World*. Notre Dame, Ind.: University of Notre Dame.

Wilkie, James W.

1967 *The Mexican Revolution: Federal Expenditure and Social Change Since 1910*. Berkeley: University of California.

1974 "Recentralization: The Budgetary Dilemma in the Economic Development of Mexico, Bolivia, and Costa Rica," in David J. Geithman (ed.), *Fiscal Policy for Industrialization and Development in Latin America*. Gainesville: University of Florida.

Wionczek, Miguel S.

1973 "El desarrollo económico y el sistema político mexicano," in William P. Glade and S. R. Ross (eds.), *Críticas constructivas del sistema político mexicano: Critiques of the Mexican Political System*. Austin: University of Texas.

Wolf, Eric

1959 *Sons of the Shaking Earth*. Chicago: University of Chicago.

1965 "Aspects of Group Relationships in a Complex Society: Mexico," in D. B. Heath and R. N. Adams (eds.), *Contemporary Cultures and Societies of Latin America*. New York: Random House.

1966 "Kinship, Friendship, and Patron-Client Relations," in M. Banton (ed.), *The Social Anthropology of Complex Societies*. London: Tavistock.

Wynia, Gary W.

1972 *Politics and Planners: Economic Development Policy in Central America*. Madison: University of Wisconsin.

Zuckerman, Alan

1971 *Hierarchal Social Divisions and Political Groups: Factions in the Italian Christian Democrat Party*. Unpublished doctoral dissertation, Princeton University.

Newspapers and Periodicals

El Día (Mexico City)
El Universal (Mexico City)
Excelsior (Mexico City)

Latin America
The New York Times

Index

213